T0407832

LIVING IN A LANDSCAPE OF SCARCITY

PUBLICATIONS OF THE
INSTITUTE OF ARCHAEOLOGY, UNIVERSITY COLLEGE LONDON

Series Editor: Ruth Whitehouse
Director of the Institute: Stephen Shennan
Founding Series Editor: Peter J. Ucko

The Institute of Archaeology of University College London is one of the oldest, largest, and most prestigious archaeology research facilities in the world. Its extensive publications program includes the best theory, research, pedagogy, and reference materials in archaeology and cognate disciplines, through publishing exemplary work of scholars worldwide. Through its publications, the Institute brings together key areas of theoretical and substantive knowledge, improves archaeological practice, and brings archaeological findings to the general public, researchers, and practitioners. It also publishes staff research projects, site and survey reports, and conference proceedings. The publications program, formerly developed in-house or in conjunction with UCL Press, is now produced in partnership with Left Coast Press, Inc. The Institute can be accessed online at http://www.ucl.ac.uk/archaeology.

Recent Titles

Susanna Harris and Laurence Douny (Eds.), *Wrapping and Unwrapping Material Culture*
Laurence Douny, *Living in a Landscape of Scarcity*
Helen Dawson, *Mediterranean Voyages*
Chris J. Stevens, Sam Nixon, Mary Anne Murray, and Dorian Q Fuller (Eds.), *Archaeology of African Plant Use*
Andrew Bevan and Mark Lake (Eds.), *Computational Approaches to Archaeological Spaces*
Sue Colledge, James Conolly, Keith Dobney, Katie Manning, and Stephen Shennan (Eds.), *The Origins and Spread of Domestic Animals in Southwest Asia and Europe*
Julia Shaw, *Buddhist Landscapes of Central India*
Ralph Haeussler, *Becoming Roman?*
Ethan E. Cochrane and Andrew Gardner, *Evolutionary and Interpretive Archaeologies*
Andrew Bevan and David Wengrow (Eds.), *Cultures of Commodity Branding*
Peter Jordan (Ed.), *Landscape and Culture in Northern Eurasia*
Peter Jordan and Marek Zvelebil (Eds.), *Ceramics before Farming*
Marcos Martinón-Torres and Thilo Rehren (Eds.), *Archaeology, History, and Science*
Miriam Davis, *Dame Kathleen Kenyon*
Elizabeth Pye (Ed.), *The Power of Touch*
Russell McDougall and Iain Davidson (Eds.), *The Roth Family, Anthropology, and Colonial Administration*
Eleni Asouti and Dorian Q Fuller, *Trees and Woodlands of South India*
Tony Waldron, *Paleoepidemiology*
Janet Picton, Stephen Quirke, and Paul C. Roberts (Eds.), *Living Images*
Timothy Clack and Marcus Brittain (Eds.), *Archaeology and the Media*
Sue Colledge and James Conolly (Eds.), *The Origins and Spread of Domestic Plants in Southwest Asia and Europe*

Information on older titles in this series can be obtained from the Left Coast Press, Inc. website http://www.LCoastPress.com.

LIVING IN A LANDSCAPE OF SCARCITY

Materiality and Cosmology in West Africa

Laurence Douny

Walnut Creek, California

LEFT COAST PRESS, INC.
1630 North Main Street, #400
Walnut Creek, CA 94596
http://www.LCoastPress.com

ISBN 978-1-61132-891-2 hardback
ISBN 978-1-61132-893-6 institutional eBook
ISBN 978-1-61132-894-3 consumer eBook

Library of Congress Cataloging-in-Publication Data:
Douny, Laurence, 1977-author.
  Living in a landscape of scarcity: materiality and cosmology in West Africa/ Laurence Douny.
    pages cm. — (Publications of the Institute of Archaeology, University College London ; v. 63)
  Includes bibliographical references and index.
  ISBN 978-1-61132-891-2 (hardback: alk. paper) — ISBN 978-1-61132-893-6 (institutional eBook) — ISBN 978-1-61132-894-3 (consumer eBook)
  1. Dogon (African people)—Mali—Material culture. 2. Landscapes—Symbolic aspects—Mali. 3. Cosmology, Dogon. 4. Architecture, Dogon. 5. Food supply—Mali. 6. Scarcity. I. Title. II. Series: Publications of the Institute of Archaeology, University College London; v. 63.
  DT551.45.D64D68 2014
  306.46096623—dc23

                    2014005345

Contents

Illustrations

Preface

To my host family in Tiréli In memory of Patrice (1951–2013)

In his fictional short story entitled *The Aleph*, Borges (1949/1974/2004) writes of a mysterious object or 'point in space', the Aleph, that 'contains all other points' in the universe (Borges 2004, 126); the Aleph is discovered in the space of a dark cellar. By looking into the Aleph the protagonist is able to see the entire universe. The Aleph contains all human experience of the infinite space-time continuum, and it conveys a deep and immediate sense of participation in the world that is felt intensely by those who experience the Aleph.

The Aleph as a cosmological literary metaphor enables me to introduce this book, which is an exploration into the contemporary Dogon cultural landscape of a village in the Bandiagara escarpment, a 'down-to-earth' point in space from which I examine the villagers' microcosmology. This book exposes Dogon shared embodied worldviews about living in a landscape of scarcity. My interest into the Dogon's perceptions of their environment came out of the context in which I conducted the core of my research in an idyllic, pictur-esque, and 'touristy' landscape that quickly turned out to be not ideal to live in (Douny 2007). It was harsh, and it was so for everybody.

My ethnography is mainly set up in a village of the *tɔrɔ sɔ* area of the Bandiagara escarpment, in Mali (West Africa), and it is grounded in my partici-patory observations of daily and seasonal embedded practices of the Dogon land-scape throughout an agricultural cycle. The Dogon microcosmology I recount is a gathering of interrelated worldviews that emanate from shared embodied experiences of a harsh environment in which the weather, and food scarcity in particular, were and still are the major problems (recorded between 2001 and 2013 and during a seventeen-month fieldwork period between 2002 and 2004).

With more than 1,000 publications written about the Dogon, some of my colleagues asked 'why another one?' My answer is simple: the Dogon daily domestic practices out of which the people's material world and thus their cul-tural landscape are shaped remain largely unexplored. In this book I attempt to show that daily practices and so techniques of 'making' and 'doing' the landscape help us to understand the ways in which Dogon people 'make' themselves in a twenty-first-century world—the Dogon perceptions and tacit knowledge about their changing cultural and natural landscapes and creative strategies that they have developed in order to cope with a harsh environment whose everyday realities are masked by the beauty of the cliffs, a UNESCO heritage site.

My reading of Dogon contemporary microcosmology stems from a material culture approach to the study of indigenous cultural landscapes. It is framed within an anthropology of techniques and it leans toward an ecological anthropology of West African landscapes. I believe that, although Dogon culture is undeniably exemplified by its impressive earth architecture, phenomenal masks, and statues, which are on display in many Western museums and art galleries, there is much more than that. I suggest that Dogon material culture, and so domestic 'containers', offer interesting new perspectives on the many ways that Dogon people perceive and experience the world in which they live and so express their worldviews. Furthermore, I believe that, by being at the crossroad of cultures and histories, the Dogon region offers inexhaustible research possibilities that remain to be explored.

My project is largely inspired by the numerous extensive research projects that have been undertaken in the Dogon region in the fields of anthropology, archaeology, history, geography, and linguistics and that I refer to in this book. I hope that my account adds some knowledge to the existing body of research by introducing some new anthropological insights into Dogon culture.

Acknowledgements

This book would never have been possible without the Wenner-Gren Foundation, which supported the core of my research with a fieldwork grant, awarded in 2003, and a great many people who encouraged, supported, advised, and assisted me throughout the years. I first wish to acknowledge an everlasting debt of gratitude to Michael Rowlands (UCL Anthropology). Mike supervised my research and gave me invaluable guidance throughout the writing process of this book. I am grateful to Chris Tilley (UCL Anthropology) for giving me insights on the phenomenology of the landscape and for his thoughtful advice on previous versions. This book also draws considerable inspiration from the work of Jean-Pierre Warnier (René Descartes/EHESS, Paris) whom I thank for his feedback on Chapters 1 and 2 and insights regarding praxeology, West African containers, and containment. Mary Douglas's (1921–2007) work and feedback were instrumental in the development of Chapter 8, on domestic waste, and Chapter 11, on food. In addition, her critical perspective on Dogon cosmology and her knowledge of Marcel Griaule and Germaine Dieterlen's work helped me to rethink the main themes of this book. I would like to thank her for her generosity and her encouragement. Also, I would like to thank Pierre Lemonnier (University en Provence, CREDO, Marseille); the Techniques & Culture group in Marseille, in particular, Frédéric Joulian and Ludovic Coupaye (UCL Anthropology, CREDO Marseille); Myriem Naji, with whom I collaborated on several conferences and writing projects that helped me to rethink my approach to 'techniques'; Paul Lane (Department of Archaeology, University of York); and Claude Ardouin (1950–2011) (Deptartment of Africa, Oceania, and the Americas, The British Museum) for their precious comments, which helped me to develop my dissertation into a monograph; also, Bill Sillar (Institute of archaeology, UCL) for his insights on concepts of seasonality in relation to techniques; Jerome Lewis (UCL Anthropology) for his feedback on an earlier draft of the chapter on cosmology in a millet grain; and Susanne Küchler (UCL Anthropology) and Paul Basu (Institute of archaeology, UCL) for their advice and encouragement.

Chapter 6 on the weather was presented at a UCL workshop on the theme of Traces: Thinking Objects through Remains (June 2010, UCL Anthropology), and I would like to thank Jan Geisbusch, with whom I coorganised it, as well as all participants and Nelson Graburn (University of California, Berkeley), in particular, for his feedback.

I am thankful to all academic and administrative staff at UCL Anthropology. I also would like to thank the Material Culture Group at UCL Anthropology—Chris Pinney, Susanne Küchler, Graeme Were, Chris Tilley, Mike Rowlands, Daniel Miller, Victor Buchli, Ludovic Coupaye, Adam Drazin, and Haidy Geismar—for their support also, thanks to Violet Diallo (GAP, Bamako/Mali) for the early, preliminary copy edit of my manuscript. I am grateful to Ruth Whitehouse at UCL Institute of Archaeology and the two anonymous reviewers for their useful comments, and to Raymond Nader, who produced the index.

Thanks to Salif Sawadogo for permission to use his photograph for the cover of the book and in Chapter 10, and Nadia Khalaf (UEA), who designed the map of the Dogon region.

Many thanks to my friends and colleagues for their support throughout the writing of this book: Myriem Naji, Frank Smith, and their daughter, May; Shaila Bhatti; Cressida Jervis-Reed; Alicia Jimenez; Charlotte Joy; Olga Lupu; Kashka Soltesova; Urmila Mohan; Susanna Harris; Titika Malkogeorgou; Nicky Mackovicky; Claude and Natasha Ardouin; Violaine and Jean Michel Courtois; Catherine Servotte; Martine Sainlez; and Muriel Mousty and her family.

Finally, I am grateful to Juan M. Felix Pérez Ruiz de Valbuena, director of the Biblioteca Olvido, and Assétou Ouedraogo in Ouahigouya (Burkina Faso) and all staff members for their kindness and technical help while I was finalising the manuscript of this book, and Youssouf Bagaya, his family, and my neighbours and friends in Ouahigouya.

This project started at the *Rijksmuseum voor Volkenkunden* in Leiden, where I benefitted from the tremendous help and generosity of Rogier Bedaux and Annette Schmidt, who provided considerable intellectual resources, including photograph archives and an ethnoarchaeological database on Dogon built environment that significantly helped me to develop my project and fieldwork. Rogier and Annette also provided outstanding feedback on multiple drafts, and they offered me their hospitality at the Museum. I am grateful to Polly Richards for sharing with me ideas and her experience of the Dogon region and Eric Jolly for sharing his encyclopedic work on Dogon millet beer. In Bamako, Mali, I would like to thank Samuel Sidibé at the National Museum in Bamako, Dr. Haidara, and Dr. Kléna Sanogo at the ISH (Institut des Sciences Humaines) for their guidance in the field; Dr. Guindo and Dr. Maiga at the CNRST (Centre National de la Recherche Scientifique et Technique), from which I received full permission to conduct research in the Dogon region, each year. I am exceedingly grateful to Violet Diallo and her family for their kindness and generosity and to 'professor' Yobi Guindo for his precious advice; Abinou Teme at the FLASH (Faculty of Humanities, Languages, Arts, and Social Sciences, University of Bamako) for sharing his work on Dogon religion and territoriality; Issaye Dougnon at the FLASH (University of Bamako) for his insights on Dogon migrations; Mamadou Diakité at Sahel Eco (Bamako) for sharing his experience and knowledge about issues on scarcity, water, and desertification in the Mopti region. In Bandiagara, I would like to thank the Mission Culturelle and in particular Lassana Cissé, Adama Dembélé, Pierre Guindo, Binet Douyon, Nohoum Guindo, and Elizabeth Ermert, who advised me considerably while I was carrying out my fieldwork. I also owe a great debt to my friend Atiamba Tembely, who guided me as an interpreter in the last stages of the core of my fieldwork. I would like to thank all my friends in Bandiagara and, in particular, Anne-Gaelle Jehanno, Youssouf Karambé, Moussa Guindo, Mohammed Haidara and his family, André Tembely, and Andrea and Gunther Göddecke.

My warmest thanks go to my host family in Tiréli, with whom I shared unforgettable moments: Balugo Saye, who assisted me throughout the core of my fieldwork; Yabému Saye; Akasom Saye; Domu Saye; Brama Saye, Yasiwe Saye, and their children; and Andra Saye. My research would not have been possible without the help of the villagers—in particular, Yaouro Saye, Yapono Saye, Yabudu Saye, Yabému Saye, Yadiné Saye, Ogobara Saye, Amasagu Saye, Moni Saye, Eli Saye, Amaga Saye, Segu Saye, Amasom Saye, Amadigue Saye, Amatiguemu Saye, Enam Saye, Dogulu Saye, Atimé Saye, Apomi Saye, and their families. I also thank Atémélu Dolo and Ali Dolo in the village of Sangha; the villagers of Pélou, Kamba Sendé, in particular Dolu Wollogem, as well as the villagers of Ouroli Téné, Soroli, Tintam, Wedjé, Iréli, Amani, Pégue, Banani, Nombori, and Endé—in particular, Boubacar, Alpha Thiam and their families. I wish a heartfelt thanks to my friends in

Bankass: Nohoum Togo, Boureima Guindo, 'Dédé' Djibo and his family, Amadou Guindo, Commandant Ba and his family, Aminata, Madi, Alpha and Koumou, Dicoré Dia, Amadou Bocoum, and Alpha Lougé and his family in Kani. Finally, I would like to say a special thanks to Salif Sawadogo for his support and assistance while I was completing the writing of this book. Last but not least, I owe much to my family: Marie-Claire, Isabelle, Jacques, and Morris Douny; Patrice (1950–2013), Miette, and Renaud Jandin.

Laurence Douny
October 2014

Transcription Notes

All Dogon terms are expressed in the *tɔrɔ sɔ* dialect, otherwise stated and with variants when known. The extensive use of Dogon terms (in phonetic) is justified by the importance of the role of indigenous vocabularies, concepts, and the wealth of their semantic contents in the construction of anthropological knowledge. As shown by French ethnolinguist Geneviève Calame-Griaule (1928–2013), *tɔrɔ sɔ* dialect is embedded in particular sociocultural contexts from which cultural meanings about the Dogon world arise. Dogon terms, which I collected through my participation in people's daily practices, inform about their local worldviews.

For transcription purposes I have relied on the *tɔrɔ sɔ* dictionary written by Calame-Griaule (1968), Eric Jolly's lexicon (1995), and Denis Douyon's work (2010). The phonetic system I have used throughout is adapted from Calame-Griaule (1968) and Eric Jolly (1995, IV), which was also used by Polly Richards (2003, 8). Finally, village names and places are spelled as they are known today, and 'v' is transcribed by 'w'.

Accent Marks[1]

Acute accent (´) corresponds to rising tone and grave accent (`) to falling tone.

Vowels

Short vowels are i, e, ɛ, a, ɔ, o, u.
Long vowels are i:, e:, ɛ:, a:, ɔ:, o:, u:.
Nasal vowels are ĩ, ē, ẽ, ã, ɔ̃, õ, ũ.

Correspondence in English[2]

e = é as in fete [fête]
ɛ = è as in fair
g = g as in gate
j = dy as in jar
ŋ = ng as in singing

ɲ = ny as in new
o = as in low
ɔ = as in chop
u = as in tool

I translated all quotes expressed in French and found in academic literature. I used endnotes to indicate all Dogon quotes that appear either in French or in Dogon language in the interviews I conducted.

I Living in a Landscape of Scarcity: A Materiality Approach

Grounded in an ethnography of a Dogon village of the Bandiagara escarpment, this book explores the Dogon people's ways of living in a landscape of scarcity. The village of Tiréli (Figure 1.1) is located in the *tɔrɔ sɔ* area (for pronunciation guidelines see the transcription notes, p. 15) of the Dogon region, southwest of the Niger River bend, in Mali (West Africa). By taking a critical look at long-lived Western idealised views about the Dogon as a mythical, harmonious, and isolated people (Ciarcia 2003; Doquet 1999, 287) and by breaking away from the popular yet widely questioned Dogon cosmogony exposed by Griaule, I examine the 'micro'cosmology of the Dogon of Tiréli. I describe the ways in which people make themselves at home in a twenty-first-century world through processes of dwelling and building (Heidegger 1971 in Ingold 2000, 172–88) in a landscape of scarcity. From the perspective of the Dogon's daily collective embodied practices or taskscapes as 'an array of related activities' in the socially constructed landscape (Ingold 2000, 195), I investigate Dogon villagers' experiences of their harsh Sahelian environment and the strategies they have developed over time in order to cope with its vicissitudes. By bringing local perceptions of their landscape into a broader materiality argument, I examine the Dogon's structures and meanings system about their microcosmology of scarcity in the light of their material practices about various forms of containers. These containers range from the landscape that is symbolically bound through earth shrines to the bound village and its enclosed architectonic, which is held by the scree and includes the compounds and granaries, to the cooking pot, a bowl of food, and finally the body.

In a landscape of scarcity, the main concerns of the villagers, who are agriculturalists, are inevitably water, the fertility of earth, and millet. Water, earth,

Figure 1.1   The village of Tiréli is located on the Bandiagara escarpment scree in the *tɔrɔ sɔ* area.

and millet are living materials and substance, which constitute the materiality of their landscape-container and therefore stand at the core of their microcosmology. As I detail in Chapter 2, this cosmology is an epistemological framework for Dogon worldviews that encompass people's experiences, attitudes, beliefs, and knowledges—and thus meanings systems about their landscape of scarcity. I propose that as Dogon worldviews are shaped and reshaped through time and an agrarian cycle, they gather into a microcosmology 'in-the-making' (Barth 1987). I envisage this microcosmology through my participant observations of Dogon daily taskscapes, with a focus on body techniques and, in particular, the tactile experience of the materiality of containers and of their contents, such as earth, millet, and water. Within an anthropology of techniques I examine 'efficacious body actions on matter' (Lemonnier 1992, 4, following Leroi-Gourhan 1943, 1945) and thus the material but also the natural and symbolic transformative processes by which matter results. The daily and seasonal taskscapes that I frame within a sequence of 'makings' and 'doings' encompass the ritual and symbolic making of the territory, the settling of the village, the making of the home, the building and storing of crops in granaries, and finally food preparation, through bodily experiences of matter in a context of shortage and unpredictable weather. Finally, I suggest that Dogon microcosmology, being materialised in the landscape-container and the multiple forms of smaller containers it holds, reveals itself as a containment model and philosophy that bring an ontological security (Giddens 1991).

Containment defines itself through boundaries making and thus containing practices in a landscape of scarcity, in which it creates a sense of order and continuity of life. Life in a landscape of scarcity is in many ways loved and celebrated by Dogon people for what it brings them; yet it remains a daily struggle.

The Research Landscape

Scarcity impoverishes Dogon daily life in dramatic and multiple ways. Yet, in Western eyes, scarcity is often masked by the stunning vistas of the Bandiagara cliffs, a popular tourist destination, in part because in 1989 UNESCO classified about 150 km of the Bandiagara escarpment area as a worldwide cultural heritage site (Cissé 2003; van Beek 2005b, 68). Its selection is due to the originality and authenticity of its unique cultural landscape, which encompasses the impressive cave dwellings of the Tellem (eleventh–sixteenth centuries) (Bedaux 1972; Bedaux & Lange 1983) and the Dogon earthen architecture hosted by the cliffs. Dogon people form one of the most celebrated West African communities; they fascinate Westerners with their material culture, such as their eminent masks (Richards 2003).

Dogon were made world famous by ethnologist Marcel Griaule, who was a student of Marcel Mauss and the founder of French field ethnology (Jolly 2001, 149). For decades, Griaule and his interdisciplinary team extensively researched the region in a holistic and systematic way, and in particular the Dogon cosmogony (Chapter 2), which consists of a corpus of myths that recounts the creation of the world. This controversial account of Dogon metaphysics has been widely discussed in Francophone and Anglophone academic circles, following, in particular, the English translation of *Dieu d'Eau: Entretiens avec Ogotemmêli* (Griaule 1966). This Dogon cosmogony remains today a heritage left by ethnologists and revived by tourism as Ciarcia demonstrates (2003). Griaule's work has certainly largely contributed to the commodification of Dogon cultures and, in particular, that of the Bandiagara escarpment, a highly exploited tourist spot that received between 20,000 and 80,000 visitors in 2004 (Bedaux & van der Waals 2004, 12).

The core of this research took place in this extensively studied and touristy *tɔrɔ sɔ* area of the cliffs, with a focus on the village of Tiréli (14° 23′ 0″ North, 3° 21′ 0″ West) (Figure 1.2). This village is located in the Sangha commune, in the administrative district of Bandiagara (Cercle), where I lived for 17 months with a host family in the quarter of Teri-Ku Dama, situated at the top of the scree (Douny 2007), while conducting research for my Ph.D. dissertation and which I have since visited on many occasions. The *tɔrɔ sɔ* area is named in relation to the language *tɔrɔ sɔ*,[1] which is mainly spoken from the areas of

Figure 1.2 The Dogon region and ɔɔɔ ɔɔ linguistic area (map designed by Nadia Khalaf)

Yendouma to Idiéli located alongside the cliffs. This language, which includes six dialects, signifies 'the language of those who slid down'—referring to dwellings set up on the escarpment scree. Calame-Griaule explains that the Dogon of the Séno Gondo plain call *tɔrɔ sɔ* speakers' areas *bomu*[2]—'the edge of the cliffs' (Calame-Griaule 1955, 65). The escarpment that characterises the *tɔrɔ sɔ* area appears as a sandstone chain that crosses the fifth region of Mali (Mopti) from southwest to northeast. The cliffs, which are over 300 km long and 777 m high in Bamba (northeast), stretch from the province of Kossi in Burkina Faso to the Grandamia massif, comprising Hombori mounts and Hombori Tondo, which reaches a height of 1,150 m (Brasseur 1968, 18). The Dogon region is characterised by two contiguous and distinct geological zones: an arid rocky plateau that is discontinued by cracks that host water holes around which gardens extend, and the sandy plain called Séno (Gondo and Mango), which is strewn with thorny shrubs and bushes trees; the presence of trees beyond villages space is rare. For the Dogon of the cliffs the most important features of this landscape are the land, which is cultivated to a maximum, and the cliffs, which retain rainwater throughout the dry season and which also provided natural hideouts at times of war and slavery raids.

The Dogon landscape constitutes the harsh ground of local daily routines that men and women have embodied through relentless hard, communal, and socially organised labour, always being alert to weather conditions; thus life is a constant struggle owing to long-term environmental and human challenges. In the Dogon region, daily and embodied taskscapes (Ingold 2000, 154) as techniques (Sigaut 2002) predominantly collective are seen as part of a heritage. These taskscapes are ritualised according to a protocol called *atɛmu* (the ancestors' laws) and ruled by the Dogon's traditional system of beliefs, or animism, called *ɔmɔlɔ*. These two, which I define as a social memory (McIntosh, Tainter, & Keech McIntosh 2002), are however, challenged by practical worldviews that Dogon villagers acquire from their systematic observations and embodied experiences of their landscape and that arise from new situations and events. Over the long term, the Dogon experiences and traditional knowledge enable the people to cope with the uncertainty of the place and so to adapt to and master the harsh environment.

The Dogon region is plagued historically by drought, famines, and localised floods that inhibit the growing of crops and that inevitably lead to humanitarian crises. Hence, the Dogon semi-arid Sahelian landscape generates severe needs for water, fertile soils, and food. It also causes humanitarian and environmental concerns about infant malnutrition, malaria, epidemic outbreaks such as cholera, and impoverishment of the soil and thus of crop production, all in a context of demographic pressure (in addition, premature rains favour locust infestations). Dogon people, who are exceedingly dependent on the natural environment, constantly face rain shortfalls and delays with immense courage and tenacity. Since 2001, when I started doing research in this region,

I have witnessed repeated food shortages caused by droughts and flash floods that resulted in crop failure in many places (Chapters 6, 9, and 10). These food shortages were more difficult for certain families than for others—for instance, than for those who make money through small trade business alongside millet cultivation or for families that possess cattle to be sold to buy foodstuff in times of need.

In the Dogon region and throughout the Sahel (de Bruijn, van Beek, & van Dijk 2005; Gonzalez 2001), the continual scarcity of natural resources is worsened by human impact, causing impoverishment of soils, overexploitation of timber/shrub resources as fire wood, and increasing need for arable land. In addition, the native fauna has substantially decreased. The Malian government and NGO aids supplying farm inputs, including chemical fertilisers and pesticides, have proved to be insufficient owing to the complexity and size of the problem (Mamadou Diakité, Sahel Eco, pers. com.). In 2012 the situation of scarcity has dramatically worsened in the Dogon region because of the drought and the Malian political crisis, initiated by conflicts among Touareg rebels and separatists, Islamists groups, and the Malian army in the north. The Dogon of the Séno plain and of the Douentza area have been subjected to exploitation and violence perpetuated by these various armed groups, including cattle rustling, the looting and destruction of granaries and of cultural heritage, the robbery of local shops and market stalls, assaults on women, and the killing of traders. Finally, since 2011, the economy of the Dogon region and the cliffs area, such as in the village of Tiréli, has dramatically suffered from the decline of tourism caused by security issues, in particular the kidnapping of Westerners in Mali and neighbouring Niger.

The Landscape of Scarcity: An Overview of Climate and Historical Events

Food-crisis records[3] date back to the seventeenth century (Gado 1993, 27). Gado (1993, 67–68, 178–79) provides accounts of twentieth-century famines that ravaged the Niger River bend and that were marked by a high death toll and children being sold for a few cowrie shells. During the first half of that century, and in particular in the northeast Dogon region, successive periods of famine were caused by droughts and floods (Cazes 1993, 27; Gallais 1975, 103–05, 109, 111; also in Bouju 1984, 240). During the second half, Cazes describes two periods of drought, in 1973 and 1983–1984 (Cazes 1993, 28). From his long-term experience of the Dogon region and of the 1982 famine events, van Beek describes the Dogon notion of scarcity as 'normalcy' that is 'the sudden arrival of the rain and the unexpected aftermath' (van Beek 2005a, 41). 'Scarcity' is expressed by the Dogon as *naun*, a term that describes the struggle or misfortune in one's life triggered by drought, *ánrā mà* ('the dry rain').

Drought causes the absence of millet (hunger, or *giyɛ*) and of material means, since millet as the ultimate Dogon wealth can always be sold at high price.

Such dramatic events add to the tumultuous history[4] of the Dogon region, which materialises in the landscape. The cliffs and the scree that host the Dogon villages function as a natural defensive geomorphologic structure (Brasseur 1968, 18; Huet 1994) that in the past, in the north of the Dogon region (Hombori, Douentza), somewhat protected its inhabitants against slave raiders—led by the Songhay under Sonni Ali Ber in the fifteenth century (Gallais 1975, 142) and then under the reign of the Askia in the sixteenth century (Cissoko 1985, 219). From end of the fifteenth century to the sixteenth century, the Nakomse (Moose/Mossi) twice attempted to occupy the Séno Gondo plain, forcing the Dogon to retreat to the cliffs (Izard 1985a, 21–22, 1985b, 27–28). Izard writes that, in the second half of the eighteenth century, King Naaba Kango of the Yatenga seized the areas of Yoro and Dinangourou, on the Burkina/Mali border (Izard 1985a, 96–97). As Martinelli points out, the Dogon Guru of the plain (the actual Koro district) are also integrated into the Kingdom of the Yatenga and have become part of the Moose political space (Martinelli 1995, 385; see also Huet 1994, 42–43, 167 about Moose invasions). In the nineteenth century, the Macina Empire (1818–1853) and then the Tokolor Empire of Bandiagara (1848–1890) took control of the Dogon region and enslaved and forced the Dogon to convert to Islam (Gallais 1975, 98, 111, 118). However, the Dogon of the Bandiagara cliffs resisted Islamic conversion. From 1893 until 1960, the Dogon region was under French colonial rule and Dogon people were forced to pay heavy taxes.

During these periods of invasion Dogon inhabitants could escape enemies by using hideouts in the cracks of the cliffs and barely adequate paths that are still used today by locals and tourists and that entail strenuous climbing. In some places, these paths are interconnected by forklike wooden ladders, which enable progress to the top of the rocky plateau, where the Dogon could find refuge in underground shelters. These famous ladders could be easily removed to stop the invaders' advancement.

Over time, many trails were created by repeated passages of people, such as invaders on horseback, travellers on foot, transhumance, carts, motorcycles, 4×4 tourist vehicles, and caravans. For instance, the well-known pathways called *Bella ódiu* going through Douentza and running parallel to the cliffs via Madougou down to Koro have been used for centuries during the dry season by the Bellah of the north, who come to the Dogon region to buy cereals and to sell or trade salt (for example, salt of Taoudenni, north of Timbuktu). In 2012 these trails were rematerialised by the repeated passage of Islamists fighters who seized the key town of Douentza and attempted to move farther south in the Séno plain. In 2013 they were followed by convoys of the MINUSMA (United Nations Multidimensional Integrated Stabilization Mission in Mali) troops. Thus the Dogon landscape of scarcity engenders a particular dynamic out of the perpetual flow of people across the land and within daily, historical, and recurring climate events, all of which generate a sense of continuity and discontinuity of life.

The Materiality of the Dogon Landscape

As I have described, the Dogon landscape stands as 'both a medium for and the outcome of action and previous histories' (Tilley 1994, 23). Taking on Ingold's definition of materiality[5] as the ' "brute" materiality of the world' and 'the ways this world is appropriated in human projects' (Ingold 2012, 439), I propose that the materiality of the Dogon landscape consists of the many ways by which its 'physicality' is shaped and reshaped by human agency and climate events.

As Ingold (2007, 2012) rightly points out, *materiality* should also include the plurality of materials that constitute the fabric of the world and that he characterises as 'matter considered in respect of its occurrence in processes of flow and transformation' (Ingold 2012, 439). Thus materiality as ensemble (Coupaye & Douny 2009, 24; Knappett 2012, 195–96) implies both social and material relations and transformative processes (Knappett 2012, 188–92). It is within this perspective that I consider the materiality of the Dogon landscape. I suggest that important to our understanding of Dogon worldviews is the Dogon people's perception and use of culturally significant materials, substances, and thus matter that constitute their landscape and on which the Dogon act in the course of their daily and ritually embodied activities in the landscape—that is, through its 'making and doing' (Chapter 2). I focus in particular on two significant materials, earth and millet, and one substance, water, which, I argue, stand at the core of Dogon microcosmology. First, water—and more specifically the rains in combination with other atmospheric events such as the winds—is obviously central to life. Second, the earth that hosts life and thus millet are also employed to build compounds and shrines. Third, as a staple crop, millet is cooked as daily food and used as libations on shrines, and remnants of the spikes and stalks are turned into a field fertiliser (Chapter 8).

To clarify, in my analysis the concept of materiality in relation to the Dogon landscape of Tiréli as a humanised container embraces four interrelated dimensions: (1) materials and substance as matter constituting the landscape; (2) symbolic and physical transformations of the landscape and of its matter into container forms by human actions and by the weather; (3) webs of relations between people and the natural and spiritual world; and (4) meanings that materialise in the landscape as a result of these transformations and relations. Consequently, the changing materiality of the Dogon landscape that unites these four aspects constitutes the ontology of their cultural landscape.

Dwelling and Building Perspectives Defined

Through an examination of the materiality of Tiréli's landscape of scarcity (matter, transformations, relations, and meanings) and the multiple container forms that it holds, I attempt to gain insights into the Dogon microcosmology; that is to say, I explore some of the ways in which Dogon people collectively engage with their landscape, by acting on it (Ingold 2000; Tilley 1994) and thus by continuously reshaping its materiality through dwelling and building (Heidegger 1971 in Ingold 2000, 172–88). From this perspective I investigate Dogon ways of living, making themselves at home in a landscape of scarcity. In *tɔrɔ sɔ* language, these concepts reveal as *adurɔn woyoji* (*wohyi*), 'inhabiting the world' *adurɔ* [*adunɔ*][6] referring to nature or the world), in the same way as inhabiting a house (*gínu woyoji*).

I employ the notion of dwelling in the sense of the making of 'a small chosen world of our own' through daily life experiences and the sharing of common values (Norberg-Schulz 1985, 7). The aspect of dwelling in the Dogon landscape that I examine concerns the social and therefore symbolic construction of the landscape and in particular that of the territory of the village of Tiréli. Following Zedeño's definition, which emphasises 'human-nature interactions', I propose the Dogon territory as a (semi-)domesticated space that is 'as object aggregate (land + natural resource + human modifications)' (Zedeño 2008, 211) and that is circumscribed by recognised boundaries. Therefore, territories are socially, politically, and symbolically (Bouju 1995a; Teme 1997; Vincent 1995) constructed and thus are bounded spatial entities within the landscape. As I demonstrate in Chapter 3, the Tiréli territory's inside and outside spaces are symbolically bounded by a system of earth shrines through which people appropriated and fixed the place and that convey a sense of ontological security. While its inside, or village (built environment), constitutes the space of the living, its outside, which corresponds to the cultivated bush, forms 'a life-giving reservoir' (van Beek & Banga 1992) from which Dogon people extract their daily resources and on which they intimately depend. Hence, by using the notion of territory, I emphasise, on the one hand, the sociocultural construction and control of parts of the Dogon landscape and of their resources and, on the other hand, the creation of an ontological security through symbolic boundaries.

Dwelling implies both the experience of the place and the material action taken on the landscape through architecture. In Chapters 5 and 7, I explore the building process as an act of residing and nesting by drawing an analysis of the Dogon village and of compounds seen as the nexus of daily agencies. By following Tilley, I propose that the Dogon built environment constitutes 'an attempt to create and to bound space. It creates an inside, and outside, a way around, a channel for movement' (Tilley 1994, 17). Being invested with the body (Blier 1987; Tilley 1994), Dogon architecture forms an absolute, finite, and fragmented entity that is constitutive of places and filled up with objects. It stands as 'a moulding of the landscape and the expression of a cultural attitude towards it' (Johnson 1994, 170). Dogon architectural space acquires its meaning from the activities and objects that it contains and the particular network or shared agencies of its occupiers (Lane 1987). Consequently, by focusing on various forms of container technologies, such as the Dogon built environment, I seek to understand the production of daily worldviews from a 'lived world' (Weiss 1996, 5) and therefore as a 'lived' landscape or an active ground that is appropriated, bounded, mapped out, transformed, and consumed through praxis.

Containers Matter: Water, Earth, and Millet

The Dogon landscape is made of living, life-bearing, and thus active materials and substances that are brought together into new matter through transformative processes and techniques, which, to follow Mauss (1936) and Leroi-Gourhan (1943), concern 'efficacious actions upon matter' within a making process through which matter is therefore physically and socially formed. This matter is then acted on and shaped into various forms of containers and contents. Materials and substances are extracted from the landscape to be stored, processed, and thus transformed into new forms of matter as life sustenance. From this perspective, I define substances as living and active liquids that enable natural, chemical, and symbolic processes to occur. For instance, water is a living substance that revives matter as it enables the fermentation of earth and organic matters (adobe) that are used in house making, in composting, and as millet that is brewed and cooked. Hence, wet mud, or adobe, and millet beer and porridge used as libation and consumed as food are material aggregates made of living elements that possess properties and efficacy.

As I describe in Chapter 3, the Dogon ɔmɔlɔ animist system sees people, animals, and things as bearing a reactive vital force or energy called ɲama (ɲaman, ɲawan). As it flows through the organism of things and beings, ɲama ensures their equilibrium. The concept of ɲama has been contested elsewhere (see Ciarcia 2003, 33–35 about Griaule's definition and use of the term; van Beek 1991, 148); however, in my view, this complex and multifaceted concept exists throughout the tɔrɔ sɔ region and beyond (Jolly 2004, 193), where this inherent living and active force is said to transcend people, animals, things, and parts of the landscape—for example, sacred places and shrines, perhaps a water course or a tree (Chapter 3). Thus ɲama may be seen as the landscape's essence, as being inherent to its materiality. The use of the concept is certainly restricted to the context of magico-religious knowledge curated by Dogon ritual experts such as blacksmiths, religious and traditional leaders, and hunters. In domestic contexts, people describe millet, water, and earth matter used in the preparation of food, condiments, drinks, building materials, manure, and so on as living and active (*kine dɔrɔgɔ*). In other words, fermented food, drinks, earth, and manure possess a vital force (*paɲà niɲi*) that revitalises and strengthens the body, the granary, the fields, and the crops. The properties that they attribute to matter may be part of the complex definition of *ɲama* or of a set of vital forces.

Water,[7] millet, and earth are therefore essential living and active materials and substances that stand at the core of the Dogon people's every-day and ritual life and thus of their microcosmology. In this respect, Bouju (1984) and Jolly (2004) have shown the importance of millet in the Dogon society as the main constituent of the sustenance of daily life. These authors demonstrate that millet binds social and spiritual life and acts as a factor of social cohesion. The production of millet rules domestic economies, and it structures both Dogon social relations and aspects of their social organisation (Bouju 1984).

Millet also plays a role in the location and production of the built space— for instance, in the design of storage space and facilities dedicated to its conservation. Additionally, millet as well as water generate temporalities based on agrarian cycles, which intrinsically rely on the rain and millet cultivation. Furthermore, in an animist view, they determine a ritual calendar marked by sacrifices devoted to God *Áma*, in return for sufficient rain and a successful millet harvest. Millet and water bridge the human and natural life cycles and the visible and invisible world as well as produce a space-time continuum. They both create particular ways of thinking, making, doing, and living in a harsh environment. Within a precarious context of unpredictable rains and drought, water and millet remain representative of a fundamental survival concern.

As a complementary element to millet and water, earth as a 'viable' force (Prussin 1999, 425) is also a fundamental matter that ensures the continuity of life in the Dogon, since it hosts the millet seeds. However, the impoverishment of the soil, mainly due to intensive cultivation of the land in tandem with a lack of fertiliser (and of rain), constitutes another major preoccupation, because fertile soil is crucial to human life and survival. In addition, clay, wet mud, and silt intervene according to their properties and qualities in the manufacturing of pots, granaries, wall coverings, house bricks, altars, and shrines. Therefore, earth, as the main component of these domestic containers and receptacles and in the manner of a folded surface similar to a 'skin envelope', forms a system of material interfaces between people and the environment. As I explain shortly, Dogon earth containers mediate and interrelate the surrounding natural environment to the individual's self and the society, through their own materiality, through people's praxis of these containing forms, and finally through the material and substantial content, such as millet and water, that they preserve.

In summary, Dogon worldviews forming a microcosmology are built on the relationships between individuals and the landscape substances and materials (water, earth, and millet) through their daily and ritual practice, as a means of ensuring the continuity of life in a scarce environment.

Living Matter and Transformative Processes

Central to the processing and transformation of millet and earth matter is fermentation. This biochemical and symbolic transformative process, which requires specific techniques, is common in the daily life of the Tiréli Dogon. For instance, it intervenes in the making of manure or compost used to fertilise the fields and gardens (Chapter 8) and in the preparation of beer and condiments that result from the fermentation of seeds, which are used in that form as medicine. As Steinkraus notes (1996, 3–4), fermentation has many benefits, since it reduces cooking time and fuel requirements, it preserves food and enriches it with protein, essential vitamins, and acids, and, finally, it adds flavour and texture (for example, strong and slimy; Chapter 11). Fermentation is produced by water and potash, which the Dogon obtain from ashes or domestic animal dung. Potash resulting from the filtering of millet-straw ashes is used mainly in food preparation; animal dung is used in building work.

As I explain in Chapter 9, wet-mud (adobe) is produced through the fermentation of mud mixed with straw and animal dung, which increase the strength of the building. The smell of fermentation, such as from rotting seeds, reminds one of death (Calame-Griaule 1996, 81, 85 note 2), yet it is also perceived as a living process made possible because of water. Yet potash—for instance, donkey dung—also plays a central role in preparing adobe, and potash made with millet-straw ashes is used to prepare condiments. Natural potash activates the fermentation process, strengthens the matter, and enhances the taste of food.

In the Dogon region, fermentation is conceptualised as a life cycle that symbolically relates to fertility (*bɔdɔ* ['to ferment'] and *ɔmɔgu* ['to rot'] mean 'to bring something back to life'). As Jolly explains, brewing millet beer enfolds as in a birth-life-death-resurrection cycle. Similarly, it is perceived as a form of gestation, regurgitation, and digestion as metaphors of birth found in oral literature (Jolly 2004, 176–77). In its malting stage grain germinates and is brought back to life by being watered. The green malt is left to dry in bright sun for a couple of days (kilning stage) and then is ground in a technique described as 'destruction' (the grain dies). The fermentation stage that enables millet to turn into beer and thus alcohol through the use of potash and millet bran symbolises the resurrection of millet, and the fizziness of beer is seen as a sign of life (Jolly 2004, 176). For the Dogon, fermentation is a living process that, as said, strengthens building matter, energises the soil, and heals the body. It is a process of transforming substances and materials into a new matter that at the end of the process becomes stronger, tastier, richer, and overall alive. Hence fermentation is a means of bringing things back to life, because it denies its linear temporality and defies death. If life is reinstated or recovered in many aspects of daily and ritual life, it is also contained as a means of flourishing and being protected.

The Landscape-Container: Material Practice and Epistemologies

Materials, substances, and matter of the landscape that serve to make container forms are also temporally retained and stored in these multiple forms of containers. In my ethnography, containers stand as both material forms and metaphors about the landscape and the multiple container forms it holds. First, containers are defined as material practice—that is, the Dogon's embodied practice about material forms and from which implicit meanings are revealed. In other words, material practice about Dogon ways of 'making' and 'doing' (Douny 2007; Naji & Douny 2009) container forms are ritualised by Dogon *atɛmu*—the ancestors' protocol that rules customs and practices (*dɔgɔ sɔ*), but also techniques and knowledges. Second, containers are material epistemologies that help us to think about Dogon ways of living in a landscape of scarcity. I argue that Dogon containers objectify cosmological principles in their own materiality as well as in their material and ideological content. In other words, through their daily making and uses of containers, Dogon villagers dwell in the landscape and make themselves at home in a landscape container.

Containers Are Good to Work with

In the manner of a 'life-giving reservoir' (van Beek & Banga 1992), the bounded landscape holds the main resources that the Dogon of Tiréli consume in their everyday lives. On a different scale, the built compound features made of earth, stone, and wood that are extracted from the surrounding landscape shelter people, resources, objects, and other forms of containers. For instance, gendered mud granaries, which I describe in Chapter 10, are used to store and to preserve food resources as well as personal belongings, including ancestor shrines, which also fit within the category of receptacles. These are solid and inverted receptacles that receive sacrificial substances in exchange for God's benefits.

As portable work tools, domestic containers are traditionally found in the form of calabashes, clay pots, baskets, wooden mortars, and carved bowls. Containers as customary material forms assist men and, mainly, women in their routine activities. Acting as symbols of intensive and straitened exertion as well as of the sustenance of life, containers assume the role of transporting goods, processing matter, facilitating consumption of meals and drinks, and storing water and food supplies. As the Dogon people frequently stated: 'without them we cannot work.' Consequently, Dogon containers form a self-contained system that enfolds multiple scaled material forms; they assist and protect men and women in their daily life. However, I suggest that containers also define through their content. People, things, matter, and substances such as earth, millet, water, and domestic waste enable us to understand the ways Dogon people live within and make their cultural landscape. Containers' varied content connects the multiple forms of containers and therefore people's lives.

Containers Are Good to Think with

Containers not only concern material forms and their content but also stand as material metaphors (Tilley 1999). In fact, Ogotemmêli's basket in Griaule's *Dieu d'eau* (1965) is grasped as an object to explain his view on the world (on a macro scale). The basket as a mnemonic device is in the old Dogon philosopher's narrative a material metaphor. From this perspective, I suggest that containers and their material practice help to uncover aspects of Dogon reality and thought. Thus, containers as material metaphors serve as an active ground for Dogon agency. In other words, material forms of containers do not really matter so much as the idea of the container as a means for people to contain substances, matters, people, activities, and ideas. Indeed, the clay pots of deceased women are left to disintegrate on the cemetery path; families leave their mortars in the habitation when they move out; old calabashes and *baɲá* wooden and clay pots are sold to tourists for cash; and when a granary is destroyed by weather, it will not be renovated if it is no longer useful, that is, practical or meaningful. Here containers as material forms are not cared for in the long term as cultural heritage, because they do not relate to an immediate use. In other words, containers in the Dogon landscape are not part of a tradition that is perpetuated by necessity, such as sacrificing.

In summary, Dogon containers, such as the bounded landscapes, the compound, granaries, plates, food, and the body, as material metaphors objectify worldviews that encompass people's daily practice and experiences of their world. Containers also stand as material and symbolic interfaces between the natural environment and people that enable people to act in their own world as well as to think about it. As they create an inside/outside dialectic (Warnier 2006) with the world, containers as material interfaces are also developed and built against the outside world as a means for people to interact with it and to protect the inside contents. Yet containers always remain porous—in the sense that things always get in and out of the containers, against people's will.

Finally, along with ideas of sociocultural transformative processes about materials and materiality, I suggest that Dogon microcosmology and so *tɔrɔ sɔ* identity are a product of transcultural processes that transcend regional distributions. That is to say, they meet the specifics of the transmission of technical skill and implicit knowledges that have long-term historical duration in West Africa. In other words, I propose that techniques and knowledges forming

Dogon microcosmology are found in a Mande or broader West African symbolic reservoir that is 'a long-held reservoir of symbols, myths and beliefs . . . [which] different subgroups of a society dip into . . . in order to extract, craft and visually display a legitimating tradition to serve their own sectional interests (McIntosh 1989, 77). In my view, the symbolic reservoir contains the cultural forms common to the various communities known today as Dogon and other West African or Mande groups. Therefore, this deep symbolic reservoir supplies Dogon microcosmologies (Chapter 2).

The Materiality of Containers: Dogon Microcosmology as Containment

In this book I attempt to develop an interpretative framework for understanding Dogon dwelling and thus living from the perspective of a philosophy of containment, which I have identified in Dogon worldviews and practices. The concept of containment is found in Warnier's 'king-pot' (Warnier 2006, 188–91, 2007, 210). In his study of the politics of governmentalities in the Cameroon Grassfields, the author develops a socio-anthropology of containment that highlights the historical and political events that shape people's subjectivity and ways of living. Warnier shows how through history the Grassfields kingdoms have forged forms of containment that are grounded in various interrelated material forms of container that are scaled, made of openings, and the contents of which transit between them. Warnier suggests that containment is a tool developed through history by the Mankon's sacred kings as a means to ensure the control and social reproduction of his kingdom.

Inspired by Warnier's work, my notion of containment is socially constructed and historically situated. Containment serves as a model that frames Dogon's microcosmology, which describes indigenous ways of making the Dogon people at home in a landscape of scarcity, which I have, as described earlier, conceptualised as a container that holds multiple material forms of scaled containers. Dogon's containment model develops through their practices of containment, which encompass their ritual and daily embodied makings and doings of material and symbolic containers that are stacked or self-contained in a successive and contiguous way. In other words, containment materialises through, first, the making of the social, political, and symbolic boundaries of the territory and of domestic space and, second, the building of a female granary—both for protection purposes. The containment model reveals itself through the gathering of living matter such as millet, water, and earth within these multiple bounded spaces and containers forms.

Containment occurs through people's ritual and embodied practices within daily and seasonal temporalities as well as through episodes of drought, famines, and wars that recur over time in different ways but with similar patterns and devastating effects. Therefore, the bounded landscape, cyclical temporalities, and recurring significant events characterise the Dogon of Tiréli's framing landscape of scarcity in which their microcosmology 'in-the-making' objectifies in its materiality through Dogon agencies.

Containment Practices as an Ontological Security

Containment as material practices about container forms is equally a protective device designed on the basis of the Dogon's individual and collective experiences of scarcity and the strategies they developed to cope with it over time. Therefore, containment is a mean by which an ontological security is achieved. In Giddens' terms, an ontological security refers to 'a sense of continuity and order in events, including those not directly within the perceptual environment of the individual' (Giddens 1991, 243).

From this perspective, containment as Dogon ways of living in a landscape container of scarcity consists of a unifying principle that creates a sense of cohesion, unity, and solidarity among Dogon villagers through their shared embodied knowledge, stemming from their taskscapes and the gathering and curation of the resources of the landscape and of the village's land shrines. Containment as a model is perpetuated through routine and seasonal containment practices through which Dogon villagers seek stability. In that sense, containment is a fixing, an ordering of Dogon's world, to which they attribute meaning through their continuous experiences of container forms as so as to feel secure or at home in their landscape of scarcity. Furthermore, containment as a form of fragmentation of the world through scaled boundaries is a means by which the land, people, and resources can be better controlled and curated. In this way, the act of containing conveys a sense of stability as it gives a sense of being in control. Protecting space, places, things, and bodies is a means for the Dogon to feel reassured and prepared when events of the past are revisited, as they always are, in their thinking.

The Spatial and Temporal Dimensions of Containment

The first aspect of containment that I explore is that of domestic forms of containers as scaled boundary-making devices that create particular locales. The emphasis here is on the reversible inside/outside spatial and temporal dialectics (Warnier 2006) that are created out of embodied praxis and thus movement within these contiguous container boundaries. The symbolic and political boundaries of Tiréli's territory are created by land shrines that circumscribe the village's territory, legitimise villagers' ownership of the land, and mark the field borders. In addition, they protect the inside/outside of the village from multiple epidemics, invaders, and witchcraft (Chapter 3). Similarly, the compound's walls, and in particular their openings, are protected by magic (Chapter 6); so is the female granary (Chapter 7). The social boundaries of the village increasingly expand owing to demographic pressure and the search for living space near water resources and communication ways (Chapter 5). Finally, the built-features openings act as control behaviour—such as maintaining privacy and the secrecy of food resources—to avoid thievery and psychological collapse.

Second, containment involves a process of gathering water, earth, and millet resources. It refers to the way that these materials and substances that sustain life as well as the knowledges and things associated with them (such as domestic waste as a by-product of activity) (Chapter 8) are gathered mostly in collective tasks around the body and through containers as active agents. It shows how the living matter of the landscape is retained inside domestic boundaries, in land shrines, and in built features such as female granaries (Chapters 9 and 10). Last, a gathering process also concerns bringing the villagers into unity and thus to the way in which Dogon men and women relate to each other as well as to the outside 'other' through embodied praxis of land shrines, gendered granaries, and through hard collective, coordinated, and socially organised labour.

Third, the temporal dimension of containment is cyclical, whereas space is seen as an expansion. This dimension is articulated by environmental and human rhythms and temporalities that imply segmented daily human tasks of a relative *durée*, synchronised and repeated day after day with the same constancy and therefore aggregated into cycles. These tasks are coordinated by the seasons and therefore the life cycle of the fields, which in a similar view symbolically refers to human life cycles. Also, droughts, famines and epidemics, jihads, wars and political conflicts with the neighbouring villages, colonialism, and more recently the Malian crisis are historical events that have changed the Dogon practice of containment by creating a ontological insecurity and thus a climax of uncertainty.

I suggest that the Dogon landscape's symbolic, political, and social boundaries are fixed but porous; that is to say, certain things get inside the boundaries at certain times that the Dogon may expel through ritual practice or that they retain, appropriate, adapt, or transform to make them their own (Bayart 2005, 71) as a consequence of modernity. The Dogon systematically remake the symbolic boundaries of the territory, of the village, and of the home, which they rebuild according to new situations and which may, however, be disrupted or failed.

Organisation of the Book

This book uses a 'containing metaphor' structure developed from the topic and content of my research. The system of containers I develop in the narrative is reflected in the organisation of the different chapters. In the introductory chapters, 1 and 2, I examine the ethnographic background of the

Dogon microcosmology, my methodology, and the concept of containment; the subsequent nine chapters are structured within two containment scales. Chapters 3, 4, and 5 concern the cultural and symbolic construction of bounded territory as a container. Chapters 7, 8, 9, 10, and 11 concern Dogon life within the home or compound.

Chapter 6 is the articulation of the book; it deals with the weather that transcends the entire landscape, and it focuses on the rain as the substance of the landscape that stands at the core of the Dogon cosmology and therefore at the core of this book. Chapter 3, which deals with the Dogon space divisions of the bounded territory, acts as a container for Chapters 4 and 5, which concern, respectively, the inside and the outside of the village. In the same vein, Chapter 7, which introduces the Dogon compound, provides containment for Chapter 8, on domestic waste, Chapters 9 and 10, on the making and doing of granaries, and Chapter 11, about the scarcity of food on a plate and the hungry body. In Chapter 12, I conclude with some cosmological matters concerning the Dogon's philosophy of containment.

2 'Making and Doing' Dogon Microcosmology: Some Ethnographic, Methodological, and Conceptual Background

The Dogon region of Mali covers some 55,000 km² and comprises a cluster of 700 patrilineal villages with a population of over 250,000 (Bedaux & van der Waals 2004, 7). The villagers of Tiréli, whose family name is Saye (*Say*) and may today number about 1,500, rely on a self-subsistence economy. Dogon men and women grow millet, the staple crop, and various subsidiary cereals, such as sorghum (Chapter 5). In addition women grow pulses, hibiscus, and groundnuts, from May to November. Onions, which were introduced during colonial times as a cash crop, are grown from December to March to be mainly sold in town. In Tiréli, Catholicism and Animism, the original worldview system (*ɔmɔlɔ*; Chapter 3) are the main religions practised, with Islam followed to a much lesser extent. The oldest man of the village is the highest authority of Tiréli (*ámiru*), and the quarter of Teri-Ku Dama is ruled by the council of elders (*àna kɔse*). They deal with the social and political issues of the quarter and of the village; they also run ritual ceremonies, set up the agrarian calendar, administer the mask society, and forecast the weather.

Dogon's Material Identity:
Cultural Unity through Diversity

As van Beek points out, the outlines of the Dogon region were drawn in colonial times—that is, at 'both a period of expansion and closure of Dogon territory' (van Beek 2005a, 65). Colonial boundaries prevented the Dogon from setting farther down in the plain, and during the colonial period the Dogon were also discovered. Beyond accounts written by French colonial adminis-trators (Arnaud 1921; Desplagnes 1907), the Dogon gained significant fame owing to the holistic work of the French ethnologist Marcel Griaule and his followers as well as the efforts of the Dakar-Djibouti Mission (1931–1933) led by Griaule. However, Griaule's influential literary enterprise resulted in establishing the Dogon as an immutable society and overall as an ethno-graphic model of purity and authenticity (as demonstrated by Doquet 1999, 2002). Since Griaule's time, the Dogon have enjoyed great popularity thanks to UNESCO, Western scholars' publications, museum exhibitions, and their exposure to worldwide media, tourism, and multiple websites. Yet, the Western idealised view is also nurtured by the Dogon themselves in tourist areas as well as by Dogon traditionalists. In this regard, since 1992, the NGO *Ginna Dogon* seeks the protection and promotion of Dogon culture and ancestral traditions, or *atɛmu* ('tradition' or 'law'), and it recognises the Dogon's Mande origin. *Ginna Dogon* has been seen elsewhere as a political and economic strategy to legitimise the practices of the Dogon elite's (Bouju 1995c, 95–117). All these factors have clearly contributed to the construction and consolidation of Dogon as a cultural unity.

However, Dogon ethnicity can be said to be an ongoing endogenous politi-cal, social, and historical construct (Bouju 1995b, 2003). Mayor, Huysecom, Gallay, Rasse, Ballouche (2005), Bedaux (1988), Bouju (1995b), Martinelli (1995), Holder (2001), and Jolly (2004), to name but a few Dogon specialists, have challenged Dogon cultural homogeneity and Griaule's work by showing the complexity of Dogon ethnicity that results from a long cultural mixing with nearby ethnic communities—notably, through war and intermarriages (see Appendices A and D).

Sense of 'Dogonness' and Mande Belonging

Rather than being an isolated and self-contained ethnic community forming a unified culture, Dogon communities exhibit many internal cultural diversi-ties. Yet, a certain Dogon 'ritual' unity is undeniable, as Jolly observed. The same Dogon cults are performed throughout the area of the cliffs, across the multiple linguistic areas (Jolly 1995, 74). This can also be observed with mas-querades (Richards 2003). In addition, a sense of unity and of 'Dogonness' is claimed in many parts of the region; Dogon people acknowledge a common origin that appears as a 'fixing' of identity (Rowlands 2003) and that they locate in the Mande[1] (in the southwest of Bamako, in the heart of the Mali Empire [thirteenth–fifteenth centuries C.E.] that is called the 'fruit of the per-son') (see Appendix B). This origin remains unquestioned by the Dogon in the most touristified and over-researched places where I worked and collected information. It is maintained through oral tradition, cultural ceremonies, and at national festivals, such as *Ginna Dogon*. This Mande identity, which the Dogon say is shared with other communities, such as the Marka-Dafing, Peul

(Fulani), and Bambara and that is recalled by oral history, often conveys the need for knowing one's origin and past, for a sense of belonging and overall of national unity in a highly culturally diverse country.

The recurring stories about Dogon settlements in the Bandigara cliffs and their spread in the various parts of the region that would have occurred through multiple migration waves may aim at legitimising Dogon occupation of the land (Appendix B). In addition, they may help to reaffirm networks of solidarity with neighbouring communities and may have a peace-making function, in particular in regard to issues about the land. Although Mande origin is widely claimed by the Dogon people, origins other than Mande should be taken into account (Mayor et al. 2005, 31).

Positioning: Dogon Shared Material Identity, Symbolic Reservoir, and Heritage

In the village of Tiréli[2] as well as across the Dogon region, where I have been conducting research since 2001, people self-identify as Dogon and Mande while they express their unity in terms of a common heritage called *atɛmu*. Yet, a sense of 'Dogonness' may have originated in the Bandiagara cliffs, seen as the heart of the Dogon region in colonial times, when the area was administrated by the French colonies (1895–1960) and was extensively studied by ethnologists led by Marcel Griaule. However, by moving away from a normative concept of ethnicity and ethnic categories, I see 'Dogon' as a material identity (Sofaer 2007)—by this I mean the ways by which Dogon identity is shaped through people's daily and ritual embodied practice about their cultural landscape in which this identity materialises[3] (Gosselain 2000). Thus I see the material identity of the *tɔrɔ sɔ* Dogon of Tiréli as shared and 'in-the-making' (Douny 2014). In my view, the villagers of Tiréli share ideas, techniques, ritual practices, usages, and customs with other Dogon communities and with Mande and other West African communities. These, I suggest, are found in a symbolic reservoir (MacEachern 1994; McIntosh 1989; Sterner 1992) in which they all have immersed themselves over time (Chapter 1).

It seems to me that today the Bandiagara cliffs and parts of the plateau remain a place of worship where ancestors' shrines within an animist tradition (called *ɔmɔlɔ*[4] in *tɔrɔ sɔ* language) are curated by ritual leaders who are responsible for sacrifices (Chapter 3). The *tɔrɔ sɔ* area is recognised by the Dogon as a place of heritage, but not in UNESCO terms. In a *tɔrɔ sɔ* Dogon's view, 'heritage' is defined as *atɛmu*, referring to the laws of the ancestors that rule Dogon practices, usages, and customs called *dɔgɔ sɔ*. Its implementation in Dogon daily and ritual life is executed by the *ɔmɔlɔ* magico-religious system, the principles and name of which may vary from one region to another. From this perspective I acknowledge the Dogon's sense of unity through their cultural and cosmological diversity. Thus, I conceptualise Dogon knowledges about living in a twenty-first-century landscape of scarcity in terms of a micro-cosmology that is developed and therefore specific to one Dogon village but that shows many cultural commonalities with other villages of the same linguistic area and beyond.

Beyond the Dogon Cosmology: Daily Worldviews as a Microcosmology In-the-Making

The term *cosmology*[5] often refers to the array of views, thoughts, beliefs, and knowledges—scientific, religious, and philosophical—on the cosmos that are found in many cultures of the past and the present. Within an anthropological view and broad definition, Western and non-Western cosmologies seek understanding about the origin, development, and existence of life within the universe and the human world, as well as formulating hypotheses about the end of the world. In other words, people express themselves cross-culturally in cosmological terms and in multiple ways—for instance, through religion practice, material culture, rituals, and artistic performance, and through narratives in oral literature. Indigenous cosmologies provide an insight into people's social world and the ways by which people relate to the environment and the invisible world. These relations are socially embedded through practice and form complex systems of local knowledge (Douglas 2003; Forde 1954).

The Dogon Cosmology and Its Ethnographic Legacy

The Dogon concept of cosmology has its roots in colonial times, when substantial research was conducted by Marcel Griaule and his research team, in a systematic way, about what he described as the Dogon cosmogony.[6] Current notion of Dogon cosmology refers to Dogon beliefs systems or religion and knowledges, including astronomy and metaphysics, about human life on earth that are embedded into cosmogonic myths that were mainly collected and interpreted by Griaule. In other words, Dogon cosmogony as presented by Griaule accounts for the mechanisms of the creation of the universe, of earth, and of humankind, and it reveals itself through graphic systems or visual metaphors (Griaule 1949, 1952, 1966; Griaule & Dieterlen 1951, 1954, 1965), which are 'the expression of a correspondence between (this) the social organisation and the world as they (Dogon) conceive it' (Griaule & Dieterlen 1954, 83).

Graphic systems that form a repertoire of signs that schematise the creation of the world by God *Áma* would systematically materialise on granaries walls, in the geometry of fields and gardens, in building structures, divination tables drawn on the sand, and shapes of baskets, to name but a few things. In other words, the holistic cosmogony integrates, according to Griaule's interpretation, all aspects of Dogon life. As a result, the cosmogony elaborated by Griaule ends up as a static imaginary ethnographic model that is an intellectualised and large-scale abstraction of Dogon people, that is throughout what is known today as the 'Pays Dogon'. In this respect, Jean Rouch's film *Cimetières dans la falaise* (1951) constitutes an example of the materialisation of this cosmogony, which has functioned to create a particularly authoritative Western, Griaulian, and colonial view of the Dogon world (Clifford, 1988).

Griaule's Dogon cosmogony—which as such remains unknown by the inhabitants of Sangha and has never been found in other areas of the Dogon region (van Beek 1991)—remains today a historic or cultural heritage left by the French ethnologist. Yet the Dogon still trigger Western fascination and curiosity for their 'Griaulian cosmogony', which is too often still taken for granted (see Appendix C), while the concept of cosmology has been dismissed in Dogon studies (see Appendix D).

In this book, I do not undertake a reevaluation of Griaule's work; this has been done many times in the past (notably, see Lettens 1971; van Beek 1991, 2004). Rather, I envisage the Dogon people's perceptions and ways of living and 'being' in a twenty-first-century landscape of scarcity, in the light of both concepts of cosmology and worldviews. I contend that these conceptual tools help to further our understanding of people's ontology and that they are key concepts to the development of anthropological theory of knowledge.

Dogon's Worldviews as Embedded and Embodied Knowledges

The microcosmology that I examine here provides an epistemological framework for Dogon worldviews.[7] These I see as a set of knowledge, attitudes, and values, and thus cultural meanings, about the world that emerge from Dogon people's perceptions about and interactions with the world in which they live. These worldviews gather into a microcosmology that translates *tɔrɔ sɔ* Dogon of Tiréli ways of living and relating to their environment of scarcity through containment (Chapter 1). In other words, I describe Dogon *tɔrɔ sɔ* microcosmology as a structuring of worldviews within a small-scale village community and that brings the self, nature, and culture (Descola 2005; Geertz 1973, 127) into a same cultural paradigm of containment.

Contrary to Griaule's examination of Dogon cosmology based on creation myths, in my analysis, Dogon microcosmology is made of worldviews that encompass the dimensions of social memory (McIntosh, Tainter, & Keech McIntosh 2000, 24) and practical worldviews. I envisage the first as a long-standing system of dynamic worldviews that concern Dogon past experiences and knowledges as a form of heritage framed by the Dogon's traditional animist system *ɔmɔlɔ* (Chapter 3) and *atɛmu*, or laws of the ancestors. *Ɔmɔlɔ* as a system of beliefs encompasses moral values, prohibitions, and ritual practice. It functions primarily as a way of restoring social and political order and of ensuring the continuity of society, of life that in this case means coping with intertwined social and environmental challenges.

I propose that the *ɔmɔlɔ* system, which maintains the ancestors' laws (*atɛmu*), which stand as the foundation of Dogon society, is therefore, like the *atɛmu,* supplied by a deeper symbolic reservoir (Chapter 1). The ancestors' laws, often referred to by the Dogon as the *tradition,* transcend Dogon daily life practice, which is therefore ritualised according to the tradition's precepts. Negative consequences such as bad luck, disease, or death follow the non-observance of these laws, as prescribed by the ɔmɔlɔ system, which also enables the remedy of such situations, through sacrifices. I suggest that the laws of the ancestors, or the tradition, are largely unconsciously embodied by the Dogon people in their daily routine. Yet, they are also consciously perpetuated by knowledge specialists and transmitted through performances such as oral tradition, initiation rites, and sacrifices.

Ɔmɔlɔ animist worldviews stand within a dialectic with practical worldviews, which include shared practical and tacit knowledge of the world that stems from Dogon's men and women's daily embodied experiences of the materiality of their landscape container. Practical worldviews arise from an array of related activities, or a taskscape (Ingold 2000), such as walking in and cultivating the land, setting up the village and the home, building and storing in granaries, recycling waste, and, finally, cooking. I suggest that Dogon practical embedded worldviews inform about the villagers' changing perceptions and actions and thus their beliefs and attitudes toward the environment. Last, I suggest that although ɔmɔlɔ animist worldviews as an established magico-religious system of power shape Dogon practical worldviews, these animist worldviews are in turn continually challenged and thus altered by the latter worldviews, which imply more factual, detailed, and maybe more personal forms of embodied knowledge, acquired through observations, evaluations, and choices (van Beek 1993, 56). The Dogon ɔmɔlɔ system endures because it manages to adapt to new situations and practice in a twenty-first-century world. Yet, it is also reinvented through time as knowledges are not transmitted to younger generations and ritual paraphernalia are sold to antiquarians.

Consequently, I propose that Dogon practical worldviews, which I focus on in Chapters 8, 9, 10, and 11 and which emerge from the Dogon's making and doing of the landscape and other container forms (Douny 2007), are therefore (1) changeable across time and space; (2) relational as they emerge from social webs and individuals' relationships to nature and the invisible/spiritual and material world; (3) variable from one group of individuals to another based on their gender and age; and (4) grounded in the tradition—ruled by it but also challenging it.

A Microcosmology In-the-Making

As I have explained, Dogon microcosmology as a containment model and structure for worldviews functions as a conceptual tool that allows me to uncover implicit forms of knowledges and thus the systems and order by which these knowledges are organised, stratified, and produced as well as how they have changed over time (Barth 1987). By drawing on Barth's thesis (1987) about the production of the cosmology of the Baktaman of Papua New Guinea, I suggest that Dogon microcosmology, as in-the-making, is generative. Using this concept, I underline the ways in which Dogon practical worldviews are generated—in particular, domestic settings—and so produced and reproduced in the course of everyday life, through shared embodied material practice about making and doing container forms.

Writing from a similar everyday practice setting, Weiss (1996) demonstrates how the Haya of Tanzania engage in the world through their everyday life practice inside and outside the home. He shows how Haya make and unmake their cosmology through their shared embodied experience and in pursuing their daily living in a context of a global economy, modernism, and thus a changing world. Likewise, I suggest that these dimensions contribute to the definition of a Dogon microcosmology that relates to how Dogon people make themselves at home (Jackson 1995) in the twenty-first-century changing world as their microcosmology is being reshaped through modernisation, religious conversion, tourism, and an overarching Malian political crisis. Throughout this book, I expound this perspective on change through continuity with the ɔmɔlɔ animist system as it relates to material practice about making symbolic, political, and social boundaries that, however, remain porous.

Here I suggest that Dogon microcosmology and cultural landscape in-the-making open the way to new forms of embodied worldviews that emerged from rapid adaptations to new circumstances of life perceived by Dogon as fatalistic and in the hands of God. Yet strategies that the Dogon develop to cope with the harsh environment are creative, allowing them to make themselves at home in a landscape of scarcity. Living in a landscape of scarcity exposes fundamental issues about territoriality (for example, land tenure for cultivation) and about resources such as water, fertile earth, and millet, in particular. The matter produced from these materials and substance that form the materiality of their cultural landscape lie at the centre of Dogon microcosmology in-the-making—the means by which the Dogon dwell, build, and so live in the twenty-first-century landscape of scarcity.

Making and Doing Containers within an Anthropology of Techniques

My examination of a Dogon microcosmology as objectified in the landscape and related containers forms stems from a praxeological approach (Julien & Rosselin 2009; Julien, Rosselin, & Warnier 2006; Julien & Warnier 1999; Warnier 1999, 2001), which I frame within the Anthropology of Techniques (Coupaye & Douny, 2010; Haudricourt 1968; Lemonnier 1976, 1992, 1993;

Leroi-Gourhan 1945; Sigaut, 2002). Here I see production as 'making' and consumption as 'doing' in the same continuity and within the same operational sequence of extracting raw materials, transforming them into matter, forming matter into containers, and using containers and recycling or discarding them (Douny 2007; Naji & Douny 2009). In other words, 'doing' is grounded in a principle of 'efficacious action upon objects and people' (Warnier 2009)—thus in the bodily experience of material forms. 'Making' concerns 'efficacious actions upon matter' (Lemonnier 1992, 4, following Leroi-Gourhan 1943, 1945) and thus the bodily experience of matter. Consequently, the 'making' and 'doing' of Dogon containers are envisaged as part of a technical system in which all elements remain interdependent and so constitute a system that encompasses the actors, matter that is acted on, tools and energy required to perform technical actions, efficacious body techniques (movements and gestures), knowledge, intended purposes, representations, and, finally, skills and expertise (Lemonnier 1992, 5–6). In my view, matter and objects that are part of the technical system that forms a heritage are experienced and so embodied. In addition, this system also includes the ritualisation of material actions about matter and container forms.

'Thinking through the Body': A Praxeological Approach

In the social sciences the concept of praxeology, defined as a 'science of efficient human actions' in the sense of human conducts, was introduced by Alfred Espinas (1890). Since then, the term has been employed and developed by scholars such as Bourdieu in his theory of practice (1977). By following Warnier's approach (2001, 2007), which relies on P. Parlebas's *Lexique de praxéologie motrice* (1981), I see praxeology as a method for in-depth analysis of body kinetics (for example, walking, working the land) and more specifically gestures such as handling, building (granary walls), pounding or crushing (foodstuff) (see Appendix E). All these actions are involved in domestic tasks through which practical knowledge (Bourdieu 1990; Merleau-Ponty 1962, 138) is acquired and tacit and ritualised forms of knowledges are revealed. In this sense, I see containers as a 'material symbolism'—that is, containers not in terms of 'their material forms *per se* but rather as practice and implicit meanings' (Rowlands 1985, 203). Here I suggest that gestures and body movements forming daily practices are ritualised by observing the pervasive *atɛmu* protocol, or the laws of the ancestors, which is implemented and maintained by the *ɔmɔlɔ* system. This system ensures the symbolic continuity of life through rituals and the cohesion of the society. It also deals with the curation and aspects of the transmission of ritual knowledge, practices, and techniques—through, for instance, initiations.

Containers as technologies or techniques reveal forms of implicit knowledge that are not or simply cannot be verbalised and hence are manifest through techniques of the body (Mauss 1936; Schlangler 2011, 74–78.). According to this view, praxeology enables us to understand social practices and meaning through situated motor actions that are mediated by objects and that involve the body's sensory and kinetic experiences of objects' materiality (Parlebas 1999; Warnier 2001). Thus, within a material culture approach, praxeology asserts a mutual shaping between people and artefacts through a process of objectification of bodily dynamic and likewise of material embodiment through body technique (Mauss 1936, 371; Warnier 2009) and so efficacious actions on people, objects, and matter. My interest in praxeology is here twofold. First, it enables me to underline Dogon *savoir-faire*, or knowledge, about *making* (production/efficacious actions on matter) and *doing* (consumption/efficacious actions on objects and people) and therefore *unmaking* and *undoing* things in daily life (Naji & Douny 2009). In other words, praxeology enables the highlighting of local lifestyle, as well as quotidian life organisation and temporalities. Second, by concentrating on people's bodily movements in the management of domestic and social space and forms, praxeology helps me to underscore indigenous worldviews as objectified and mediated by the material praxis of containers and of their contents.

The praxeological dimension I wish to propose here differs from Warnier's position on subjectivation and constitution of the self as a process of internalisation of body motricity and sensory-affective-experience within an individual's 'psychic envelope' that is operated through the mediation of objects (Warnier 1999, 161; see also Warnier 2001). From a standpoint different from Warnier's, I think that it is social relationships or intersubjective processes that craft the individual's self as a directed outer self. Following Bourdieu's thesis (1993), I suggest that subjectivity is founded in everyday life practice and cultural transmission. In other words, it results from the socialisation processes that I observed in the field. This conclusion is borne out by the fact that the 'making' and 'doing' of things occur in gendered, age-grouped activities that correspond to particular stratifications and organisations within African societies. Through the emulation and coordination of tasks, the individual's self becomes indivisible from those of others. Thus I do not consider agency as individualistic. On the contrary, I prefer to see it as a grounded network of synchronised and negotiated interactions mediated by the materiality of objects and matter that are viewed as corporeal and, in terms of efficacy, by the capacity they have to forge or to act on individuals in particular situations (Rowlands & Warnier 1996). Therefore, I employ praxeology in tandem with phenomenology, which considers the tactile experience of matter and therefore sees matter as the result of transformative processes led by efficient actions—for instance, through gestures on materials and substances.

'Thinking through One's Fingers': A Phenomenological Approach

In my view, phenomenology situates itself within the continuity of praxeology. Phenomenology postulates the knowing of the world through the body's senses (Merleau-Ponty 1962; Schutz 1967). In other words, it consists of knowing the world of 'others' through our own perception and experience of their world (Jackson 1996, 29). It is a dialectical process of knowing that occurs between a perceived object world and a perceiving subject toward which we project ourselves through our senses and actions. This process of knowing the world is defined by Merleau-Ponty (1962, 138) as practical knowledge (see also Bourdieu 1990). In other words, phenomenology consists of a practical lived experience made of shared intentionality (Sartre 1958) and agency (Schütz 1967). By placing emphasis on the body kinetic grounded in a systematic daily-life praxis of matter and of objects and their sensory experience of things, I stress the relationships between the materiality of containers, their contents, and the body. In other words, I am interested in how Dogon people make themselves at home in a landscape of scarcity through their body sensory experiences of containers and of their content. The body in Dogon society that is used as a tool to perform daily tasks constitutes a fundamental source of knowing, learning, and thinking about the landscape container. The body is the *loci* for motor actions and intersensorial perceptions that Berthoz defines as the 'sense of movement' that brings into consideration body movement, perceptions, emotions, and cognition as part of a same 'culture of motricity' (Berthoz 1997, 9; Berthoz & Petit 2006).

In my account, praxeology as phenomenologically oriented facilitates insights into indigenous understandings of the materiality of their world through an examination of gestures. The anthropology of gestures has its distinctive schools and approaches, influenced by the work of Mauss (for example, Bril & Roux 2002; Jousse 1974; Kawada 1991; Leroi-Gourhan 1945). Gestures involve the tactile experience of matter in the production and emulation of material forms. These processes create particular material ontologies—that is, the ways individuals make themselves and thus relate to their own world through matter. The haptic experience of earth matter enables evaluation of the consistency, texture, and weight of building materials necessary to build up the granary walls as well as to measure their thickness and strength—a process that Warnier, quoting Mauss and Halbwachs, calls 'thinking through one's fingers' (Warnier 1999).

Here I want to emphasise the importance of hands and tactility in the transformation of or technical action on matter such as earth and millet, the use of the pestle seen as the extension of the body and the tactile experience being involved in eating with one's hand. I seek to understand implicit forms of meanings and material symbolism attached to gestures and thus to embodied techniques. By following Lemonnier's thesis and quoting Leroi-Gourhan (1992, 4), I propose that these embodied techniques, as 'efficacious actions upon matter' that result in the extraction, processing, and transformation of materials into matter, through shared body rhythms are practical means to maximise and control resources. Technical efficacy is also partly achieved by Dogon people through observing the ancestors' protocol that engenders the continuity of daily routine and of life. To a lesser extent, I provide meanings relating to techniques of pounding and grinding that lead to understanding Dogon symbolism attached to millet as bringing within its own materiality the life cycle of the people and of the environment.

Making and Doing Processes as Embedded *chaînes opératoires*

As proposed by Ingold, artefacts are defined as the product of human agency and are, therefore, a 'coming-into-being' through human practice (Ingold 2000, 168). In other words, the basket that he describes emerges through its 'making'—that is, through its being woven or as a material/technique/action relationship (Ingold 2000, 339–48). From this perspective, in Chapter 8 I look at the making process of an earth granary that is designed by the body and is without plans. The container is shaped day by day through the tactile experience of the earth matter and the builder's body dynamic, or body technique (Mauss 1936; Schlangler 1991), as objectified in the material form. The shape and measure result from learned skills in practice, and the making of this earth container requires the full body's engagement with the matter. Building a granary occurs fundamentally, through the emulation of forms, the pounding, grinding, and crushing, as well as through the haptic experience of matter in which body rhythms, such as its motion inside and outside the container, are objectified. I suggest that the Dogon sense of materiality is generated and constituted at its most fundamental level by body rhythms, which attribute particular configurations to containers (for example, successfully shaping or breaking containers while they are being made).

The notion of 'using' or *doing* containers consists of a series of embodied experienced and participatory daily life habits defined by shared body rhythms that are expressed in collective or semicollective activities by walking in the landscape (Ingold 2004; Tilley 1994, 2004) and in the weatherscape (Ingold 2004), cultivating the fields, storing food in a granary, or recycling waste. In other words, I propose that, on the one hand, making containers consists of a creative and generative or 'coming-into-being' process (Ingold 2000, 168) through which material forms take shape, while, on the other hand, doing things concerns the daily practical uses of an object through which the object decays, that is, goes through a process that is a 'coming-to-an-end'. Consequently, both processes of making and doing occur through body motricity and the sensory experience of the materiality of containers. I suggest that through making and doing (Douny 2007; Naji & Douny 2009) the Dogon make themselves in the world. I expose these processes through sequences of manufacture and uses of containers with particular reference to the making and doing of a female granary. These visual and descriptive sequences are called *chaînes opératoires*, or operational sequences (Lemonnier 1976; Leroi-Gourhan 1943, 1945).

Thinking through Sequences of Operations

As a means to identify the different operational stages in the processing of materials such as millet and earth, the shaping of granaries, or a meal and the uses of containers, I frame my in-the-field observations within a *chaîne opéra-toire* scheme that encompasses other sequences of related operations (Coupaye 2009, 443). These sequences allow me to highlight the technical stages of the manufacturing process and the use of materials and material forms through visual recordings of activities as well as through detailed and empirical ethnographic descriptions. These sequences reveal the step-by-step transformation of matter employed in the seasonal and daily making of receptacles and their content as well as their daily uses.

Introduced by Leroi-Gourhan (1943, 1945), the founder of the French *Anthropology of Techniques*, the concept was further developed as an in-depth fieldwork method and theorised by Lemonnier (1976, 1992). It constitutes a checklist and key analytical tool (Gosselain 2000) in identifying and understanding situated practice such as extracting, processing, transforming, preparing, practicing, using, repairing, recycling, and discarding objects and matter. Hence, containers and their contents are framed within a life-cycle sequence by recording their processes from their birth, or making, through the transformation and shaping of matter, then on through their life, or domestic use, and, finally, right up to their death, or after death, to their recycling. In that sense, the idea of a *chaîne opératoire* constitutes a way of underscoring networks of implicit relationships between the life cycle of people, the environment, and objects as part of one and the same cultural process.

The *chaîne opératoire* is proposed from a perspective that views the multiple tasks that occur in the making of a Dogon female granary, or in cooking a meal, as a gathering process that denies temporal linearity. It attempts to cross-reference the manufacturing stages revealed in the local terminology with their Western transcription. Thus the *chaîne opératoire* schema constitutes a self-reflexive way of showing how indigenous technical knowledge is usually conceptualised and understood by the researcher via a process of analysis and reconstruction that tends, to borrow an everyday phrase, to 'go without saying'. Moreover, the sequence of operations gathered in schemas proposed in Chapters 9 and 11 presents a further challenge to this 'unspoken' way of working by conceptualising local cyclic temporalities in terms of a time of gathering that transcends daily shared or participatory agencies.

Sequences of Operations as a Gathering Process   What I propose is a vertically oriented, syntagmatic sequence of actions that translates the synchronic series of steps in the making of the container and a meal. Each level is crossed by a horizontal, paradigmatic gathering-of-activities that happen within one and the same operation. The vertical sequence is an inventory of the succession of actions as I have been able to observe them systematically;

the horizontal paradigm renders the Dogon ways of 'doing' and 'naming' the routine steps in terms of 'what has to be done'. Finally, this structure seeks to set up, metaphorically and spatially, the whole underlying notion of the containing and gathering process as being cyclical. In other words, by framing the multiple technical levels within a cyclical framework that encompasses both daily and seasonal temporalities (the building task prior to the agrarian cycle), I present this epigenetic sequence as a gathering of tasks conceived as relative doxic modalities.

Sequences of Temporalities: Life Cycle, Synchronicity, and Sense of Duration   As mentioned, the method of presenting actions within a sequence tends to put across a much more routinised and therefore repetitive sense of duration. Thus duration is locally denied while the task is being performed. Here I have endeavoured to resolve the ambiguity of the linear or synchronic intervals of the recorded sequence by reflecting, in my writing, the time spent on each activity. In short, the sequence gathers interconnected sociocultural and domestic durations that are brought into the temporality of a wider landscape and ritual life. Thus my aim is for this description to express the particular sense of continuity and life cycle that transpires through my analysis of the material I have collected in the field—and to do this by adding to the making of the granary the dimensions of its repair, recycling, and discarding. Similarly, as I show in the making of a meal, while being processed millet spikes are turned into grains and flour that are cooked into a cake while daily leftovers are dried, pounded, and re-cooked as a new meal. Matter is always being given another life through recycling as well as through fermentation processes (Chapter 1).

Discontinuity in Operation Sequences   A similar continuity shows through the learning process at stake in the making and shaping of a granary, owing to the increasing frequency with which, now, there is a danger that only partial transmission and exposure to the praxis will become the norm. In addition, this rupture in the transmission of the techniques is exacerbated by both the tendency not to build granaries, owing to a drastic reduction in crop yields and the increasing replacement of granaries by modern concrete storage facilities, and the replacement of clay pots by metallic or plastic materials. Thus changes in practice create changes in knowledge transmitted. Similarly, disruption caused by a wooden pestle that breaks during the pounding of millet symbolically signifies an interruption (illness, death, divorce) in the woman's life, while foodstuff (millet) is said to 'disappear' (through food shortage, famine) if a sacrifice is not performed to remedy the 'broken situation'.

Shared Embodied Tasks and the Transmission of Knowledge   The making of granaries (Chapter 9) and the pounding of millet (Chapter 11) act as a social gathering in which young apprentices, children, relatives, friends, and neighbours take part in the process by advising and/or practising as well as being entertained. Participation in this consists of an act of identity that reunites and consolidates the relationships between people as well as constituting a form of heritage through the technical knowledge that is transmitted (for instance, see the work of Marchand 2009). In fact, pounding millet is a shared embodied practice that coordinates multiple synchronous body rhythms that are not verbalised but transmitted through emulations of movements and repeated exposures to sound.

Consequently, my observations of Dogon daily and seasonal activities that concern acting on the materiality of the landscape through walking, cultivating and harvesting, sacrificing, recycling waste, building, storing, and cooking as I experienced them result in a sequence of operation about making and doing containers, which as unifying principle in some place (Chapters 10 and 11) materialise in two *chaînes opératoires*. These intertwined sequences reveal that the life cycle of people is meshed with the life cycle of the natural and material environment in which they live. Then they show daily temporalities and the Dogon's perception of time as cyclical—that is, the Dogon's denial of the linearity of time and therefore of the end of things. The regeneration of life is symbolically celebrated through annual sacrifices, and matter such earth and millet are revitalised through daily practices and, as I explained in Chapter 1, through fermentation.

The Materiality of Containers: Embodied Knowledges and Material Metaphors of Containment

This book focuses on the relatedness of containers through domestic praxis by considering containers as embodied material metaphors (Lakoff & Johnson 1999) and from which a metaphor of containing develops into a form of containment—that is, a Dogon's microcosmological model. Through an anthropology of techniques about making and doing (Naji & Douny 2009), I envisage containers as part of action of containing, which is concerned with the material and immaterial structure of Dogon containers as boundaries and which involves on the one hand their landscape of scarcity and on the other the built environment, the bowl of food, and the body. Containers are seen as folded surface of contact that interconnects the individuals to the external world by means of their bodily sensory experience of material forms. I suggest that, through containers, people draw the boundaries of their lived environment and engage themselves in their own world. Containers create locales in which social networks, transactions, and, also, sociocultural meanings about the landscape of scarcity develop. The *chaîne opératoire* in particular helps me to uncover these implicit forms of meaning that reveal through people's embodied and embedded daily and ritual tasks and that gather into a microcosmology that is in-the-making. An understanding of the Dogon's ɔmɔlɔ system in tandem with Dogon everyday practice enable me to shed some light on a Dogon microcosmology as made of worldviews—that is, the ways the Dogon perceive and conceptualise their relationships to their social and natural environments and therefore the ways they act on their cultural landscape in their everyday and ritual life—for instance, in making and reactivating the symbolic boundaries of territory and of the village's built features, forecasting the weather, rain making, and ensuring the fertility of soil and full granaries.

Consequently, central to the Dogon perception and understanding of the environment in which the Dogon dwell, build, and live, is their experience of the materiality of their landscape container that, as I argue, defines through praxis about its material and content, through Dogon agency and containment; that is, as I have explained in Chapter 1, an enframing model that develops from practices of containment about making boundaries and the gathering of resources such as water, earth, and millet as they both constitute the materiality of the Dogon's landscape. Containment creates an ontological security (Giddens 1991) by conveying a sense of order and of continuity of life, which I explore in the following chapters, starting with the social and symbolic construction of the Dogon territory.

3 Conceptual Boundaries and Inside/Outside Dialectics: A Dwelling Process

Earth Shrines: Spatial Enclosures and Inside/Outside Dialectics

The landscape of the Dogon village of Tiréli is conceptually bounded by two contiguous enclosures in which people dwell and gather the world around them. These encircling symbolic structures create particular liveable configurations by forming a system generated through a series of shrines that map out the land. They are ruled by the ɔmɔlɔ system, which expresses the relationships between people and their god, the spirits of the land, and the ancestors who founded the territory. On the one hand, the system of symbolic enclosures institutes a network of protection for its material and human content. On the other hand, it constitutes a social behaviour control device, a gathering process and material identity making, as well as attempting to act on the unpredictable environment. The symbolic protections of the Dogon landscape generated by a series of shrines that enclose its territory involves a particular philosophy of action that concerns the reactivation of ontological boundaries and thus of a series of earth shrines.

This chapter explores cosmological ideas of containment as the Dogon principle of dwelling in the world as it is framed by ɔmɔlɔ system and through embodied experiences of land shrines.[1] I describe Dogon's making of space in terms of the conceptual bounding that remains porous and the division of Dogon village space. Furthermore, I examine the particular ontological security (Giddens 1984, 1991) that this system generates to ensure the continuity of Dogon society. I propose that the shrines preserve a certain sense of local unity by acting on nature through the control of boundaries. Through their materiality, the shrines fix these social and existential principles, revealing a primary condition of Dogon microcosmology: the relationships between the surrounding environment and the local community that define itself through a process of 'making oneself at home in the world' (Jackson 1995).

Earth Shrines of West African Landscapes

Earth shrines,[2] which are prominent sacred elements in African ritual life (Prussin 1982) and which very often appear in the form of an artefact or a natural feature of the landscape, such as a significant tree, rock, or watercourse, are widespread phenomena in Africa (Dawson 2009, XII). As described by Antongini and Spini, the Lobi of Burkina Faso possess an earth shrine called *Dithil* ('spirit of the land'), a term that also refers to the object described as 'a heap of stones placed in front of a tree, which is supposed to "keep buried" all the evils which may attempt to harm the community' (Antongini & Spini 1997, 755).

The *Dithil* as a territorial mark for Lobi identity signifies the political and geographical unity of the village (Antongini & Spini 1997, 755–56). Insoll (2007, 140, referring to Courtright 1987, 299) proposes that shrines are both material fixed elements and dynamic or active containers or receptacles that accumulate power and meaning in their materiality during seasonal sacrificial practices. Shrines as objects of power are often located away from the houses and surrounded by an enclosure as a means of preventing people from approaching them and where they blend in with the surrounding landscape. As Lentz underlines, shrines can serve as a landmark for a community that convey a sense of rootedness and therefore spell out an ownership for their land (Lentz 2009). In addition, these artefacts—cared for by ritual specialists—act as a means of cosmologically organising space, controlling and protecting the people against the circulation of malevolent entities, as Bouju (1995a) and Teme (1997) have demonstrated with regard to Dogon land shrines in villages of the *dɔnɔ sɔ* and *tɔrɔ sɔ* areas. Therefore, shrines used by humans as means to harness and mediate with spiritual forces that dwell in the landscape are evidence of the domestication of the landscape (Mather 2003), which is never complete, because the spiritual forces that inhabit the land cannot be domesticated. This landscape also becomes wild again as soon as human activity and control cease.

The ɔmɔlɔ System: Managing the Living Landscape

Earth shrines as bearing active principles play a part in the making of Tiréli's microcosmology. Based on a close-knit human dependency on natural resources, the *ɔmɔlɔ* Dogon complex of worldviews rules both the sacred and the profane. This spiritual doctrine orders and regulates much of society as well as the land by interconnecting their life cycles. The invocations that the

Dogon of Tiréli dedicate to their god, *Áma,* relate to everyday life concerns such as the unpredictability of the weather, the successful growing of crops, good health, having a large family, and thus fertility of the land and of people as well as maintaining social cohesion. This system endures changes and is always sought after by people of all faiths when the rain is failing or if social conflicts or land tenure issues cannot be resolved on friendly terms or through legal justice and as a means to maintain the cohesion of the society. This *ɔmɔlɔ* system, as the ancestors' tradition, underlies Dogon culture, beyond all faiths, which in Tiréli are predominantly Catholicism/Christianity and Islam. The *ɔmɔlɔ* system constitutes an important aspect of Dogon identity. People who do not partake in the actual rituals and ceremonies that are coordinated by the *ɔmɔlɔ* system undoubtedly recognise the ontological importance of the tradition and shrines.

Shrines are feared because of their inherent power and because they materialise people's relationship to their ancestors—that is, also to the land that remains their property. In other words, all villagers benefit from the *ɔmɔlɔ* system's protections and solutions. As people say 'we are all Dogon and all from this land'.

Ɔmɔlɔ is a polysemic and totalising concept that encompasses internal logic of Dogon monotheist thinking (Teme 1997, 3). In this context, *ɔmɔlɔ* designates the array as well as the management of both collective and individual ritual practices dedicated to *Áma* and to other supernatural beings. As Teme, who is a native Dogon and anthropologist, suggests, the concept of *ɔmɔlɔ* refers to a system of beliefs that legitimises action of power within social organisation and by ruling human relationships to nature (Teme 1997, 127–28, 136–39). *Ɔmɔlɔ* as faithful to the *atɛmu* or ancestors' law is the legitimate foundation of Dogon society. It rules social relationships and all institutions from the political management of the land to matrimonial laws, social behaviour, and hierarchy (Teme 2002, 44). The precepts or laws of the ancestors that this traditional system supports are largely unconsciously embodied and reproduced by people in their everyday life who justify and legitimise their practices by virtue of their inception in time immemorial—'what we have found with our ancestors'.

Ɔmɔlɔ can be translated as 'sacrifice' that locates itself at the core of Dogon ritual practice and that determines its efficacy. *Ɔmɔlɔ* may indicate bad luck or punishment inflicted by the spiritual world on humans. In that sense, through *ɔmɔlɔ* ritual practices order is reinstated. For instance, *búlo* (*ɔmɔlɔ búlone, búlu*) as the name of the sowing-feast for the village of Tiréli means 'to revive', 'to make something living again', or 'to regenerate' (Calame-Griaule 1968, 49–50). This term implies the practice of protecting and regenerating society through sacrifice. The term *ɔmɔlɔ* also refers to the ritual objects, including *áma* altars (movable) and shrines (fixed), as well as to their function. Therefore, the concept of *ɔmɔlɔ* encompasses the actual ritual practice as the result of rule-breaking (or prohibition called *damá*), a state of impurity (*pùru*), and the apparatus activated to reinstate the correct order (the state of purity [ɔmɔ]). I suggest that ɔmɔlɔ should not be restricted to a religion but rather is a system of worldviews that encompasses beliefs, knowledges, attitudes, and values—that is, cultural meanings about the world. In addition, ɔmɔlɔ as 'a spiritual weapon of the social project' (Teme 1997, 138) defines Dogon ways of living in the landscape of scarcity. Therefore, this system enacts as a cosmological principle of dealing with and acting on the visible and invisible world through magico-religious ritual practice. It may thus be constitutive of what it is to be Dogon people existing and living in the world.

The Village's Territory: Physical Limits and Divisions of Space

As part of the thirty villages of the Bandiagara escarpment, the village of Tiréli extends over a scree slope approximately 400 m in length that creates a natural protective niche. The settlement comprises two main districts: Sodanga in the northeast and Teri-Ku in the southwest (Figure 3.1). Each of these is subdivided into three areas: Sodanga, Tatara, and Gujoguru and Dama, Sabo, and Komangua, respectively. The distance between the two farthest points of the village is about 1.3 km. Tiréli is delimited by a series of prominent features that make its landscape unique. The village is located on the scree of a

Figure 3.1 View of the territory of the village of Tiréli from the top of the cliffs showing Dogon settlements in the quarter of Teri-Ku, the gardens and fields of the cultivated bush

450-m-high escarpment (*koko*) that faces the dune (*dudum*) that physically bounds the territory. These natural features create a furrow running parallel to the escarpment as well, stretching along the edge of the Séno plain. The field boundaries of Tiréli border those of the villages of Ourou (1 km) and Komankani (4.5 km) to the west and the village of Amani (3 km) to the east.

These unmarked borders are known to the respective owners of the fields and regularly generate lively conflicts between villages. The zone sandwiched between the escarpment and the dune is a patchwork of fields. These wet-season fields are turned into gardens during the dry season. They contain dispersed trees, and the cultivated fringe in the vicinity of the settlement is sliced in two by the river that is straddled by a number of Dogon villages. These boundaries are crossed daily by people moving vertically and horizontally along paths that are in constant use. Paths in the sand are also marked and consolidated into wider routes by the frequent passage of four-wheel-drive vehicles that bring tourists to Tiréli; these wider routes are also used by local mopeds, bicycles, and carts. These natural limits stand as reference points in space that are redesigned through human movement as well as the change of seasons.

As Teme proposes, in the *tɔrɔ sɔ* area the notion of territory called *sala* (or *sara*) refers to the nourishing land, space owned by the ancestors and that legitimises its present occupiers, as well as a space in which 'cosmic' order is managed and restored. Therefore, it is the locus of political stakes (1997, 112). By following Teme's definition, I propose Tiréli's territory as a humanised portion of the landscape that is symbolically bounded as a result of a long process of appropriation and settlement. Although it is humanly occupied and transformed, the territory is owned by the ancestors and spirits that animate the land. Thus, the inhabited and cultivated areas constitute what I call the territory of Tiréli, whereas Tiréli itself is defined by the villagers as the built zone, or the village (*àna*). In fact, as expressed by the villagers, the fields, gardens, and orchards located in the cultivated bush (*ɔru*) 'belong to Tiréli', and Tiréli is 'where we live'. It is worth noting that the materiality of the landscape, of its content and thus of land shrines, is perceived by the Dogon as living and active. First, the land as the property of their ancestors is believed to be inhabited by various forms of benevolent or malevolent spirits who act as intermediaries between humans and God. Second, within an *ɔmɔlɔ* worldviews system and thus in the context of experts' ritual knowledge— for instance, of blacksmiths, religious and traditional ritual leaders, and also hunters—it is believed that people, animals, things, and matter possess vital force or inherent energy called *ɲama*[3] (*ɲaman, ɲawan, yawan*) (Chapter 1). As mentioned in Chapter 1, this 'vital force' flows through the organism of beings and things such as earth shrines; *ɲama* ensures their well-functioning. The harmful consequences of a loss of *ɲama* (as a dangerous reacting force) for a human were often described to me as madness, death, or a trauma that can be generated, for instance, by the breaking of a prohibition, approaching earth shrines, or engaging in a violent verbal or physical conflict (also described in Calame-Griaule 1968, 205–06; Dieterlen 1941). Hence, the Dogon ɔmɔlɔ system places particular emphasis on the vitality of the materiality of things and beings, their order and their cohesion. The force, vitality, positive or negative energy, longevity, and strength of people, things, and animals are emphasised in people's everyday life practices and thus practical worldviews, which are shaped by the ɔmɔlɔ system.

The limits of the territory of Dogon villages as proposed by Petit 'are characterized by altars or fétiches (often a conical bollard made of earth) that protect the village against epidemics [and] bad spirits' (Petit 1998, 39). In Tiréli, the village space that contains at least forty different types of altars (shrines) (van Beek 1991, 145) and that is bounded on the east and west by the protection shrines is also physically delimited by the escarpment located to the north of the village. As proposed by Petit, Dogon's territory schema, which applies to Tiréli, can be conceptualised 'by considering the village as a point that stands in the middle of concentric circles. As moving away from the central point, one leaves the civilised, known world, to penetrate into an unpredictable, dangerous world' (Petit 1998, 39).

Hence, a first symbolic boundary is materialised by three shrines that distinguish the wild and 'dangerous' space of the bush from the 'safe' cultural space of the village and its surroundings, where most social and domestic activities take place. Tiréli people refer to this 'semi-domesticated or cultivated bush' as the 'outside' of the village that is passed through in order to reach the 'wild bush'. Hence, the village's territory is contained by a symbolic boundary within which the surface of the settlement and the cultivated space around it are delimited and protected. A second symbolic boundary is generated by a shrine located inside the village that protects its built surface. This boundary is physically materialised by the limits of settlements. In other words, the definition of the Dogon territory involves a conjuncture of physical and symbolic space.

Inside/Outside Dialectics
and Spatial Container Metaphors

As described by the inhabitants of Tiréli, the space they occupy is defined conceptually in terms of an 'inside' and an 'outside'. The 'inside' is commonly designated as the village, which is defined as 'the place where people live. That is where you find our compounds'. The village, therefore, corresponds to the built area called àna kóro (the area around the site of the foundation of the village), which is also called àna bɛrɛ (the broader inside of the village). Its verb form translates as 'to surround with' as in this example provided by Calame-Griaule: 'surrounding a plant with a hedge of thorns to protect it or from the same perspective, to surround a herd with a fence to prevent it running away' (Calame-Griaule 1968, 162–63).

Whereas *kóro* refers to a container such as a calabash, *bɛrɛ* signifies the village as its stomach or entrails. I suggest that the metaphor of the village as a container can say something about the physical, defensive qualities of the site and therefore how Dogon people benefit from the relative natural protection of the scree as well as of their own built environment. In fact, although the rocky slope is difficult to access, the Dogon compounds and in particular their granaries function as ramparts that have prevented assaults from humans and wild animals. The 'outside' is called *àna kɛrigu*[4] (*kɛrgu*), which refers to the areas 'on the side of' the village. On the one hand, this outside portion includes the fringe situated between the village and the dune cord that contains, notably, the gardens, fields, and trees; on the other hand, this area also includes patchy cultivated areas among the rocks that weave through the top and sides of the 'inside village'.

The *Pɛgu* Earth Shrines: Fixing, Appropriating and Protecting the Village's Territory

The territory of Tiréli, made of the inside of the village (*kóro*) and the outside (*kɛrigu*) is framed by four mud shrines: one called *lɔbɔ* and three others termed *múnɔ* (the *gínu múnɔ* and two *ɔru múnɔ*). Blending into the landscape, the three *múnɔ* shrines located on the dune and in the scree take on the camouflage qualities of the landscape. The four shrines are commonly designated by the term *pɛgu*, which refers to both the act of fixing and the act of maintaining the continuity of life in the village. These *pɛgu* shrines are *áma* shrines made by men, as opposed to those provided by supernatural beings. *Pɛgu* designates the village or collective shrines that found and 'fix' the village and are often located at the strategic entrances to the village. They serve as a protection for the village's community and thus its territory (Teme 1997, 173). In Tiréli, they mark the divide between the territory of the village and the wild bush. The first shrine that was fixed, the *gínu múnɔ,* is located where the settlement was founded and is also the most important for protecting it. These *pɛgu* mostly reaffirm the idea of a shared common ancestry and therefore the unity of the Saye (Say), or the people.

Located in a relatively inaccessible area, the *pɛgu* shrines are planted in the sense of being fixed in a place and of fixing people to the place. The term *pɛgu* also relates to a particular process of constituting the object and was described to me as follows. The foundation of a *pɛgu* is reported to have been accompanied in the past by the sacrifice of a person standing in a hole in the ground and in whose skull a metallic hook had been 'planted' (also, see Bouju 1995a, 355). Then, this hook would have been integrated to a mud bollard, standing upright on the ground. The hook as a hidden part of the shrine would canalize the male victim's *ɲama*, that is, the vital force or energy that flows through his body. Released from the victim's body, the vital force empowers the artefact in which it is embedded. The empowered shrine is sited on a location generally out of reach, such as in the escarpment scree, on a promontory, or surrounded by bushes.

Before sacrificial practices take place, land shrines undergo a process of repair similar to that used for the built environment, but with different materials and substances added to it. The seasonal replastering of these artefacts consists of adding a new layer of mud to the shrine. The matter is dug from the bottom of a pond, because it possesses good material strength. Furthermore, the soil of the ground of the shrine's immediate surroundings is gathered and added to the fresh mud, because in the previous year this soil would have been impregnated by the blood of sacrificed animals. Last, blood of sacrificed animals and/or cracked eggs are blended in the mud, before the shrine is plastered. Thus earth shrines are made of layers of 'living' and empowered mud as a means to strengthen and regenerate the object and thus also symbolically the society and the environment. All sacrifices on the *pɛgu* of the village occur before the start of the rain season, generally toward the end of May.

The *Gínu Múnɔ* Shrine: Protective 'Wrapping' of the Village

The first village shrine described to me was the *gínu múnɔ*. It constitutes an inner-area protective device that covers or 'wraps' the inhabited space, as a kind of protective shield. A similar concept is described by Kuba in referring to Dagara-Wiile's concept of *tengan*, meaning 'the crust or skin of the earth', a term that 'refers to the territory under the protection of a particular earth shrine' (2000, 417). As the term *gínu* indicates, the shrine refers to the place where the houses or compounds stand. The shrine protects the inside of the village against the various forms of evil influence that infiltrate the village or that are generated in and live inside the village. These malevolent forces trigger conflicts between the villagers by, in their words, 'mixing up' their souls. Social distortions are therefore seen as external to the individual, and they are not necessarily humanly produced. Rather, they intrude into the village space and, by seizing people, compel them to act negatively. These beings possess the capacity to cross the village threshold. Similarly, witchcraft (*duŋo duŋu*) is seen to occur between compounds or within them.

In comparison with the three others, *gínu múnɔ* is described as generating a shield that extends from a unique point to completely cover the whole settled area. This shrine marks the place of the foundation of the village from which the village developed and was the second to be fixed after the *lɔbɜ*.

The *Lɔbɜ* Shrine: The Regeneration and Continuity of the Society

Another *pɛgu* that was established by the ancestors at the foundation of the village is called the *lɔbɜ*, marking an act of appropriation of the place by the founders of Tiréli. This artefact is considered by the villagers to be an element that serves to maintain the cohesion of society, which is disturbed by evil forces coming from outside the village. It creates a dividing line between the village of the living and the escarpment in which the dead are buried. The *lɔbɔ* stands on a prominent rock that overhangs the escarpment scree in the district of Teri-Ku Dama. The *lɔbɔ* promontory, called *lɔbɔ dalá*, defines the place on which stands the small shed where the ritual paraphernalia are preserved.

As previously stated, the *lɔbɔ* is considered to be the oldest shrine in the village (see Appendix F). It legitimises the village because it was created when the village was founded. *Lɔbɔ* refers to the mythical ancestor *lɔbɔ*, a chtonian entity who 'incarnates the fertilizing force of nourishing earth' (Jolly 2004, 37) and by extension of nature; therefore, it constitutes an element of regeneration. According to de Ganay, the first *lɔbɔ* brought from the Mande was made of the soil of the tomb of the ancestor from whom the three Dogon clans— *Dyon*, *Ono,* and *Arou*—descended (most *lɔbɔ* shrines throughout the Dogon region were made from a fragment of the initial shrine) (de Ganay 1937, 205).

The *lɔbɔ* shrine can also be seen as a symbol of identity that relates people to the ancestors who founded the village. The shrine objectifies two types of temporality in its materiality. First, it constitutes a symbol of ancestor worship that reminds the villagers of the history of Dogon migration and of the origin of the foundation of their village. Second, it materialises the natural cycles and, by so doing, the seasonal activities relating to the land. This function is demonstrated by the fact that the *lɔbɔ* cult meets yearly and is the most important element in the villagers' ritual life. As part of the cult ritual, a sacrifice dedicated to the ancestors is enacted before the first rains. This is termed the *búlo* period. A rooster, a sheep, or sometimes an ox is sacrificed, and the blood and heart of the animal are offered to the shrine. The cult celebrates the regeneration of nature and therefore of the agricultural cycle. Thus, it corresponds to a rebirth of the earth, of the vegetal environment, and, more specifically, to the growing of millet with the coming of the rain. Symbolically, this ritual serves to re-engage the regeneration or the reordering of society—that is, to reinstate good social relationships and therefore to maintain as well as to strengthen its cohesion (van Beek 2003b, 95). According to the villagers, this shrine guarantees good health, regeneration, and fertility of the families of the village—the fecundity of the earth and of women—and, finally, it ensures the longevity of the elders. Thus, the continuity and the prosperity of life lie at the core of the *lɔbɔ* agency. The village celebration of the shrine institutes a breaking of daily routine and re-engages the seasonal cycle of cultivation tasks. If the shrine can be conceived as binding together the past and the present, the *lɔbɔ* can analogously be considered to play a central role in both the production of space as well as in the creation of a sense of boundedness. Indeed, as a principal element of the foundation of the village, the shrine is revealed as an act of appropriation of place.

The Ɔru Múnɔ Shrines: Protecting the Bush

The two other *múnɔ* shrines, *ɔru múnɔ*, are planted beyond the cultivated bush, outside the village. One of them, known as *sógu múnɔ*, situated on the east side of the *àna kɛrigu*, is fixed in the escarpment scree, where it is hidden by trees. The other one, known as *ɔru múnɔ*, is settled in a similar fashion on the west side of the bush, in the dune. If one follows the literal meaning of the term, the *múnɔ* would symbolically wrap the village's territory, enclosing it from all directions, including from above. However, the term also signifies the 'scream of the fox', a name that was given to the shrine after the pale fox, a mystic animal that plays a part in the divination process following the annual sacrifice on the *ɔru múnɔ*, which also conjures the falling of the rain.

It is noteworthy that each *múnɔ* shrine supports both protection and rain making, and in that they are complementary. The shrine of the dune facilitates requests for abundant rains to God, whereas the shrine of the scree serves to forecast, provoke, and/or stop the rain. Furthermore, the *ɔru múnɔ* of the dune performs the function of encouraging the establishment of male age groups through initiation as networks of solidarity in sharing tasks. Both *ɔru múnɔ* insulate Tiréli before the start of the rainy season against malevolent entities such as sorcerers that roam in the cultivated bush—the *jabu* or souls of those who died in particular circumstances such as suicide and epidemics such as meningitis (brought in by bad winds—and the evil spirits of the bush [*jinu*]), which compromise social relationships and kill humans. The shrine also protects against insects such as locusts that destroy crops and birds that eat crops. Last, both *ɔru múnɔ* are also used as protection against the wild animals owned by the bush spirits.

During the rainy season, when these malevolent entities intrude into the domesticated zone, they prompt accidents, which happen to people while they work in the fields as well as when they travel to the plain, where they are found unconscious in the bush or in a state of convulsion and then lose their minds. In the local conception, the two *ɔru múnɔ* shrines that protect the cultivated bush create a symbolic boundary that separates the wild space of the bush (*ɔmna*) from the cultural space of the village (surrounding cultivated bush [*gòrò*] and village [*àna*; see Figure 5.1, Chapter 5]). The shrines objectify a conjuncture of temporalities that are ritual and seasonal, since they are related to the agrarian cycle and the renewal of nature. Similarly, they recall the history of boundaries through the multiple threats against which the Dogon protect themselves.

Hence, the two bush shrines form an initial barrier to block the entrance of malevolent forces by containing them within these obstructions of external obstacles. However, this symbolic enclosure remains porous, since the malign entities still penetrate the boundary if their power is stronger than the protection provided by the shrines. Therefore, sacrifices are made on these specific shrines in order to repair the impurity or a broken situation caused by these entitites.[5] Finally, the *sógu múnɔ* located in the scree also has the function of invoking as well as stopping the rain and so protecting against drought and against downpours that destroy crops and houses and that kill people and cattle. The cattle are protected by a shrine called *ɛ̃nrɛ̃ girun amá*. The shrine of shepherds, who are children, is located at the foot of the scree in the quarter of Komanga and is meant to protect cattle from accidents, predators, and miscarriages and to promote their fertility and the good health of the shepherds. A libation of millet cream and fresh milk are poured onto the shrine by the *bà: iré*, a 60-year-old man.

Ontological Security and the Symbolic Mechanism of Earth Shrines

As suggested by Bouju, malicious invisible elements occupy a parallel world that also constitutes the space of the ancestors, sorcerers, and wandering souls. In other words, when this invisible world interferes with the bush space, it dramatically affects human life (Bouju 1995a, 354–55). This interesting point raised by Bouju emphasises a dual conception of the environment that rests on the coexistence of the human world, including the physical space of the bush, with a second, invisible world of the dead and the spirits that is tangential to the first. As these two worlds communicate, it becomes necessary for people to control the boundary and thus to prevent, through symbolic protections such as shrines, the entrance of negative elements. In his account of Dogon territoriality, Bouju proposes that the meeting points of these two worlds are materialised by the two bush shrines located at the eastern and the western ends of the Dogon village. He conceptualises these two shrines as two doors, through one of which malevolent entities enter the living space (shrine at the east) and through the other (shrine at the west) they are expelled (Bouju 1995a, 354–55). In Tiréli, malevolent entities entering the territory are expelled from the *gínu múnɔ* located inside the village.

Bouju describes a linear current of malevolent entities that he defines as an inverted modality of space and time. As he puts it: 'Dogon people attribute to the invisible space (more precisely to the trajectory of invisible forces) a property that in the visible world . . . belongs [only] to the dimension of time, i.e., the irreversibility of its orientation' (Bouju 1995a, 355).

The unbound, invisible world as fundamentally temporal exists, however, outside human time, which is made up of, for instance, daily seasonal cycles of activities. The meeting point of these two tangential worlds is often described as an inside/out passageway that is operated through particular initiations, witchcraft, hunting, and mask rituals (van Beek 1992, 68). Through this reversible movement from one sphere to the other, people who possess the capacity of seeing or experiencing the invisible in the bush space may benefit from particular forms of knowledge such as about the medicines they bring back to the village.

The fact of being enclosed by this system of overlapping protection reinforces the ontological security that is partly and naturally provided by the site of the scree, which does indeed constitute a natural defensive system, by making access to the village particularly problematic. Furthermore, the shrines exist to fix and guarantee principles of social cohesion through prohibitions associated with reordering the world and averting chaos. This order creates a conformity comparable to the objects as the system of prohibition that ensures good functioning and stability, forcing people to adapt to and respect their own intrinsic principles. Thus the shrines create a generational continuity through the embodied transmission of the rules or the ancestor laws applied in everyday practice. They materialise and recall the authority of the ancestors and the power of the invisible world by standing in the landscape. Interrelated as they are, these shrines complement one another and maximise the strength of the field of protection. As proposed by Bouju, the malevolent entities are contained by these shrine-obstacles (Bouju 1995a, 363). Hence, the shrines act as receptacles that canalize negative elements and subsequently have to be repaired and purified. This process occurs before the rainy season and therefore before the sacrifice. Beyond offering protection, these shrines symbolise the cohesion of the village as well as renewal of social networks. And, finally, the *múnɔ* and the *lɜbɜ*, which facilitate a gathering process, convey a sense of collectedness.

Formation of the protective boundaries starts with the establishment of the enclosed interiors of the village. The enclosures of Tiréli have been created over a long time, beginning with elements from the foundation of the village (Appendix F). The whole system of enclosures, or 'wrappings', consisting metaphorically of a series of circles, was originally generated from the inside of the settled space. Therefore, these boundaries were set up over time. As seen from above, the built surface or village of Tiréli is bounded by the *gínu múnɔ*. The village designates a place of social cohesion—that is, a place to live in (community). Such cohesion involves obligations to recognise reciprocal and complementary assistance between people. The village shrines materialise the attachment of the villagers to one another, since through one another they recognise a shared common origin that stems from a long history of migration.

Earth Shrines as a Sense of Unity and Legitimation of Dogon Identity

The Dogon village of Tiréli possesses a common story of migration spread over centuries that led to the foundation of the village (see Appendix B). The multiple versions of this story (Dieterlen 1941, 23–72; Huet 1994; Petit 1998) testify to a common Mande ancestor origin for all of present-day Dogon.

The story is of a complex journey, a perpetual movement toward the northeast part of the country. In the tale, the Dogon migratory group divides into multiple subsets as the clans, often because of quarrels, separate and spread over the land and eventually establish their own villages. The general plot of the Dogon migration is based on one family that became divided and subdivided as people moved along the escarpment, the plain, and the plateau (*tíbi kú*), settling in the areas that would become the Dogon villages as we know them today. The story reveals a state of continual movement, based on clan logic, of fleeing one place and finding refuge in another. As a form of containment, the uneven escarpment would have been chosen in particular because of its defensive nature; it comprises fissures and caves (Chapter 5) where people could hide and hidden paths they could follow to escape, as well as the impassable scree (Walther 2010, 14–16), which made access to the villages particularly difficult for such invaders[6] as Fulani horsemen (Huet 1994, 25). The migration schema is characterised by a context of threats and escape.

The formation of the village of Tiréli was initially defined by installation of the *lɔbɔ* and *múnɔ* shrines as well as the naming of the village's quarters as the village developed. The toponyms of Tiréli quarters (see Appendix F) constitute a way of appropriating the land in order to fix or legitimate a people's occupation of it. As the name Tiréli indicates, clearing a site by felling trees is a direct and efficient way of appropriating the site. This action is also expressed in the family name Saye, which connotes the act of uprooting, concretised by the scattering and deportation of the former *Ongoeba* occupants. From this perspective, the appropriation of the site is a political act that generates conflicts and migrations. The village shrines objectify the foundation of the place in the same way as the architectural elements do. Together they objectify the long-term establishment of the place and ways of dwelling as they fix its history and material identity. In particular, the *lɔbɔ* shrine constitutes the element through which the villagers legitimate, according to the principle of lineage and ancestry, the appropriation of the place by their ancestors. It fixes them conceptually to the land. The *lɔbɔ* thus materialises an act of dwelling. It mediates the establishment and expansion of a community in a place made viable by having been cleared and by already having satisfactory water, land, and game resources. Furthermore, the shrine materialises particular ancestor affiliations that relate all Dogon to a common mythic Mande origin—although this point is debated (Chapter 1). Thus the shrine as a material identity creates a 'sense of Dogon-ness'.

The *Lɔbɔ* Shrine: Sense of Rootedness, Mande Heritage and Social Cohesion

I have suggested that the *lɔbɔ* shrine, as a founding element of civilisation, brings particular senses of attachment to the place, conveying a sense of rootedness. Equally, it materialises a shared Mande heritage and identity by standing as a guarantor of ancestral Mande origin. Similarly, it objectifies the genealogies of the village families that stem from the common ancestors who founded the village. It creates particular networks of solidarity between the Dogon villages of the same *Arou* clan. Notably, such alliances exist for ritual practices as well, to mitigate conflicts with external communities. Hence, the villagers who share a common origin find allegiance in the *lɔbɔ* name.

The *lɔbɔ* also stands as a symbol of cohesion on a village level. In the words of a young Muslim of the village, the shrine, because it is the oldest, functions as the most important element of the village. As he explained: 'the *lɔbɔ* keeps people together whatever happens, whether you are Muslim, Catholic, or Animist. It is for everybody together. It stands for the amity between the villagers. But the day the *lɔbɔ* is left by the villagers, that will be the end of the village'. By this, the young man indicates that the *lɔbɔ* constitutes an important element of solidarity between the villagers and the multiple religious groups of Tiréli. Hence, the day the sacrifice on the *lɔbɔ* stops, the village will lose the values of the community, such as the good relationships between people, the reciprocation of help, and the sense of unity, which are essential to survive in a landscape of scarcity. In other words, the *lɔbɔ* shrine ensures the cohesion of the village, which is politically divided by long-term conflicts between the two main quarters of Teri-Ku and Sodanga, as well as by quarrels among the lineages—notably, about field limits, ownership, and distribution. On a wider level, the *lɔbɔ* reiterates the unity of the Dogon people of Tiréli as part of the Mande world. Finally, it conveys a sense of ontological security of 'staying together', that is, of maintaining social cohesion that they reaffirm through common practice at village shrines.

Conclusion

The shrines of the *lɔbɔ*, the *gínu múnɔ,* and the two *ɔru múnɔ* mark the foundation of the territory of Tiréli, as well as the protection of its space. As fixed inside and outside the village, Tiréli's shrines map out the living landscape and divide its cultural space, including the separation of the domesticated bush from the wild space. As I have demonstrated, these objects of power and control define a particular model of containment through symbolic enclosure and protection of the cultural and domesticated space of humans against the world of the invisible. Tangentially, these two worlds interface through two openings that are materialised by the bush shrines. The protected surfaces I have described are made effective through a process of 'wrapping' the territory's surfaces that is generated by Tiréli's shrines, creating a particular ontological security.

Through this account of the mechanism by which enclosures are achieved by Dogon people from Tiréli, I have also underlined the conjuncture of temporalities that is objectified in land shrines materiality. Land shrines endow the temporality of the environment—that is, the regeneration of the land and of ritual practice, as well as the history of people. Consequently, the model of containment, as a process of making oneself at home in the world, is defined as flexible. In other words, the boundaries have to be understood here as a device for protection that remains relatively open, since they may always let bad things enter, depending on the efficacy of the shrines. Finally, the shrines materialise Dogon cultural identities. In fact, their reactivation through ritual practice constitutes a gathering process conveying through ritual a sense of collectedness and 'Dogon-ness'—that is, of the unity of the villagers with other Dogon and Mande communities to which Tiréli relates through ancestor affiliation.

4   The Inside of the Village: Material Symbolism and Building Process

Because it has retained its natural colours and textures, the village of Tiréli blends with the surrounding landscape of the cliffs from which stones, earth, and wood are extracted and used as construction materials. The building of the village seems to have depended on a process of containing that relates to the scree milieu, which shelters the village by disguising it, and on a process of de-containing, which concerns the exploitation of the materiality of the scree, as a means of building homes. Subjected in the past to many adversities and dangers, notably jihadi, slave traders, and wildlife (Chapter 2), the site of Tiréli offers particular defensive qualities through its elevation and the unevenness of its steep topography. Hence, the containment—the hidden and thus protective nature of the village environment—becomes defined through a natural aesthetic and the qualities of the place.

This chapter focuses on the daily dynamics by which the Dogon of Tiréli make sense of the village's landscape as a place, through a building process. To a certain extent, I attempt to contextualise and define the village, or *àna kóro*, through the daily movements of people, who, as they walk up and down the escarpment or along the furrows around the compounds, are canalized by the built features.

Movement is introduced by the villagers through daily practices that create a sense of attachment to the place and by tourists as they visit the site. From the perspective or movement and change, I suggest that although the village blends in with the scree, it is also increasingly disclosed by tourism and modernism.[1] Therefore, I center my argument on a dialectic of fixity and fluidity of boundaries that enclose the multiple built elements. I focus on the spatial relationships between built features and the paths that connect them.

Living in a Landscape of Scarcity: Materiality and Cosmology in West Africa by Laurence Douny, 67–80 © 2014 Left Coast Press, Inc. All rights reserved.

I examine the architectural system that operated in the past as a control device. It was effective notably in the maintenance of social organisation and gender boundaries, which have become more flexible. I propose that the Dogon built-environment stands as a material symbolism that does not imply material forms *per se* but all that the built environment enfolds in terms of *implicit assumptions and practices* (Rowlands 1985, 203). Although the architecture of the village is physically and conceptually fixed in space, its temporality and agency are recreated daily through its use by men, women, old people, children, and foreigners. Here, I consider the inside of the village as a living cultural matrix defined through specific active processes of movement. Thus, by walking readers through the village of Tiréli/Teri-Ku Dama, starting from the top of the scree, I look at how the village has been configured over time. Then, by examining the spatial layout of Dogon architectonics, I show how this built and lived environment frames daily social life and thought.

Spatial and Social Organisation of the Village

The village of Tiréli is divided into the two main districts of Teri-Ku and Sodanga. These are designated by the term *tógu* ('district'), which also refers to its subdivisions. Both *tógu* are subdivided into three. Thus the first district is composed of the subdistricts of Dama, Sabo, and Komanga, and the second includes Gujoguru, Tatara, and Sodanga. As a result of migrations several families left the escarpment, installing themselves on the plateau and founding Daga, while others, including Gimeto and Binesoy, congregated in the Séno Gondo plain. The top of the escarpment scree forms a surface that contains people's dwellings and that offers an interesting spatial layout, in which the development of the village—its demographic logic—can be read. The top of the scree is occupied by the oldest known built elements that founded Tiréli. The spatial layouts of times past, a few troglodyte Tellem sites (c. eleventh–fourteenth centuries C.E.), can also be seen on the face of the escarpment; however, these are not considered to be part of the village. The complex social organisation of Dogon villages (Paulme 1988) is objectified in the distribution of the compounds. In fact, as Bourdier suggests, the notion of village and built environment in West Africa refers to 'a plural entity formed by a number of households organised on the basis of agnatic descents cultivating separately and/or collectively the farmland, and residing in the same composite habitat' (Bourdier 1997, 2116).

In her work on the Kasena of Burkina Faso, Liberski-Bagnoud proposes architectural space as a compelling way of reading and understanding lineage and thus kinship structure (Liberski-Bagnoud 2002, 67–89). Regarding the Dogon, Lane (1986, 1994) has explored the relationships between social organisation and built forms. His work raises the question of the temporalities of Dogon material forms as well as the active role of architectural space *in the reproduction and the transformation of the society* (Lane 1994, 196). Therefore, as Lane proposes, architecture allows an insight into the way the *Dogon perceive and construct their past* (Lane 1994, 210).

In Dama, the two *gínna*, or ancestral houses, generate the village district's architectural matrix. These family houses, or 'big' houses, located near the sacred sites and multiple sanctuaries, are the first built elements found right at the top of the scree. The compounds that stand below the *gínna* form a *tire tɔgú*. In the broadest sense of the term, *tire tɔgú* refers to a cluster of compounds or patrilineal groups that originate from a common ancestor. In other words, they relate to the same *gínna*, from which the district of the village has developed. As proposed by Paulme, the term *gínna* is a contraction of *gínu na*, which means 'big house' (1988, 123). Therefore, the *gínna*, or parent company, standing for the whole group, materialises all the genealogies of the descendant part of an extended line of agnatic groups that relate through intermarriage (Lane 1986). In theory, the *gínna* constitutes and maintains the solidarity and the cohesion of its members on the levels of ritual practice, economy, management, and field tenure (Paulme 1988, 47–49). The *gínna* is a powerful political institution that is governed by the oldest man of the district. His age is always strongly debated among the families, since everyone wants to enthrone his or her own father. As a result, virulent conflicts break out among the families leading to internecine wars and the division of the *gínna*.

The *gínna* of the district form a *tire gínna*. This term originally applied to a group of families or compounds of common descent, thereby designating a kernel of *gínna*, which originated from a common ancestor. The *tire gínna* therefore gathers several *gínna*, and each of them divides into a series of a *tire tɔgú* (Palau-Marti 1957, 58; Paulme 1988, 48–49). *Tire* means the known ancestors, going back three generations, according to Calame-Griaule (1968, 275). The *tire tɔgú* designates the family in the strictest sense of the term. It comprises a father, his wives, their children, and their own compounds. Thus it refers to a patriarchal unit whose organisational design is based on the same model as the *gínna*.

The specificity of the *tire gínna* system and *tire tɔgú* is that they interrelate people on a kinship as well as on an economic level (Lane 1986; Paulme 1988), which concerns, as mentioned previously, the distribution of the fields and their exploitation. The *gínna* houses of Teri-Ku gather the families that stem from them on the same scree area. However, owing to a lack of space and interest, the *tire tɔgú* schema that initially reproduced the logic of being surrounded by either the sons or the brother of the patriarch has ceased to function. In the upper part of the scree, the schema seems to be applied; however, as we move farther down, the *tire tɔgú* and the simple *gínna dagi* and *gínu* units, as well as *gujɔ*, share the same space randomly. The origin of the *gínu* is found in the *gujɔ*, or the smallest unit of the Dogon habitat, which corresponds to a room that a young man occupies on his own or shares with his wife and small children. The term *gujɔ* refers to the basic element from which a compound is generated materially, although its meaning also relates to the lineage of its inhabitants (Chapter 7).

Today, the top of the scree is being deserted by the villagers. In fact, it is sparsely occupied only by older members of the family and by ruins that are not reused and are allowed to decay, because of the uneven topography and the difficulty of access to resources. But these sites still constitute the property of the ancestors of the place. The foot of the scree is being increasingly built up. The ways in which these compounds relate to one another tends to be random, owing to the occupation of convenient places and because of the availability of space. The people of Tiréli fear that one day the base of the scree will be overpopulated, and they will have to spread out into agricultural space. As indicated, elements of the demographic logic of Teri-Ku Dama[2] can be visualised vertically, as it is animated by a movement down toward the foot of the scree. Overall, when walking through the village and referring to individuals, the villagers operate a distinction between the 'people of the top' (*dà* or *dàran*) and the 'people of the foot' (*dóɲu*); the first term refers to the 'old families', the second refers to the 'youth' of the village.

The 'First' House of the Village: Architectural Matrix and Generative Process

The first *gínna* of Tiréli corresponds to the first house of the first district (*tógu*) of the village, which is said to be *Tatara*. In that place, the village's founder, called *Enẽ* (Appendix F), would have first built a shelter[3] under the *gínu múnɔ* rock. On one side of it, a mud cone has been affixed to protect the village as well as to indicate the place that, in the past, sheltered the ancestor of the Saye people who first discovered the site and founded Tiréli. However, I was also told that the house of the ancestor from which all the compounds of the village descended existed on the plateau. It reportedly was a small house with a low ceiling or a rock cavity that was used as a temporary shelter for the original ancestor, a hunter. It was replaced by a proper compound, or *gínna*, he built at the top of the scree, where nothing of it remains. The precise location of the 'first' house has been contradicted by other sources, which maintain that it was located farther down and would have been abandoned over time. (The multiple versions about the history of the foundation of Dogon villages support internal politics and cause conflict among the villagers.)

From the multiple conversations I had with the elders of Tiréli and elsewhere, it seems that the idea of the 'first' house of the village operates as a myth that provides information about the appropriation and political validation of origins and also as a form of prestige. As observed by Paulme (1988), the idea of a common ancestry is a way of gathering people to ensure the continuity, cohesion, and, therefore, strength of the group. Furthermore, the fact that there is competition over the location of a first house suggests rivalry between the districts. In fact, the myth empowers a system of rules and social organisation, as well as determining coalition in case of war. Although the myth serves to constitute a relatively coherent whole, it can be observed in Tiréli that the more the group ramifies, the less united the unit becomes. If the *gínna* house originally constituted a form of unity that was reproduced, on a different scale, through the *gínna* houses of the village, the present evolution of the built environment translates into a sort of splintering of the social structure and relationships.

The *Gínna* of Teri-Ku Dama: The Fixing of Material Identities

A 'first' house was built at the foundation of each Dogon village, from which stemmed all the existing *gínna* of the village. In theory, each *gínna* enables people to trace the genealogy of their families (Lane 1986), as well as the demography of the village. Extrapolating from the villagers' discourse on the development of the built environment, one could say that the concept of the 'first' house fixes local identities and the ontology of the village. This idea is supported by one of the functions of the *gínna*, which is to define, through multiple altars and protection systems, a particular sense of attachment to the past, rootedness in the place as well as a sense of relatedness. Thus, the *gínna* conveys a sense of containment through the spatial logic of fixing and bounding families. It also creates and maintains a sense of unity among the families of Teri-Ku Dama.

Among young people, the *gínna* is important for those who follow the (animist) 'tradition'; those who convert to Islam and Christianity do not contribute to the family ceremonies and, in particular, to sacrifices. Such links to the *gínna* are generally perpetuated by the old people. Although the young people maintain and verbally express their relatedness to and descent from a particular *gínna*, this affirmation is contradicted in practice by an increasing sense of individualism, autonomy, and personal growth. As young people often put it: 'Here, everybody looks to his/her own future. It's up to you, and it's every man for himself'.[4] Therefore, the transmission of knowledge regarding family affairs, genealogies, and ritual practices—as well as the allocation of the fields and the harvest—is gradually controlled less and less by the *gínna*. Imported religions and modernism have, indeed, introduced new ways of relating and new forms of socialising, as well as new values.

The *gínna* building distinguishes itself from other houses by its location. It stands in the oldest part of the village, which can be the village centre or, in the case of the escarpment, the top of the scree that was first occupied. The other significant characteristic lies in its architecture, which offers a particular style that sometimes varies according to the escarpment or plateau. While only one *gínna* may be found in some village districts, in others several buildings of this type can be observed. Tiréli Dama comprises two houses, the *Ginédoɲu* and the *Banɔgu*. Thus, as detailed in a simplified verbal schema by my sources, the people of Teri-Ku originate from the common ancestor, *Ko-u*, who founded a *tógu* and from whom the descendants of the three *gínna* listed earlier can trace their origins. The ruin of their ancestor's house stands, according to them, at the very top of the scree. This assertion constitutes an abstract site or reference point that testifies to their common origin rather than offering material evidence. While the oldest *gínna* of the *Ginéku*—that is, the 'head house'—stands at the top the escarpment scree, the *Ginedoɲu* ('the house below') is located a few metres down. The *Banɔgu* is located even farther down, in the middle of the scree. I was told that the locations of these houses relate to their order of foundation. Therefore, as mentioned, the oldest would be the *Ginéku* standing at the top. This building has two characteristics. The first one relates to its particular architectural style of successive terraces leaning against the rock. The second concerns the coexistence of two *gínna* on one site. In fact, the *Ginéku* comprises two families, whose houses are semidetached. The reason given to me for the coexistence of two *Ginéku gínna* was hypothesised as a quarrel within the family. It was extremely difficult to gain details about these houses, since long-term tensions still exist between the families.

The Ancestor's House: Materialising Genealogies

In many areas of the Dogon region, the Dogon *gínna* are said to be founded by the construction of a shrine, or *áma na*, which in most places takes the shape of a prominent rock on which the foundations of the house are erected. This shrine emphasises the notion of attachment, or the fixing of the house and hence of the family, to the place. The house highlights the establishment and the future development of a district. Along with the family shrines that symbolise the cohesion of the family and ensure its prosperity and well-being, the house often contains a series of clay pots called *búnɔ*, which are aligned. They materialise similar principles of fixing and continuity of the family, that is, of the lineage. The containers are dedicated to the *wagem*, or ancestors—to 'those who are far away' (Calame-Griaule 1968, 293).

The pots are filled with nonfermented millet beer during the *Buro*, or celebration of the end of the harvests. People go to pray and to address the ancestors to thank them for their assistance in transmitting the people's will to God. The pots are refilled before the rainy season, at the time of the *búlu*. This activity celebrates the regeneration of the environment, as well as the start of the sowing period (Chapter 3). It signifies the revival of social networks, remembering the ancestors from whom protection and goodwill for the coming agricultural cycle is requested. In other words, the *búlu* constitutes a re-reconnecting of the people to the ancestors in order to gain their support for the cultivation season, fertility, and prosperity of the lineage. Hence, every time a patriarch dies, a *búnɔ* is placed in the *gínna*. These pots symbolise the genealogy of the family continuing back, in theory, to the ancestral founder of the place (in reality, most of the pots are broken). The container, filled with nonfermented millet beer, enables members to host the soul of the ancestor, who is invited to alight on the liquid and to drink it. As Jolly writes, the purpose of this libation rite is to refresh and to appease the ancestors with a 'white beer' that does not get them drunk (Jolly 2004, 206). The pot, and more specifically the liquid it contains, consists of a receptacle destined to receive the ancestor's soul. I was told that if the pot breaks, it is said that the house manager will die. Therefore, to repair the offence done to the ancestors, he has to sacrifice a goat and apologise for the incident while a new *búnɔ* is brought in to replace the broken one. Consequently, the pots that represent the ascendant agnatic members of a lineage fix the genealogy as well as the cohesion of the families by hosting the ancestors during significant moments of the agrarian cycle. It was also reported to me that the *gínna* house possesses a protective system laid in the foundation of the house. It consists of medicine made of plants that act as magic to prevent attacks by malevolent spirits and witchcraft. At the same time, it symbolises the fixing, continuity, success, and peace among the families.

Spatial Containment: Material Relations, Boundaries, and Social Control

Using the paths designed for tourists to walk around the village and between the compounds, I now examine the built features that stand along the way in Teri-Ku Dama, Tiréli. By focusing on the architectural content of this district, Tiréli, I investigate the Dogon spatial logic of the fixed and bounded built elements, which are used by all the villagers. The built system is symmetrical but not identical for each district of the village; that is to say, in each subdistrict it has more or less the same features. One of the reasons is that the architectural elements and their style are relatively fluid, owing to increasing modernism. The schema of spatial relations proposed here enables us, first, to highlight the demographic, gendered, and geographical divisions of the community, as they are reproduced in each area of the village. Second, it underlines some implicit structures of control and of regulation that are objectified in the built environment and in their spatial and visual relationships. Third, the system delineates the material limits of the inhabited surface; thus, it gives an indication of the expansion of the village of Tiréli.

The Village Paths: Canalizing Daily Life and Tourism

Although the cliff appears as a fixed and stable container element, the escarpment scree and in particular its large rocks are the result of the collapse of sections of the escarpment that, in some places, still threatens to fall. Large flat rocks located away from the houses are used as platforms on which onions are pounded (*gaw[a] nɔmɔ*) by relatives, often the young people, in a circular choreography (Figure 4.1) accompanied by singing (*gaw[a] nɔmɔ ní*, 'singing for the onions'). The blows produced by the pounding and the songs add to the Dogon's daily soundtrack. The onion juice covers the young men's feet, its acid smell diffuses in the air, and the onion paste leaves permanent stains on the rock. The onion traces left by this seasonal task shape the materiality of rocks (Tilley 2004) and become a testimony to everyday life.

On a symbolic level, the rocks that are located outside the village and that constitute the escarpment slope are said to be 'living'. In fact, in their materiality they host benevolent but formidable spirits, in the same way that the trees do. Thus, rocks and trees are said to move at night: 'When everybody is asleep, the trees and the rocks gather in the bush where they chat'. Thus the villagers avoid walking near the tree areas early in the morning, in order not to disturb the trees' intimacy. As discussed in the next section, because they endow life, rocks and trees function as a metaphor for humanity and social life.

The built environment is interlaced with paths that weave around and through the compounds, connecting them, and through which they communicate with one another. Although most paths are eventually abandoned because the compounds they enclose are in ruins, the main arterial paths are used daily

Figure 4.1   A large flat rock in the scree is used by young men and the author as a platform for pounding onions in a circular choreography.

by both tourists and locals. These are regularly maintained to maximise safety as well as to facilitate visits by tourists and are, therefore, being considerably improved. In contrast, the paths that only the local inhabitants use are less accessible and not well maintained.

As shown by Walther (2001, 73), paths are redesigned and created over time to ensure that tourists move among the various elements they come to see in the manner most convenient for the villagers. Hence the paths guide visitors in particular directions to guarantee that they do not miss elements but also to make sure that they do not enter sacred places. As Walther notes, the mobility of the villagers through the village does not necessary correspond to that of the tourists (Walther 2001, 73). There is here a reinvention of Dogon architectural culture at work, which is characterised by a redesign of space, creation of new spatial logic, and, as I show later, of built forms that demonstrate particular practices of doing and undoing the environment as a means to promote a certain image of local culture. As suggested by Walther, referring to Balandier (1988, 1992), Dogon people have over time appropriated and learned 'to interpret the dynamic of modernity and transformed it under an appearance of continuity' (Walther 2001, 111).

Interconnectivity: Built Forms as a Control Device

In Tiréli the built features concentrate horizontally on the top of the scree near the *gínna* houses. However, in many villages on the plateau, the spatial layout of the built environment starts from the centre and expands outward like a circular maze, revolving around the first house of the village. The public place interconnects the different parts of the district as a juncture point from which the multiple paths radiate to access the compounds. The *tógu na* ('shelter with a low ceiling') and the public place, as part of the same site, constitute the physical core of the subdistrict of Dama. (As mentioned earlier, the actual centre of the village of Tiréli is said to be the place where it was founded, that is, in Tatara.) The public place, called *táy gonó*, is characterised by a baobab tree that stands at its centre. As a species that survives for over a century, the baobab commonly symbolises the longevity of the elders, who stand as the guarantors of Dogon culture. The public place is defined as the cultural centre of the village. It is where young people gather at night; they play under the moonlight while the elders watch from the *tógu na*. Indeed, the place itself plays a crucial role in the socialisation of youth, as well as in the meeting of future spouses.

The place is physically divided into various locales in which young people and children gather according to age groups; one side is assigned to the girls and the other to the boys. They play at night, separately, as each gendered group possesses its own games. While the youngest of both groups play continuously until late at night, the older ones sit on the sides of the *tógu na* on large flat stones to rest or discuss serious matters. Although in the past this use of the space meant that the elders could easily control the meetings of teenage boys and, particularly, those of girls, today the youth of the village tend to meet in new places at the foot of the scree. Slightly set back from the compounds, these are seen as free places appropriated by the youth and therefore not imposed by the system. Out of reach of the gaze of the elders, they chat freely, smoke, and court each other. The main gathering in the Dama public place generally constitutes the last step of a series of meetings. These start in Sâpo or Komanga's public places or alternatively in a deserted and site of a former compound. In these locations, two or three young people start a game by singing and clapping their hands, ŋiŋ pomu for the girls and the *bambam* for the boys.

The *táy gonó* also acts as a ritual site where funerals take place during the dry seasons. Men and women are assigned their own corners while they perform rituals; women stand opposite the men. The *táy dumo* rock is dedicated to the dead body that is lying on it during the funeral before the body is taken to the cave.

In Tiréli masquerades in the public place, the *imína dumodɛ̃* is the place where the masks sit, and the *tiɲe tãŋa paɲi* is an elevated place dedicated to the stilt mask. The public place is the most attractive area of the village for tourists. In fact, in the last twenty years, before the Malian political crisis, the Tiréli masquerade has become a tourist attraction as visitors arrive once or twice a day and as many as four days a week to watch it. (Since the end of 2011, tourism industry in the Dogon region has collapsed.)

The public place and its elements thus serve to organise the society spatially and distribute people while they are meeting for leisure as well as during ritual activities. Through its purposeful spatial division, the public place acts as a system of control. In other words, it reminds people, whether occupying it or just crossing it, that, as part of the community, everyone occupies a particular place and plays a particular role. These roles must be maintained in order to ensure the cohesion and continuity of social life.

On the southeastern side of the *táy gonó* stand the ruins of the smithy. In the mid-1990s, the smithy was reestablished at the foot of the district for practical reasons. Next to it, facing the public place, stands the *tógu na*, which is considered to be the first public element of the village's foundation (Spini & Spini 1976). The edifice is a thick roof of stalks supported by pillars. It functions as a 'palaver house', because it is used in the evenings as a place of rest where the older men tend to stay, swapping daily news items and various tales, gossip, and information; and it acts as a court of justice within which conflicts are resolved and decisions made. Its particularly low ceiling protects the inside from the sun and heat, and this restricted space contains any violence or aggression, which are perceived as a sign of extreme disorder. Thus problems are kept within and sorted out inside this container.

The *tógu na*, which is referred to as the 'men's house', as an emblematic element of the Dogon village that stands at the core of the village quarters is constantly reappropriated by the locals to emphasise Dogon culture. Because the building attracts the curiosity of the tourists, it has been elaborately redecorated over the past five years. Its environment and pillars are covered with symbols that represent Dogon culture, such as the hunter, the blanket of the dead, and the masks. Mythical symbols such as the *lɜbɜ* snake, a group of stars, and the wild fauna that used to be found in the bush, as well as the architecture of Tiréli, such as the house and the granary, are all represented on the pillars and plastered rocks surrounding the *tógu na.*

The symbols located in the environment of the *tógu na* act as miniature visual representations of Dogon village culture that highlight the Dogon habitat and tradition. These graphic elements constitute markers of identity as well as validation of the tourist economy. The house located near the *tógu na* in the district of Sodanga is also elaborately decorated. Being constantly photographed by the tourists makes it a source of pride to its owner, and thus it functions as a source of income for the owner, since he can ask the tourists for money to take pictures of his house.

Given its distinct, perched vantage point, the *tógu na* acts as a panopticon, enabling a 360° surveillance of the activities in the district. The thick, low ceiling, which darkens the inside, and the pillars hide the men seated within the *tógu.* Therefore, all movement occurring in the village can be observed by them without being seen. This function is the reason why, in the past, it was used as an observation site for hunting. As a lookout point from which nighttime intrusion into compounds could be detected and therefore prevented, it also constituted a safeguard against raids and notably against witchcraft. It was also used as a means to control the women's house located behind it and to help intervene in kidnappings and to identify witches who are said to live on their own. Today, however, the practicality of visual surveillance is considerably reduced owing to extensive building activity. In fact, because all the space surrounding the *tógu na* of Dama is inhabited, only distant views of the foot and face of the escarpment are possible. However, the visual control function is now largely irrelevant, because most of the recorded scourges have disappeared, with the exception, perhaps, of witchcraft. If the *tógu na* remains to some extent occupied by the old men of the village, most men tend to gather at the foot of the scree under a tree in a place called *ŋamarã*—another place that seems to be occupied more for chatting while weaving baskets, ropes, and mats or carving wooden pestles and mortars.

As we leave the public place and walk into the northeast side, we end up at the *yápùnu gínu*, or the women's house. Women stay here during menstruation because their blood is perceived as impure. As a polluting element, it affects water as well as the power of magic and ritual objects. The house is enclosed in a circle of stones, indicating the impurity of the place. At the time I visited the house a bed had been made with a plank fixed on four piles of stone. I was told that such beds are used by women in an 'impure' state so that they do not

touch the ground and thus make it infertile. Within the *yápùnu gínu* enclosure stands a small stone house in which women keep their cooking utensils
(Chapter 8). In the past, the house stood outside the village. Now, owing to the
expansion of the village, it is surrounded by several compounds. A series of
dòmolo, wooden hooks that are symbols of virility, are hung on the façade by
the young men of the village. In association with these, as seen in the village of
Pèlou, the side walls of the house are covered with male and female figurines.
These generally constitute a sequence, by symbolising the start and continuity of a family. Because this house symbolically relates to reproduction, the
figurines on the walls are ritual traces that signify the situation of people who
cannot have children.

The house is repaired only when the building has been extensively damaged—for example, when the rain starts to get in, or when women simply ask
the elders for its repair, which occurs before the rainy season. The task is conducted by young bachelors of a specific age group. The more young men that
participate, the better, since male youth represent the potential demographic
increase of the village. When the job is done, the young men who are looking
for a wife sculpt female figurines on the outside wall with a small quantity of
wet mud. Then they bring a *dòmolo* that they leave hanging on the rooftop
above the door and hope to find a wife during the coming year.

This rite is also carried out by men who hope their wives will give birth
to a child of a particular sex. Over time, figurines, which signify fecundity
and therefore life, accumulate all around the house. This system is, therefore,
gendered. It concerns the wish for offspring or a spouse, and it concerns men.
The building is repaired when nature 'revives' at the end of the dry season as a
sign of regeneration and fertility. The enclosed place represents the reproductive cycle of women. Its surrounding stone boundaries contain the 'impurity'
within it and thus prevent 'contamination' of the village. The walls provide
space to express a vital need or lack. Therefore, each *dòmolo* expresses the
need of obtaining either a wife or a child. The figurines are made directly after
the repairs, when the wall is still wet, in order to increase the grip between the
mud figurine and the wall it is pressed on to. Similarly, the moisture also signifies fertility. If over time a *dòmolo* falls off the front of the house, the women
gather it and burn it as firewood.

Leaving the site and walking straight toward the east, we reach the *bínu
gínu* houses. A *bínu gínu* building acts both as a bounded container and a
receptacle for the shrines dedicated to the cult of the *bínu*. The need for purity
is the reason why this building is always constructed far away from the menstruating women's house. Finally, its shape, generally round and comprising
a single room, is said to 'preserve the secret in its inside'. As mentioned, the
oldest elements of the village are located at the top of the scree. These are
gathered on a horizontal strip that is framed by two main paths used by tourists
to visit the village. The *bínu gínu* and the *yápùnu gínu* as well as the *tógu na*

were elements that constituted the former limits of the village, since they were located on its fringe. However, with the considerable expansion of the village, the compounds started to congregate around these elements. Hence, it is possible to draw the former physical boundaries of the place and thus, to some extent, to trace its expansion.

A final element that manifests itself on our journey through the village of Tiréli is the ruins. The upper part of the scree of the village of Tiréli constitutes a wide horizontal strip of deserted settlements. This part of the village is being abandoned owing to significant migrations to town, on the plain as well as in neighbouring countries. In fact, according to Petit, since 1945 significant numbers of villagers have drifted away from Tiréli in search of arable land (Petit 1998, 123). Referred to as *Àna yana*, 'those who move far away from the village' or, as translated by Petit (1998, 173), 'those who move far away from the Dogon Land', these people settled in local towns, such as Bandiagara; in the capital, Bamako; in Ivory Coast; in Ghana (Dougnon 2007; Petit 1995, 173); or in Guinea Conakry, where women may work as maids and men work as builders, warehousemen, on plantations, or in gold fields. For most of these people, the lack of food resources and harsh living conditions force them to leave Tiréli. Although most of them eventually return to cultivate the land of their ancestors, some never come back.

Also, because of population pressure the village has expanded and people have either drifted away or progressively extended the settled area on the scree to facilitate access to basic resources such as water. As mentioned earlier, many young men have no interest in reoccupying their father's house after his death or even to settle next to it, as was traditionally done in the past. The lack of space, the discomfort, and the substantial physical investment required for seasonal repairs to the wet mud habitat largely discourage young people, who would rather live in one of the new, long-lasting, modern concrete houses. As pointed out to me by one of my local sources: 'When the father dies, we will leave the compound. Nobody wants to live up here. It is too complicated. . . . Also, all the friends have gone down now'.[5]

As the village expands at the bottom of the scree near the church and the mosque, new neighbourhoods based on social friendship networks have taken shape. As stated by an old man who lives near the *gínna* ruins and whom we met on our way to Sodanga to examine a series of compounds, these sites 'belong to those of the past'.[6] Most young people never make the effort to pay a daily visit to the elders even though they live in the same village. This neglect is perceived as a total lack of respect that demolishes the authority and power of the patriarch, as the family dissolves. As proposed by Walther, the ruins validate the authenticity of Dogon ancestral culture (Walther 2001), an authenticity that, as observed in Tiréli, makes them another 'photographic' target. By building new houses, the young generation is expressing its desire for emancipation and freedom from the traditional social system. As I show in Chapter 7, the 'modern' house testifies to new values and a regeneration of local identity.

Note that despite the fact that some villagers temporarily migrate and others settle at the foot of the scree, most villagers believe that leaving the scree to settle down elsewhere, such as in the plain, is a mistake, because certain events of the past, such as razzia (raids) and wars, may happen again.

Conclusion

Through a depiction of the dynamic of built forms that compose the village of Tiréli, I have shown that the spatial layout of buildings and compounds enfolds a sense of attachment to the place. It was originally created through their building processes and particular modes of fixing and bounding the built elements. This sense of attachment to the place manifests itself through, and is surely reinforced by, tourism and the concomitant promotion of the village's built units. Similarly, annual village celebrations contribute to the revival of the built environment, consolidating existing bonds among the villagers as well as reinforcing a sense of attachment to the village. The bounding system constituted through bodily action and comprising the built units, in particular, those of the compound, is becoming increasingly porous owing to modernising influences, such as the young people's increasing detachment from the authority of the patriarch. The system remains, therefore, relative, since young people do not use, conceive of, or make space in the same ways as their parents. Hence we are witnesses to a progressive form of decontainment; as the inside of the village and its multiple internal boundaries extend, the village becomes more and more fluid with the passage of time and of people.

5 The Outside of the Village as a 'Life-Giving' Reservoir

This chapter provides an analysis of the contiguous zones, and therefore elements, that compose the outside of the village, an area called *àna kɛrigu* (*kɛrgu*), the 'side of', or the outside of, the village (Figure 5.1). In the villagers' view, the *àna kɛrigu* functions as a framing device for the village because it contains life resources. I propose that the village territory can be defined as a humanised landscape shaped and reshaped through the seasonal embodied experiences of villagers' working in and crossing the territory. In other words, human action on the land, such as the exploitation of natural resources as well as its ritual management, confers particular configurations and meanings to the territory. By drawing on van Beek and Banga's (1992) work, I conceptualise the outside of the village—and more specifically the cultivated bush—as the 'life-giving reservoir' of the village, that is to say, a place from which the Dogon people extract their daily means of subsistence and therefore on which they are greatly dependant. It is certainly the most important aspect of the territory of Tiréli, because it contains the fields that, for the most part, host millet. Hence, I explore the dimension of the outside of the village as a form of container for the inside of the village, by looking at the elements of which the outside is composed through the Dogon people's seasonal and daily activities.

I suggest that the inside/outside spatial dialectic of Tiréli does not function within a system of oppositions conceptualised as a 'safe cultural' inside space versus a 'threatening natural' outside space. Rather, I argue that these two space reveal themselves to be contiguous and reversible through people's daily embodied and to some extent ritual practice of space. Thus, through seasonal tasks, travelling, and also modernism and tourism, Tiréli defines itself by daily movements and does so through the circulation of people and/or things.

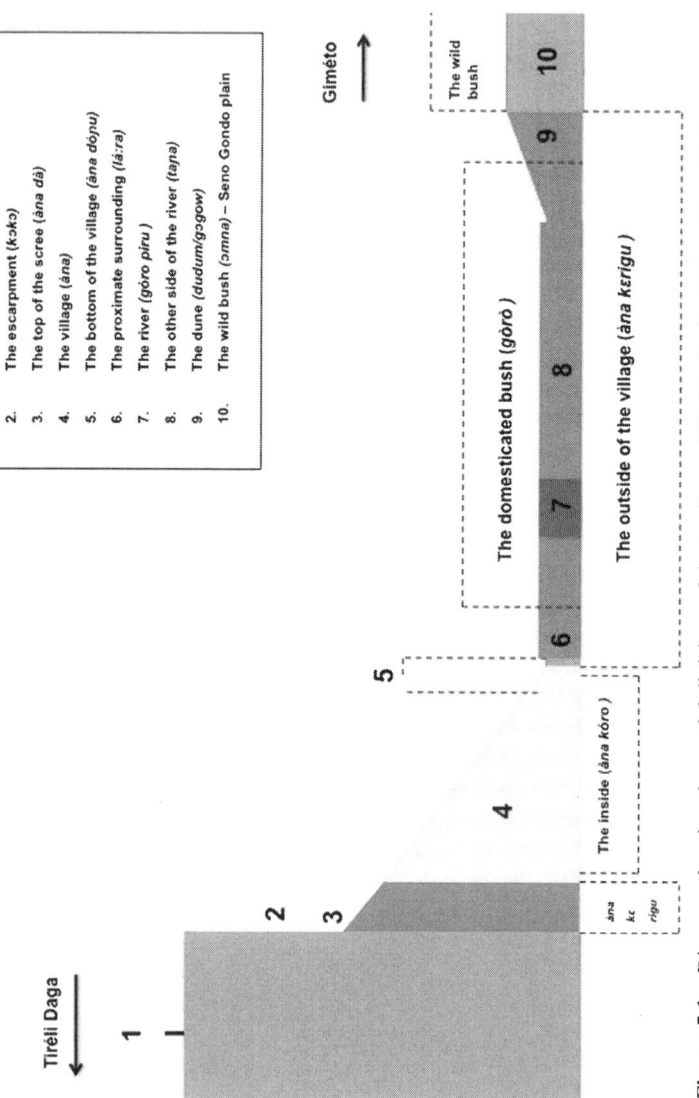

1. Gardens/ bush – The Bandiagara plateau
2. The escarpment (kɔkɔ)
3. The top of the scree (ana dǎ)
4. The village (ana)
5. The bottom of the village (ana dɔɲu)
6. The proximate surrounding (lǎ:ra)
7. The river (gôro piru)
8. The other side of the river (taɲa)
9. The dune (dudum/gɔgow)
10. The wild bush (ɔmna) – Seno Gondo plain

Tiréli Daga

Giméto

The inside (ana kóro)

ana kɛ rigu

The domesticated bush (gôro)

The outside of the village (ana kɛrigu)

The wild bush

Figure 5.1 Diagram showing the spatial divisions of the territory of Tiréli—its 'inside' and 'outside'

Therefore, I propose that the boundaries of the Dogon landscape as a container in which people dwell remain flexible. As we have seen in Chapter 3, although the Dogon concept of space reveals a certain form of containment that functions as a protection mechanism, the control and overall the efficacy of the symbolic boundaries of the inside and outside of the village are challenged by the intrusion of malevolent entities. Therefore, the boundaries remain porous. In addition, the porosity of the mechanism very much depends on contingencies and the course of events; the modernisation of communication paths that traverse the Dogon region and that are emulated for tourist purposes increase the accessibility and, therefore, the busyness of the place. This factor of modernisation, paired with intensifying levels of cultivation that lead to an increasing and totalising occupation of the cultivated bush and beyond, tends to push at the existing physical boundaries, expanding them and, in the process, reifying the dichotomy of the inside and the outside. Inevitably, shifting boundaries increase existing long-term conflicts about field borders with neighbouring villages and communities; the spatial divisions remain fundamentally mutable. Finally, as we shall see, human overexploitation of the resources of the landscape is also life-threatening and is generated from the inside by people themselves.

Introducing the Escarpment Container

The escarpment, face, called *kɔkɔ*, materialises the limit between the scree, which is inhabited and cultivated, and the Bandiagara plateau (*tíbi kú:*). It is endowed with a particular geomorphology made of fissures and hollows. The villagers of Tiréli have used these over time for multiple mobility and storage purposes, as well as to a lesser extent as a time keeper; for instance, the passage of the Milky Way (*yàlu úlo*) above a noticeable vertical crack of the escarpment toward the end of October indicates that Bambara groundnuts (*vigna subterranean*) are ready for harvesting.

The escarpment offers multiple winding and precipitous paths that allow villagers and tourists to reach the plateau area. Although the paths are repaired to facilitate tourists' access to the village, using these sinuous, steep, and busy routes requires particular care, since the stones often come loose. Although the villagers climb up and glide down the escarpment paths with astonishing agility and confidence, most tourists struggle to keep their balance—a contrast most eloquently exemplified by the Dogon women, who, with an impeccable synchronicity of perfectly timed and balanced movements, never falter when transporting heavy loads of goods and jars of beer that they carry on their heads. The cliff features a prominent cylindrical rock that is often used by travellers to locate the village from the plain; thus the rock serves as a landmark of the whole village of Tiréli. Some Tellem troglodyte dwellings carved from the rock can be observed there, and in this way the rock materialises the history of its human occupation. However, the visual stratification of three types of architecture of the Tellem[1] and the Dogon, whose settlements occurred at different periods, can be better observed in other villages of the escarpment such as Tiréli. Ancient dwellings, human remains, and material culture discovered in the necropolis were extensively researched by Dutch human biologist and archaeologists Huizinga and Bedaux and their team in the 1960s to the mid-1980s. The Tellem architectonic located in the highest areas of the escarpment that can be observed in certain places (Bedaux 1972) appears as cylindrical containers, recessed in the rock cavities that were used as storage facilities. The areas located above these natural hollows were used as a necropolis. In his study of Tellem culture, which he dates from the eleventh century C.E., Bedaux shows that Dogon and Tellem habitats are clearly distinct and show no cross-cultural influences (Bedaux 1972; Bedaux & Lange 1983). According to him, the Dogon took over the place and settled in the area around the fifteenth century (Bedaux 1972).

Cemeteries in the Cliff: Containing and Ordering Death

The escarpment provides the base for Dogon cemeteries made famous by French filmmakers Jean Rouch and Roger Rosfelder (Rouch & Rosfelder 1950) in their ethnodocumentary *Cimetières dans la falaise*, which recounts the funeral of a man who died by drowning and was buried in the cliff the day after his body was returned by the *nɔmmɔ*, or water spirit. Dogon cemeteries are called *ɔmo sày*, which refers to 'the place where the living decompose' (Calame-Griaule 1968, 211). Despite the increasing religious conversion of Tiréli's people, most of their dead lie in the escarpment chambers. In fact, the enclosed (Christian and Islamic) cemeteries located below the dune remain relatively sparsely occupied. The original burial grounds are distributed along the escarpment in its cavities, where the dead are buried separately according to the cause or circumstance of death (Dieterlen 1941, 187). The Dogon separate the dead by category, interring the 'ordinary dead' and the 'extraordinary dead' in the distant hollows of the cliff. The 'exceptional dead', those who did not grow to a height considered normal (for example, a witch), are taken far away in the wild bush, where the bodies are placed into the hollow of a baobab tree trunk (Bouju 1995a, 363). Whereas the main, larger fissure in the escarpment is dedicated to 'ordinary' deaths, smaller hollows are allocated to horses and the Peul[2] people. In other villages, spiritually important persons, such as the *Hogon* (spiritual chief) or the *bínu kédinɛ* (priest), are also buried apart because of their status and spiritual power. In keeping with this arrangement, some hollows are allocated to those categories of the dead considered to be dangerous. The dead in these categories are placed in the *mɔɲu õŋɛ̃* or the place of the 'bad souls/dead'. The categories include victims of infanticide, stillbirth, and miscarriage, as well as deaths of women who were menstruating, pregnant, or giving birth. In Tiréli it is said that the dangerous, jealous souls of pregnant or menstruating women return to haunt the village, striking out at other women and at children. Also, those who died of leprosy and suicide are all perceived as harmful.

As explained by the son of the *bínu kédinɛ* (priest) of Kamba Sendé, who controls the village boundaries, 'bad' types of death emanate from the transgression of a prohibition. Categories of exceptional death/dead have been enumerated by Dieterlen (1941, 188–209): those who died in the bush and whose body remained unfound; people killed during a war; those murdered, burned, or killed by a spiritual force; and, finally, those who did not grow to a height considered normal by the Dogon. These categories of the dead are considered to be signs of failure and forms of impurity that threaten to repeat themselves, permanently contaminating the family. Dogon elders who possess the knowledge about the shrines perform specific ritual procedures in order to prevent contamination. The shrines called *ɔru múnɔ* in Tiréli and located in the bush enable the Dogon to 'contain' the bad deaths that attempt to penetrate the space of the living. These 'obstacles'[3] must be purified by the elders subsequently carrying out maintenance tasks before the rainy season.

Each quarter of Tiréli possesses a *íɛ kɔmɔ* that designates a fissure, a cave, or a hollow that serves as a cemetery and that is dedicated to 'ordinary death', which refers mostly to old people who died a natural death. This dark room is accessed by a forking path that zigzags across the escarpment face (*kɔmɔ ódiu*). The main branch of the path, leading to the plateau, is used daily, whereas the bottom part of the path leads to the cave cemetery. A segment of this path called *ódiu dì*, 'the road of the water', leads to a rock on which libations of millet cream are offered to the ancestors in order to attract their benevolence and good luck in whatever one might wish, such as good harvests or business. Water symbolises life and the luck of the Dogon. However, libations may also be done on the rock to drink the souls of the dead in order to appease them when, for instance, they disturb infants in their sleep.

As in many villages of the escarpment (Lane & Bedaux 2003, 89), in Tiréli, below the Teri-Ku Dama's cemetery entrance, the personal objects that once belonged to the deceased are deposited in a place called *toɲɔ̃ dàni*. Among them are small ceramics called *sá toɲɔ̃* used for containing women's African grape-tree body oil (*Lannea microcarpa*) and in which some cotton is placed along with ladles and spinning spindles, which all symbolise the deceased's work and status (for example, an old woman); all these items are left there to disintegrate naturally. In the burial area in the cliff, which is relatively full, before a dead body is interred in the chamber, the bones of a dead person are dug up to make space for the new body. The dug-up bones are then piled up on top of the newly buried body, where they end up being mixed up with other bones. The stretchers on which the dead are brought to their graves are also abandoned in the scree below the cemetery entrance after use. Thus the outside of the village is seen as a place where the villagers leave the dead, whose souls can always return to the village. The rock provides a practical logic of power, containing death in the landscape, by excluding it from the inside living space of the village.

Beyond Culture: The Space of the Bush

The outside of the village, or *àna kɛrigu*, possesses an internal space division that relies on the features of its landscape, such as the river or the dune cord. In Teri-Ku Dama, the space divisions of the village territory are named according to human body parts. For instance, the village 'inside' may be designated as *àna bɛrɛ*, the stomach/womb. The term *ɔru dɔ̃y* (also *lá:ra*) indicates the hip of the bush and designates the articulation between the village and the cultivated bush. While *ɔru gobi* refers to the waist or the belt of the cultivated bush, *ɔru kú:* (*koun*) designates the head of the bush. These terms appear in the current naming of Dogon space division; however, anthropomorphic space, or the analogy between space and a human body as suggested by Griaule (1966), is denied by the villagers.

In the next section I start with an examination of the base of the scree and move progressively across the cultivated bush to reach the dune cordon, from where I take a look at the wild bush that extends beyond the territory of Tiréli.

Liminality: The Bottom of the Scree

As we walk down the escarpment scree of Teri-Ku Dama and reach its bottom, called *àna dɔ́ɲu*, we come across the first large strip of the outside of the village, called *lá:ra*, 'the village proximate surroundings', or the hip of the bush. It starts where the compounds stop, and it extends to the river. It constitutes a transitory space between the village and the cultivated bush (*gòrò*) and a social area where people gather for social events such as during the market (*iwɛ*), as well as where tourists' cars are parked. The *lá:ra* is also partly covered by fields during the rainy season. The four-by-four vehicles of the tourists regularly shatter the tranquillity of the place, as they park or depart from near the hostels. The foot of the scree is one of the most lively animated, or social, areas of the village, as people wander around and chat, especially during the dry season, which is considered a period of rest. To the side of the meeting place where men gather and drink tea in the shadow of a tree stands the water well, where women collect water at least twice a day and where they share the latest gossip. Nearby, young girls often wash the family clothes, leaving them to dry on the rocks from where they will collect them later on. The soil is affected by human movement, activities, and rubbish, such as plastic, which result from and also testify to the busyness of the place and the proximity of the market and of local shops. Some parts of the *lá:ra* are also used by the women to process millet fingers during the dry season, when the space is not cultivated.

Another element that characterises the segment of the *lá:ra* is the market place, which becomes animated once every five days from mid-afternoon, but the sellers start unpacking much earlier in the day. The stalls, filled with multiple colourful goods, release the scents of spices and soap, attracting the interest of the children, who with their sharp eyes scrutinise the candies and biscuits on display.

While the traders from the plain set up under these stalls, the women generally collect on the periphery, where they sell pulses, vegetables, cooked food, and drinks. The market is set up in a particular order, with goods in the middle of the market place and cooked food, grilled meat, and drinks surrounding this. The abundance of products as well as the animation of the place materialised by the cacophony of the crowd, audible even on the top of the scree, and the villagers' dressing themselves in their best clothes often masks any dismay due to a lack of money or things to trade. Thus the market constitutes a necessary social environment in which people alleviate the pressure of their daily constraints and overall paucity of resources, which are the norm for most of the villagers. The market is a place where men and women gather to chat and mostly to drink beer until it runs out. As suggested by Jolly (1995, 2004), the brew not only creates social networks, it also brings together the life cycles of the people with that of the fields, in both ritual and daily life, as a form of linkage and of regeneration of the individual as well as of the society. Yet, millet beer consumption also intoxicates social relations, as extreme drinking in the market and in local 'cabarets' leads to fights and indecent sexual behaviour. The market endows a longitudinal periodicity on Tiréli, linking it with the other markets of the escarpment villages that occur one after the other. Thus the markets as a network interconnect the Dogon villages through particular events that gather people socially but also for business purposes.

As we leave Tiréli's market and cross the river, we reach the local school. It is built of stone and concrete and has a tin roof. The teachers' lodgings, made of wet mud, stand next to it. The children and teenagers of Tiréli, as well as those of the villages of the plain, attend this primary and secondary school. Its buildings are also used as a meeting place for the villagers where they can discuss issues and projects—for instance, with NGO or the Malian authorities. Next to the school, which is physically isolated from the village life, is a water pump that belongs to the school and from which the villagers cannot benefit. Clean water is a precious property, and access to it is highly politicised. Therefore, the *lá:ra* is a place of transit that is characterised by movement and that tends to become the most social area of the village; thus it is a place of interaction for the villagers but also of interaction with the visitors, whereas the public place is occupied mostly by old people and young children and tends to be regarded as a place of tradition, where funerals and masquerades such as the Dama are performed (for example, the Dama funerals in 2008).

Social life during the day tends to have people congregate at the bottom of the scree and in the *lá:ra*, the places through which the trappings and practices of the modern world are introduced to the village, creating new paths toward a modern lifestyle through a greater mobility of goods and of people. Visitors; various companies, such as Coca-Cola, which supplies the hostels of the village with drinks; the consolidation of the paths to facilitate access to the village, and, as we have seen, introduction of new commodities are just some of the elements that introduce movement to the village. In this way, the village expands its social boundaries and visions of the outside world, through greater access to things and places.

The Cultivated Bush as a Life-Giving Reservoir

The cultivated bush (*gòrò, ɔru sɔmo*) forms a belt of land that faces the village and extends toward the dune corridor. It is composed mostly of fields and trees that are located on both sides of the river. As proposed by van Beek and Banga, the bush, ambivalently life-giving and life-threatening, constitutes a place where people obtain essential, daily resources for living: 'From the bush, people are fed, the sick are healed, knowledge is acquired and discipline meted out' (van Beek & Banga 1992, 69).

Note that although this definition of the bush might give an impression of abundance, crops fail regularly because of lack of water or are eaten by locusts or various parasites. Hence, the bush often turns itself into a landscape of scarcity, generating an ontological insecurity. The Dogon cultivated bush is the result of long-term interaction and adaptation by the Dogon to the physical as well as to the sociopolitical environment, which over time, as I have shown in Chapter 2, has been characterised by slave trading, colonisation, and population growth and from which the Dogon people have developed their own particular, shared technical and practical knowledges that have emerged though an embodied practice of the place. This area that stands beyond the village is cultivated but as van Beek suggests is not 'domesticated', because it hosts multiple spirits and witches and sorcerers who roam by night. Therefore, it constantly has to be 'tamed' over and over again (van Beek 1993, 53).

Millet Fields Patterns and Social Structure   The division and pattern of the fields[4] were originally modelled on the structure of social organisation within the village, which emphasises working and support networks within the families. In other words, because the fields belong to the families (Chapter 4), they are divided, as well as allocated, according to a lineage model. In addition, some of the fields belong to the heads of the main institutional structures of the village within the ɔmɔlɔ system. Therefore, the way the Dogon relate to one another from a social point of view is reproduced in the structure and distribution of the fields. Therefore, the social cohesion, hierarchy, and organisation are materialised through the distribution and spatial layout of the fields, as realised by their size, the quality of the soil, and their location.

I was told that a redistribution of land is carried out every three years, when a new head of an extended family is introduced. Also, the schema of the fields[5] seems to vary slightly from one village to another. Although the social organisation applies in the same way in most Dogon villages, certain types of fields are indeed redistributed or included within other fields, because their classification and attribution have become irrelevant. In such a case, the fields are redistributed internally on a *gínna* level.

The cultivated area called *gòrò*, which is the most important part of the territory, has been almost completely exploited. *Gòrò* refers in practice to the fields that are alternately cultivated and located in a humid area and that are in theory of good quality. However, owing to intensive cultivation, the soil is generally depleted. The west side of this area located at the foot of the dune belongs to the people of Teri-Ku. These fields extend for some 3 km and form the boundary with the village of Komokan. Some of the *minɛ poroba*, the collective, or lineage, fields, are located in the area between the foot of village and the river. These belong to the three *gínna* of Teri-Ku, and they are divided among their members. The owners of these fields, which are seen as autochthonous, had to fight within their *gínna* to obtain one of them. They are of exceptionally good quality, because they are in a humid and therefore fertile zone.

Within the *minɛ poroba* category are particular fields such as the *lɔbɔ minɛ* ('field of Hogon') and the *wagi minɛ* ('fields of the ancestors'). They are owned and therefore exploited by the head—the oldest man—of each of the *gínna*. The other fields, belonging to the *gínna* chief, are located at the top of the scree. During his first year of ownership, the members of the *gínna* help the chief. In subsequent years, he manages his fields with his sons and grandsons.

Individual fields, attributed to one family or individual are also found in this zone. They are often loaned to a member of a family in need of land to cultivate. These *woru minɛ* are of medium quality and are located on the border between Tiréli, Komokan, and Ourou in a place called *tɛɲu (tɛraɲu)*, translated to me as 'the place where *hibiscus* or *aɲu* is largely cultivated by the old women'. However, the zone consists of large millet fields that lie at the centre of an unresolved conflict between Tiréli and the village of Ourou, which accounted for several deaths in 2006 as well as arrests by the gendarmerie. Both sides repeatedly contest the ownership of this cultivated land, each claiming their exclusive right to harvest it.

The *gínna minɛ* are divided and distributed among the members of the lineage. They comprise vast juxtaposed rectangular fields located beyond the dune and around the plain village of Gimeto, founded by Tiréli's people. This zone also consists of small portions of land called *jo,* of poor quality, that are allocated by the *gínna* to young men who decide to cultivate on their own and exclusively for their compound.

The fields, and, as mentioned, more specifically the millet grown in them, constitute the subsistence economy of the Dogon people. However, because of recurrent poor millet harvests, the Dogon of Tiréli have increasingly invested their energy, money, and hopes in onion cultivation, which can earn considerable amounts of cash, since the product is transported to towns, the capital Bamako, and Mali's neighbouring countries for commercial sale. In the Dogon land, millet cultivation starts in May and ends in November, depending on the rain. Once the millet is harvested, the villagers' cattle[6] go into the fields to eat the remaining leaves as well as to trample the straw, which is mixed with the animals' dung and after a while turns into compost. Millet straws (*yù: bé:lu*) are generally cut down, and the roots, called *yù: bòtun,* are left in the soil, where they naturally turn into compost. The Dogon alternate the cultivation of millet with onions, from December through March, depending on water reserves. Thus these cultivated areas undergo a recycling of space, which operates between the continuity of two modes of culture and economy, individual millet consumption and onion exportation. Additionally, it binds the wet season to the dry one.

Multicrop Systems and Field Limits   A multicrop system is applied, combining crops such as millet and cowpeas and/or hibiscus, which can also be combined with sorghum,[7] in one field. Women grow hibiscus and beans or, alternatively, peanuts, fonio, and cotton, which often account for their personal economic income. The property boundaries are known by the owners of the fields as well as by the chief of the *gínna,* who keeps the records about field property and distribution.

The Dogon often determine field limits (boundaries) with reference to trees or stones in the area, and the outlines of the fields are marked in the soil through cultivation. However, in some places these traces vanish throughout the dry season, with the cattle roaming in the field and the wind. A plant called *yòdiu,*[8] often found at the field edges, is also used as a boundary indicator at the beginning of the rainy season. However, long-term disputes over field limits, which were set up at the foundation of the villages, inevitably resurface with the beginning of the rainy season. Similar conflicts occur regarding the demarcation of roads operated by Malian authorities; milestones are often destroyed by angry cultivators who claim that the government is encroaching on their land.

In addition, Dogon farmers have a long history of violent conflicts[9] with Peul cattle herders, whom they temporarily give grazing privileges in the dry season but with whom they fight in the rainy season, when the cattle roam in their fields and devastate the crops (see de Bruijn, van Beek, & van Dijk 1997; Thibaud 2005, 52).

In October, before the start of the harvest, the 'generous earth' is celebrated as part of the *saraka* (a Fulbe term), which is dedicated to the feeding earth. Libations of millet cream are made at the entrance of the compound. As Teme explains, this is a means to express gratitude to the ancestors when they pass through the entrance, because they own the land and cleared out the fields (1997, 151). Once the *saraka* is over, cow peas and hibiscus can be consumed.

Tree Ownership and Protective System   The trees belong to the families who own the field in which the trees stand. As is done with crops, in order to protect the fruits of a tree from theft, an *áma* artefact, possibly manufactured by the blacksmith, is attached to a branch of the tree. The artefact signifies the ownership of the tree and casts a spell on the thief. Similar *áma* are placed on the large flat rocks lying at both village entrances, so as to protect the heavy and large bush resources or harvests that cannot be brought straight back to the compound. The *áma* therefore forms a system of protection of people's foodstuffs.

Also, the sacred trees, or *timu dɔ̃*, on which sacrifices are performed are located in this cultivated bush space and in the scree, surrounded by a low fence made of stones that indicates the sacred nature of the place, which most of the time relates to an ancestor. Therefore, stepping beyond the fence endangers the lives of those who enter the place. The trees, often tamarind *omunu*,[10] *ɔr*,[11] and baobab and *ji*[12] (silk cotton tree), indicate a sacred site or a cemetery, as well as announcing the physical proximity of a village. As emphasised by one of my sources, trees often stand as a metaphor for humanity, because they always come in groups. As mentioned previously, the rocks and trees are said to be animated by vital forces that cause them to move at night; trees have their own sociability, just as humans do.

Liminality: Approaching the Wild Bush

The cultivated area proximate to the village (*gòrò*) is crossed by a sinuous river, named *góro piru*, that runs parallel to the cliff. The place name refers to the sides of the river where people work. Between the river and the dune is a space called *taɲa*, a name that expresses 'the movement of going beyond, or to the other side'. This space constitutes another transitory space that lies at the limit of the uncultivated bush space. The far end of this strip becomes less occupied as we get closer to the dune, owing to its relatively good soil quality. The tourists' four-by-four vehicles have furrowed this area with a series of tracks that are reused by the villagers and backpackers travelling from one village to another. The villagers have also created multiple paths that run between the fields, allowing access to the cultivation area. Finally, the Christian and Muslim cemeteries are located in this area. These graveyards, enclosed by bushes, are not very heavily used and coexist with the traditional *ɔmɔlɔ* system.

As we have seen, the cultivated area of Tiréli is where the villagers extract most of their daily resources, such as cereals, fruit, and water. Medicinal plants and lumber for building also count among the benefits of the cultivated bush. The space is converted strategically throughout the season, with fields being turned into gardens to maximise the cultivation potential of the land. Consequently, the cultivated bush is revealed as a form of containment through the process of gathering the means to subsist around the outside of the village, the space of which is exploited to the maximum.

The dune (*dudum*) marks the transition between the cultivated bush and the wild bush that stands beyond it. The place is used by the elders of the village to carry out the divinations (Griaule & Dieterlen 1965) that are framed in rectangular and compartmentalised tables designed on the sand and called *yugurú búmo*. In these tables, tiny elements such as stones, ground nuts, and sticks are placed that make material the questions left to be answered by 'the Pale Fox' at night (Paulme 1937).

As we continue to walk away from the village, we come to the liminal space of the dune cordon, which announces the 'wild bush' of the Séno Gondo plain. The fairly clear area of the wild bush that stands beyond the dune is known as *ɔmna* (*sɛ sámu*) and is where women collect fire wood and where the cattle roam. After this zone we come to the *kirɛ dungɔ*, which is a remote cultivated bush space that announces the village of Gimeto. It is symbolically marked by a *kirɛ* tree (*Prosopis Africana*), which is said to be on its knees (*kirɛ dungɔ*). Because various supernatural beings, such as the souls of the dead, roam in the *ɔmna*, this area is perceived as an environment more dangerous than the cultivated space, which remains protected by the bush shrine. The *ɔmna* is crossed by paths that connect the villages of the plain to villages of the cliffs.

The Wild Bush as 'Life-Threatening' Space

The wild bush area comprises three zones. The first is the scree, where various occult practices take place such as circumcision, divinations, and sacrifices and where the masks come out. The second is the plateau, which is characterised by rocky soil and by large and deep fissures, which retain rain water. The third concerns the extended sandy area (plain) located behind the dune. On the plateau and in the scree the young shepherds lead their goatherds to the edge of the escarpment, and some people cultivate onions in the remote area called *tɛgu*. As far as the plain is concerned, some villagers temporarily occupy huts there made of straw when cultivating millet in the surroundings of the villages that were founded in the plain by Tiréli's ancestors. Hence, the people of the plain have conceptually defined their own boundaries that enclose their habitat.

Increasing population of the plain has led to exploitation of the land, which, in combination with bush fires and frequent periods of drought, causes desertification of the bush space. As a consequence, hunting today represents a form of folklore, since there is really no game to catch. The bush is crossed periodically by groups of women—often young women collecting firewood (Figure 5.2) destined for cooking and brewing. The collection of firewood operates, in theory, according to specific rules, such as not collecting the green wood, which women sometimes do out of necessity. Hence, conflicts related to environmental issues between men and women occur concerning questions of erosion, because trees retain the soil that is otherwise blown away by the wind or eroded by the rain.

I was told that women always collect wood in groups as a measure of security. However, others say that it is simply more fun in a group. On the occasions when I accompanied the young girls of Tiréli Dama to collect firewood, our journey often turned into a period of recreation punctuated by singing and laughter, though it must be said that the task remains particularly laborious after the long walk to reach the site, up to 7 km according to van Beek and Banga (1992, 58). Thus long treks in the heat and exertion are involved in

Figure 5.2   In the bush, a group of young women collects firewood that will serve for cooking and brewing.

packing the wood as well as the carrying the faggots on the head. According
to van Beek and Banga, a load of wood, around 20 kg, lasts for 10 or 11 days
(1992, 63). In the village of Tiréli, very few women are familiar with *fourneaux
améliores* (improved cooking stoves), designed to consume much less wood.

The bush space is perceived as dangerous, though probably more so in the
past than today. In fact, the lack of plant life facilitates a greater visibility, and
the absence of wildlife has made the environment safer. However, as in the
cultivated bush, witchcraft and rituals are still practised in this zone, which is
also considered a place where spirits are encountered, beyond the protective
symbolic boundaries of the village.

Today, the bush space is largely occupied by Dogon villages and thus by
the associated intensification of agricultural activities. (At the fall of French
colonialisation, the political borders established between Mali and Burkina
Faso limited Dogon villages' expansion in the quest for fertile soils [van Beek
2005, 66].) However, beyond the fact that the environment has become relatively safe from wildlife threats owing to deforestation, the concept of the bush
as a dangerous space is still very much alive; for example, stories about rape,
robbery, and trafficking, notably of antiquities and drugs, circulate in Dogon
villages. Hence, the 'open' bush space still denotes insecurity even though
its cultural boundaries are constantly reified through actions. The bush space
is the home of spirits called *jinu* or *jinagu*, which are invisible, possess great
magical capacity, and move among the humans. The full range of material
things that make up the human and natural realms constitutes a potential host
for these supernatural entities.

The syncretism of Islamic and Animist thought suggested by the correspondence of the term *jinu* to the Arabic term *djin* is interesting. The *jinu*
possess a certain ability to penetrate the boundaries of the village. The bush
spirits assist people in their life by offering medicine, found by people in the
bush, or by communicating specific knowledge that enables the visualisation
of particular situations through divination processes that sort out daily life
problems by determining the cause of a problem and proposing a solution to it.
They manifest themselves as whirlwinds of dust and sand, or as a softness and
warmth. They remain invisible and signal their presence through manifestations of ringing or resounding drumlike sounds or flashes of light, as well as
through the sudden appearance of objects such as dishes, a piece of wood, or
a stone with a particular shape.

Here, although the place is 'life-threatening' (van Beek 1992), the source of
the villagers' insecurity does not seem to rest exclusively with the malevolent
supernatural qualities of the place but stems instead from a more mundane source:
the deforestation process that leads to a considerable lack of resources. As told
to me by an uncle, 'by cutting down the trees, the *jinu* leave the bush and never
come back'. This belief in bush spirits can be translated as a particular experience and attachment that the people have to the land, as well as providing us

with an insight into the way the Dogon view their society and themselves. By exploiting the bush, they imperil their own life. Hence, life-threatening situations also stem from the inside and from people themselves.

Conclusion

In this chapter I have examined the outside space of the village called *àna kɛrigu* by walking through the various continuous, fluid, and mutable zones that make this space and according to the elements that they contain. Through their embodied activities in the landscape Dogon people engage with the land as well as the living and invisible entities that this landscape hosts. While the Dogon use the escarpment outside the village predominantly as a container for death, the cultivated bush, which also lies outside the village, contains significant life resources. Death is allocated to the cliff or the dune outside the village, where it borders life. (Paradoxically, the escarpment also stands as reservoir for water and thus for life, as we shall see in Chapter 6.)

As we left the village on our walking tour, we entered the uncultivated and boundless 'life-threatening' space of the bush, from which particular forms of esoteric knowledge are transmitted to the Dogon men by the bush spirits. The two bush areas intersect in the liminal space of the dune. Similarly, the foot of the scree acts as another transitory space in which aspects of social life are set. A sense of detachment from the village can be felt as we cross the river and progress into the fields. These embodied boundaries of the outside of the village enable people to locate themselves within the world as well as to gather and to order life and death around them.

The two zones of the cultural space of the village and the natural space of the bush that make up the territory of Tiréli are conceived to be continuous rather than antagonistic. The boundaries that divide and contain these two spaces overlap and tend to fuse owing to an intensive exploitation of the land and a progressive pushing back of the limits of the village. The 'wild' bush space is also a space of change; it is being increasingly cultivated owing to its status as an intermediate zone lying between the territory of the village and the villages of the plain. Consequently, the considerably reduced boundaries of this zone, still visible today, may fuse at some point into one cultivated zone joining Tiréli and Gimeto. Furthermore, the significant touristification of the place adds to the intensity of agrarian actions.

Finally, the territory of Tiréli is undergoing continuous modifications, and its permeable boundaries are being constantly redefined over time through mobility, the forces of modernisation, religious conversions, and tourism. Consequently, the landscape of Tiréli is characterised by the circulation of things and people as well as by better access to places and consumer goods owing to the multiplicity of paths that cross the land and that offer a greater mobility, which expands social boundaries and local views on the outside world.

6 Dogon 'Weather World': Local Conceptions of Rain and Wind

Throughout the Dogon region, the erratic weather, characterised mainly by drought, triggers considerable anxiety in Dogon cultivators. The rain is their main preoccupation, because it is the ultimate condition of survival in the Sahelian landscape. Thus the weather occupies a central place in Dogon microcosmology—with rain and thus water flowing throughout the landscape in which they are temporarily contained before completely disappearing. Drawing on Ingold's view that people dwell in a 'weather world' (Ingold 2005, 2007, 2010), I propose that the atmosphere that embraces the inside and outside of the Dogon landscape acts as a container substance (Lakoff & Johnson 1980, 74). In that sense, the atmosphere as a medium (Ingold 2007, 25, referring to Gibson 1979) holds transiting winds and rains that make up its substance and that facilitate crop growth while at the same time drastically affecting the land.

From this perspective I examine Dogon conceptions of wind and rain, on which food resources and life in general completely depend in the Dogon region and thus in the village of Tiréli. The rain is important obviously because people rely on it, yet it remains unpredictable and scarce. The wind is of relevance to my argument because of the nature of elements it brings into the Dogon territory, the symbolic boundaries of which remain porous.

In this chapter I explore Dogon perceptions of the seasonality of the weatherscape throughout an agrarian cycle. I discuss Dogon interpretations and knowledge about atmospheric phenomena. In addition, I show Dogon cultural meanings attached to the traces left by the weather on the land and in conjunction with human activity on the land. This approach enables me to highlight the weather's dramatic effects on the landscape and on the Dogon people—that is, the ways they express their distress and build up strategies vis-à-vis a recurring climate of uncertainty. The weather's traces on the landscape are not just treated as evidence of the drastic conditions of the Sahelian climate; they also can be seen as an interesting material support for memory, enabling people to recall and talk about their experiences as well as their views and knowledge of the weather.

I draw on an indigenous perception of the environment of 'living in a weather world' (Ingold 2007) by taking into account multiple views on the weather, stemming from cultivators and weather specialists who spend considerable time observing the changing environment and, in particular, the sky. These 'men of crisis' have the power and knowledge to act on the weather (McIntosh 2000, 142).

Dogon people's views on their 'weather world' are grounded in their traditional ɔmɔlɔ system, which as a social memory describes 'the ways by which communities curate and transmit both past environmental states and possible responses to them . . . based on recycling or reinvention of curated knowledge of past climate experience and of economic and socio-political strategies that previously provided solutions' (McIntosh, Tainter, & Keech McIntosh 2000, 24). The magico-religious and political ɔmɔlɔ system provides ritual solutions to the erratic weather by acting on the weatherscape through rain making or halting it if it threatens to cause floods (*di: yoi*), and also by integrating over time people's embodied experiences and knowledge of the weather. Finally, a Dogon microcosmology brings together the atmosphere or the sky and the land, as a surface receptacle in which the weather inscribes itself. The weather affects but also transcends human everyday life and discourses. It emotionally and physically influences people in many ways, within historical and political contexts, and so it shapes Dogon culture.

Some African Conceptions of the Weather

For the Swahili coastal communities of East Africa, concepts of winds and their movements are intimately connected to ideas about 'life breath,' as well as smells, which are all considered as manifestations of spirits or deities (Parkin 2007, 40). For the Mwaba-Gurma of Togo, breath is seen as a creative and fundamental vital energy that is inherent to the materials that compose their magico-religious paraphernalia and that therefore ensure their efficacy (de Surgy 1994, 67). The Diola-Adiamat of Guinea-Bissau view the weather as the will of God and the wind as its breath, referring to God's unpredictability and creative power (Julliard 2000). Across the Sahel, hot dry winds that provoke prolonged exhaustion are believed to spread epidemics and mental illness, which are said to be brought by the souls of the dead and various spirits that inhabit the bush space and frequently enter the human world

(Coppo 1998; Jolly 2004, 216; Masquelier 1994; Rasmussen 1999). They are said to move through the air and also in the water.

Thus the full range of material things of which human and natural realms are composed constitutes a potential host for these supernatural entities (Griaule 1994).[1] The winds are media by which they may enter the human space, and the consequences of their actions are visible only through atmospheric elements.

Dogon knowledge about the weather is grounded in individual and collective relationships to nature that are animated by the spiritual world and largely believed to be beyond the influence of all dominant religious faiths. This world is tangential to human daily life and also transcends it. It reveals itself as an atemporal, aspatial dimension where the spirits of the land, the ancestors, and the souls of the dead reside. These invisible entities are made responsible for weather conditions and what they bring to daily life. The spirits and the souls of the dead transit and arise through the weather to stabilise or destabilise the human world.

Dogon Knowledge of the Weather

Dogon people draw their knowledge about the weather from their long-term systematic observations of the weather, their magico-religious techniques and actions on it, which constitute a heritage, and their seasonal/daily embodied experiences of working and walking in the harsh weatherscape. Over time the Dogon of Tiréli have developed rituals and pragmatic strategies to cope with the lack of water throughout the agrarian cycle—for instance, by identifying and exploiting water reservoirs in the cliff or digging water-retaining ponds in selected places in the landscape, as well as controlling the access to water. In this chapter, knowledge about the weather is also recalled by people through the help of multiple traces left on the land by the weather; thus the landscape offers surface inscriptions, or as Nelson metaphorically puts it: 'Weather is the hammer and the land is the anvil' (Nelson 1983, 33). In other words, the powerful weather inscribes and erases and at the same time creates and destroys the land, a land made by formative and transformative processes and that is therefore always 'coming into being' (Ingold 2007, 28).

In the manner of scars, traces such as deep cracks, uprooted trees, erosion (*minɛ sɔŋɛ̃*), split and burned trees, and the collapse of the dune are created by repeated passages of strong winds, rains, and lightning strikes during the hot, dry, and rainy seasons. The air causes swarms of desert locusts (*Schistocerca gregaria*) to circulate, and they feed on crops and thus devastate food resources, leaving trees bare. Locusts' eggs are mostly destroyed through heavy pounding or through insecticides, which, however, remain expensive. The wind causes the air of the village to circulate and to contain evil spirits, the souls of the 'bad dead', as well as the epidemics that permeate the village when the efficacy of the symbolic boundaries is weak (Chapter 3). Strong winds propelling occasional heavy rains, followed by long periods of drought (*ánrã mà*), eat away at the dune and the soil in the fields. Furthermore, the wind creates a dusty environment that affects people's health and generates respiratory problems. When it rains too much all at once, the planted seeds do not take; they rot in the soil owing to an excess of water, or they come to the surface and dry out or get eaten by birds. The rain also washes away the built environment made of earth, while the heat affects wildlife by contributing to desertification, which imperils the crops. However, of course, rain also gives sustenance to the land, reviving plant life. It fills up the river bed and creates large water reservoirs that are used to water the gardens during the cold dry season.

These multiple traces in the landscape also stand as material metaphors that Dogon people use to express their worldviews, emotions, and distress about the harsh conditions of their life. Hence, the Dogon's interpretation of traces while they walk through the land make it possible for one to gain a better insight into their perceptions about their environment—more generally, how they think about abstract notions of space and time and, ultimately, how they conceptualise life and death. The irreversible traces left by the weather also stand as evidence of climate changes, and every second these traces remind the villagers about the fragility of life, which primarily relies on water. Finally, multiple traces left on the land by human activity that is seen as polluting must be 'erased' before the fall of the first rain, to allow seeds to germinate (Teme 1997, 141–42).

The Weatherscape: Atmospheric Phenomena through the Seasons

It is a common Sahelian predicament[2] that many Dogon water wells and pumps are often in bad shape and do not suffice to supply water for a large population. This situation often makes people's daily life unbearable and forces villagers to rely on distant neighboring villages' water resources—a situation that inevitably creates conflict. The luckiest villages possess water pump systems that obtain pure water from water tables located deep underground. Yet, tools, spare parts, and technical competences for repairing the pumps are often nonexistent. In Tiréli-Teri-Ku, water for daily consumption is obtained from a well located at the foot of the scree (which in 2008 during the Dama funeral celebrations did not have sufficient water output to supply the quarter's population and their guests). The water of the river and ponds that serves to sprinkle gardens disappears at the beginning of March. The long-awaited rainy season is often delayed and characterised by shortfalls of rain, leaving the villagers in complete distress. The landscape is subjected to erratic weather conditions that I describe now by starting from the hot dry season.[3]

The Hot Dry Season: Waiting and Preparing for the Rain

The hot dry season, called *nay bánu* ('red sun', 'hot sun'; from mid-February/ March up to mid-May), is characterised by extreme heat that in some places at mid-day reaches 47°C in the cliffs area. The heat strikes days and night, and it results in ponds and rivers becoming completely dry, (*mà:*), creating harsh conditions of life and poverty. By the time of the hot dry season, for most people, the foodstuff is gone; stressed by this lack, women put pressure on men that often leads to divorce and/or mental breakdown. During that period, people also must prepare themselves to face the rainy season, or 'wintering', while waiting nervously and impatiently for its start. The elders observe that when the heavy hot dry winds start blowing from early March throughout April and May, rain will be premature. Thus, heavy rain falling in May guarantees abundant rains throughout wintering. However, heat with no wind indicates that wintering and thus the rain will be delayed.

The main atmospheric phenomenon of the hot dry season is the strong, hot dry wind (the Harmattan, *o:ɲɔ́ já:bu*) that blows off the granaries' tops and are identified as a dust sweeps. The wind lifts into the air particles of dust, pollen, and sand (Nouaceur 2004), which then become haze, dust whirls, and sandstorms (Gallais 1967, 64). As a result, such winds dramatically reduce visibility, causing people to lose their way while travelling in the bush. The hot wind of the dry season provokes coughs, lung and eye infections, and skin irritation, as well as meningitis. It also brings epidemics such as plague and smallpox. These are, generally, occurrences of the past, but, according to the villagers, they could always come back. Finally it can bring mental illnesses, such as forms of madness and depression.

Hot dry wind as a whirlwind, called *o:ɲɔ́ simu*, blows starting in March, at a time when the heat also starts to strike at night. This spinning column of air picks up light materials on the ground and sweeps everything away. As it is said to be generated by and to contain bush spirits, when the whirlwind is about to form, people often attempt to destroy it by beating it with a stick, observing blood coming out of it. People also believe that this passing disorder encapsulates and brings the souls of the dead to the village to harm people.

This bad wind constitutes a medium for the avenging souls of women who died in pregnancy or while giving birth (*ya pilú*) and who come back into the village to attack young women. Furthermore, this hot wind is said to make people quarrelsome, a state described as when everybody 'rises like the wind'. When a quarrel takes place, people refer to it as the 'dust coming out'. This wind is also said to announce bad news, such as the death of a relative or a fatal illness in a family. Whirlwinds are associated with magic—for example, it is believed that sorcerers have the capacity to turn into a whirlwind to travel long distances.

From the end of March, through April and May, a soft wind, or air stream, brings a light rain called *ánrã mà vɛru* that people describe as an alert to get ready for the start of the rainy season. This type of rain, which does not dampen the soil sufficiently to sow crops, is said to lift up the smell of excrement and waste embedded in the dry ground and diffuse it in the air. As this light rain tempers the heat by increasing the humidity, it facilitates the burgeoning of trees. During this period, people impatiently await the fall of proper rain and check for signs that would announce this—for instance, when millet potash liquefies. The elders forecast the weather by cowrie divination—by placing shells overnight in a calabash of fresh milk, on a crossroad. In the morning, the diviner washes his face with the milk as a means of contacting the spirits, who reveal the status of the rain. Cool mornings and hot evenings indicate delay of the rain, whereas rain falling in early May indicates a long wintering season featuring sporadic rains.

During prewintering season, Dogon men and women who have been working in local towns since the end of the harvest return home; the cash they earned helps to alleviate food shortages caused by the delay of or the insufficiency of the rain. Everybody's mind is set on the fields that the villagers clear up by burning weeds and by repairing hoes and carts; the villagers also fertilise the land by scattering compost (Chapter 8). During this particularly tense period, when people feel oppressed by the heat and tend to be moody, witchcraft is at its height; it aims at weakening people by stealing their souls to reduce people's chances of accomplishing the new agrarian cycle successfully.

The end of the hot, dry season is also the time of the *búlo* celebration in the escarpment villages, where sacrifices occur on the village shrines—for instance, the bush shrine (*ɔru múnɔ*, Chapter 3)—as a way of attracting God Áma's benevolence; people ask for protection, good health, and abundant and constant rains that will bring crops to maturity and thus deliver good harvests. Conversely, rituals are performed on the *sógu múnɔ* shrine to stop the rain if crops are becoming severely damaged by the weather. Malicious people also try to stop the rain in order to sabotage the villagers' crops.

Dogon people of all faiths perform sacrifices to make rain in their own ways. For instance, Muslims of the Séno plain leave offerings such as round, flat millet cakes while reciting Suras followed by prayers. Another form of Muslim sacrifice is to give away food to those who are in need, in order to attract the benevolence of Allah. The animist *ándugɔ*[4] cult of rain involves blood sacrifices of white animals and millet-based libations on an altar to attract God Áma's benevolence, the most powerful *ándugɔ* remaining the one performed by the Hogon of Arou, who possesses the capacity of 'mastering the atmosphere' (Teme 1997, 166). However, as Teme wrote in mid-1990s, these rituals are disappearing, because there is often no one to perpetuate the tradition, and the paraphernalia is being sold to antiquarians (Teme 1997, 168) and the spirits of the land 'are gone' (Chapter 4). Yet as I observed on many occasions, Dogon rituals considered as vital are always recovered and so are reinvented over time. Knowledge and ritual material culture are partly retrieved and reproduced from memory. Furthermore, ritual and practical knowledge about the weather is remade according to new climatic situations.

In the villages of the plain (the *Tengu* area), women who are not Dogon but married to Dogon men traditionally perform a ritual called *ya yɛrɛ* ('women who came yesterday', who are not autochtonous but who married in the village) that consists of dressing up like men, wearing men's underwear. As they gather outside the village they sing shamelessly dirty jokes, dance in an exuberant ways, mimic sexual intercourse, and denounce the villagers' crimes and misbehaviour as a means of provoking the rain.

Another type of ritual concerning rain-making was described to me as a reconciliation between people called *gɛ tóni*, meaning 'the body that gets cold' and that is 'devastated and scared'. A large quantity of groundnuts is grilled on firewood from the biers on which the dead are placed when taken to the cemetery. Then the nuts are consumed by people who have committed crimes such as witchcraft or adultery and by their victims or those they have offended. It is believed that the rain will fall, providing that conflicts between the multiple parties are resolved through honest talk and the recognition of fault and crimes that are responsible for the drought, and therefore through offering apologies. Conversely, if people who are presumably guilty remain quiet about their unlawful acts and still eat the groundnuts offered to them, sooner or later they will be struck down by thunder. In other words, the Dogon traditionally view rainfall as washing away social problems, as a time when people unite and forgive each other for past actions, according to God's will. People of all faiths confront one another in this traditional Dogon practice, as they believe that there is one God for everybody.

At the coming of the rainy season, called *korosolu*[5] or *ánrā dí*, another ritual, called *kukusum* and recounted by Teme, is performed in the area of Yenduma. It signifies the erasing of traces left on the land and opens the start of the agrarian cycle. In general, it concerns purification of the land from human soiling caused by sexual intercourse, giving birth, death, menses, men of caste seen as impure, or the presence of Fulani (Peul) cattle herders, travellers, and local shepherds on Dogon lands during the dry season. Therefore, the land must be 'cleansed' before the fall of the first rain (*ánrā pɔːlɔ*) in order that the seeds be able to germinate. The *bà: bínu* (clan priest) drags behind him a bundle of *weɲɛ̃* wood (*Ficus lecardii*) throughout the village's territory while the remains of Fulani temporary settlements are burned off. This activity is seen as a means to restore the order of nature—that is, its productive and reproductive forces (Teme 1997, 141–43).

Seasonal Transition: The Sandstorm as Anticipation

By mid-May, during the period called *ba-do*, a wind called *o:ɲɔ́ bánu* (big dust wind') blows and appears as a spectacular sandstorm followed by rain called *ánrã pɔ:lɔ* ('first rain'), after which people take the immediate risk of sowing (Figure 6.1). The passage of this wind is viewed by the Dogon people as occurring in stages. First the wind brings the anticipation that rain is 'incoming'—the air is humid and loaded with freshness. The rain is said to be initiated by the wind, which leads it and brings it down on the village. As the wind rushes into the bush, it progressively expands into a wall, massively lifting up sand, leaves, branches, and other light elements. As the rain falls on the fields, it disperses organic matter into the field soil and therefore fertilises the earth. Hence, the rain that follows the wind plays a complementary role to the wind in the fertilisation process.

As the sand wall hits the village, the light turns progressively pale yellow, becoming dark gold as the sand storm moves, reducing visibility. At this point, everyone hides where they can, because tiny particles of sand suspended in the air damage lungs, cause burning sensations in the eyes, and scratch the skin. When people get caught in a sandstorm, they are strongly advised to lie under a bush, face down toward the ground, or under a tree, with the head facing in the direction they are walking, which is a means of finding one's way after the storm and also of protecting oneself from falling branches and trees. Time

Figure 6.1   The wall of sand approaching the village heralds the arrival of rain.

seems to be suspended, until a dark brown light announces the rain that will wash the wall of sand away. Then the sky clears up, shedding a white light on the landscape. As I observed in Tiréli, after the rain passed, a group of men rushed into the fields to check water saturation of the soil. Generally, if the soil is wet enough—for instance, at a depth of between 15 and 20 mm in sandy areas or 40 mm in clay soils—they report this information to the elders. In this case, the ɔgɔ gave the signal that it was time to start sowing, so the villagers and I packed our belongings and headed off to the plain, where the sowers temporarily live during the cultivation period. Dogon men also observe that if toads croak after this first rain, then people can start sowing. However, if it rains too much at once, sowed seeds will not germinate. They rot in the soil, or they come to the surface and dry out or get eaten by birds.

The passage of the sandstorm generated by the wind and followed by rain are elements that permeate the village and introduce temporary disorder. The materiality of the air acts as a medium for movement or transport of things from outside the village to its interior, as they crossing it from east to west. The passage of light also creates a fluidity, in the same way as the sun rising in the east behind the escarpment, spreading a pink and reddish light that turns white at mid-day and gold and ochre at the end of the day, then vanishing finally into the darkness of the night, as the sun disappears in the west.

As soon as the first rain falls, a rite called *uguru* is performed through sacrifices that continue throughout the rainy season as a means to stimulate crop shoots and to erase traces of soiling (Teme 1997, 145–46). As Teme highlights, rock salt (a powerful fertiliser) is used in the *uguru* rite as a means to symbolically ensure fast crop growth and ensure the fall of abundant and regular rains. The *uguru* rite also has a cleansing function to remedy the spread of fungal disease that develops in manure, said to be caused by symbolic forms of soiling the land, such as through death or sexual intercourses in the fields, occurring during the rainy season in the village's territory (1997, 146).

The Rainy Season: Cultivating Hopes

The rainy season is characterised by the monsoon, a hot and humid wind that blows from June to mid/late October, bringing a rainfall of between 250 and 500 mm per year and temperatures averaging about 34°C. As Dogon women explained, wintering (*jinɛ*) is the time when the majority of fertile women become pregnant. As the rain is falling, nature is regenerating and literately filling up the empty space of the hot dry season. As nature regenerates, the landscape becomes thicker, reducing visibility over the land and offering space for sorcerers to move around easily.

In late June and early July, heavy rains (*ánrã gába*) start to fall, and they are critical to the germination and growth of millet plants. They are heralded by the *o:ɲɔ̃ gába*, a strong wind that very often breaks large trees and damages millet plants. This wind that blows at the end of the day is preceded by black clouds and spreads cooler temperatures on the land. It comes from the southwest, and the rain that follows waters the fields, 'bringing hope' for successful harvests, but also supports the breeding of malaria-infected mosquitoes. The wind is a constant indication of rain. For instance, as a villager explains: 'If the wind blows in multiple directions and not just in one, most of the time it brings currents of fresh air and very little rain, so we have doubts about the arrival of heavy rain. On the contrary, if the wind blows largely from the south for a while and then stops, this indicates the arrival of heavy rain'. (In 2011, an elder counted 33 rains, among which there were 13 heavy rains and 20 light rains. The air cools down to an average of 29°C.)

As a cultivator on the plain explains, the signs that announce the arrival of *ánrā gába* are the strong heat and a wind that blows starting at sunrise. Clouds, gathered in the south, move very fast. One can also notice the gathering of the birds called *maɲu* (Saddle-Billed Stork, or *Ephippiorhynchus senegalensis*), the messengers of wintering and of God, high in the sky in the east dispersing to find shelter.

During the period of *ánrā gába*, people are very anxious, because wintering conditions remain a matter of guesswork. If the heavy rains are delayed for long, then the granaries will soon be empty. Long heavy rains that water the soil also fill up the river bed and create major water reservoirs that are used to water the gardens during the upcoming cold dry season. But strong winds pushing heavy rainstorms followed by long periods of drought also have a dramatic effect on the landscape, eating away at the dune and the soil. Heavy rains also ruin the built environment and flood the fields, imperilling crops; millet rots ('turns red') and is eaten by worms that swarm in the fertiliser.[6] Sporadic cholera outbreaks can also occur. As Teme describes, a rite called *anrā pogu* ('to attach the rain') is performed in the *tɔrɔ sɔ* region to stop too-heavy rains (Teme 1997, 299–300).

In August, rain falls on and off for 15 minutes, day and night. A weather specialist explained that observing changes in the direction of the wind is important in forecasting the rain. In fact, it rains generally when the air is very hot and the wind blows for about an hour toward the east and then changes direction to blow to the west and finally stops abruptly.

The August rain is said to clean the flowers off millet stems, enabling the grains to develop. Toward the end of August or the beginning of September heavy clouds propelled by a light wind may bring moisture instead of proper rainfall. In this case, the rain, *ɔmɔ daga loso* ('the rain of lucky people'), falls only in a few places, although the rain cloud passes over all the villages. This period of the year is also very critical, as people wait impatiently for the last heavy rains, which will determine the state of final crop growth and provide sufficient water to last until the millet harvest at the end of October/early November, a period called *ba:go*.

Toward the end of September comes destructive rain, *ánrã mɔɲu*, that can eat roads away (Figure 6.2); it is said to act as a 'farewell' to winter. This rain is preceded by a destructive dust wind, *o:ɲɔ̃ mɔɲu*, that uproots trees, breaks their trunks, and destroys buildings. The *ánrã mɔɲu* rain, together with the wind, is said to sweep away even children and cattle. During heavy rainfall in a short period of time, houses and granaries break and collapse on top of people. When the rain surprises people who are travelling, they can easily get lost in the bush. Therefore, the *griot*s are called to play the drum and to search for and to fetch the missing persons. The unpredictable *ánrã mɔɲu* is perceived as God's revenge on humans for having committed adultery, divorce, thefts, and other crimes. One villager put it in this way: 'All these disasters remind us of the absolute strength of God, who calls to order people who misbehaved throughout the year, who quarrelled, divorced, or had an abortion'.

Rainstorms (*ánrã mɔɲu*) are accompanied by thunder and lightning strikes that are also interpreted as the power of God. I was told that wood burned by a lightning strike constitutes a powerful material, sought by witches. It is also reported that people who have transgressed a prohibition—for instance, gathering and consuming prohibited plants—are struck by lightning during the rainy seasons. Lightning is also said to be brought down on people through witchcraft as a form of revenge. People protect their houses against lightning by hanging leaves of the *gono*[7] tree inside; the tree is considered by the Dogon

Figure 6.2 Destructive rains erode the landscape, leaving deep cracks and damaging roads.

people as the oldest bush tree known to humanity and has vast and important medicinal properties. In the past, if a house or granary was burned down by a lightning strike, the building would be dismantled and rebuilt in a different place, to prevent it from being subjected to God's anger again, owing to the house's bad placement.

Finally, from early to late October—that is, the end of the millet harvest—a very light rain, *mí miɲɛ*, which lightly impregnates the soil, falls periodically and is beneficial for the growth of crops and pulses such as cowpeas, which are harvested after millet is stored in the granaries. This is also a time when people start making mud bricks to build houses, taking the opportunity of using the remaining water that has gathered in village ponds and rivers.

The Cold Dry Season: Resting, Gardening, and Seasonal Migrations

By the end of November, people enter the cold dry season (from December to February), called *ká:lu* (in some places, *gínna tomoŋu*—*gínna* meaning 'house' and *tomoŋu* meaning a temperature fall, indicating that the cold is creeping into the house). December is a festive period, a time when the end of the agrarian cycle is celebrated by the villagers. The temperatures drop at night, down to 15°C, and they remain an average of 30°C during the day. Cool spells are brought down by winds that blow from the northeast, and days become shorter.

The cold dry season is generally considered as a period of rest, but some people cultivate onions, an activity that does not require intensive work and as many worries as does millet cultivation. As mentioned in Chapter 4, during this time some people temporarily leave the village to find work in town. As the climate gets dryer, vegetation disappears, creating greater visibility, and people can see between the trees, making areas safer for travellers. Wind force increases until April.

The 'Filled Up' Landscape: River, Ponds, and Water Reservoirs in the Cliffs

The river (*góro piru*) segments that run at the bottom of the Bandiagara cliffs are empty furrows during the dry season but become a reservoir in the rainy season. Almost continuously interconnecting the villages of the cliffs, this reservoir is filled instantaneously during the rainy season by forceful waterfalls (*sò mò*) that crash down from the plateau and that can be heard from afar. In the Teri-Ku section of the village of Tiréli, each part of the river is used for a different purpose, such as watering the fields, washing clothes, or for separate bathing by men and women. Water areas are said to be inhabited by the water spirit *nɔmmɔ*, who represents fecundity and life forces such as rain (Bouju, Tinta, & Poudjougou 1998; Dieterlen & de Ganay 1942; Griaule

1966; Griaule & Dieterlen 1965). The *nɔmmɔ* has an ambivalent good and evil nature and can take on different human or animal shapes. The *nɔmmɔ* is believed to turn into a snake when circulating in the river, where he catches and drowns people and drinks their blood (Bouju, Tinta, & Poudjougou 1998, 68–69).

In the past, the use and crossing of the river were allowed only if several prohibitions were observed, such as not wearing red clothes or jewellery, not using soap, and not shouting, in order to prevent provoking the spirit who owns all elements of the water. For some people, these prohibitions are obsolete; however, others still apply them. The river is always crossed at places that are known to be safe to avoid drowning incidents caused by tree roots, the current, the irregularity of its sandy bottom, and the water spirit.

In 2003 a bridge was built by an NGO in the district of Sodanga to facilitate the crossing of the river. The river constitutes a social 'in-between' spatial element on the sides of which social and business activities are concentrated during the cold and hot seasons and where sorghum and millet are grown during the rainy season. Yet, the cultivated sides of the river and therefore crops can also be affected by devastating floods owing to the narrowness of the river and the dryness of the soil, as well as the powerful flow of water intensified by the waterfalls that pour over the top of the escarpment and collect in the river.

As seen in Chapter 5, the Bandiagara cliffs, as a container for death, host cemeteries, but the cliffs are also marked by their function as a water reservoir that therefore retains life. The water reservoir, called *titɛ̃* in Tiréli, is a cave that is open at the top and that therefore 'communicates' with the plateau. During the rainy season, water collects in its cavity, where it is protected from impurities and evaporation. In the past, before the drilling of water wells, this reserve was exploited throughout the hot dry season, when the ponds and the river dried up. At the start of the dry season, rituals and prayers were performed to guarantee the continuous supply of water. This practice also included fumigation using plant leaves and roots to protect the reservoir from access by insects and spirits.

The reservoir is entered from the top of the cliffs by a platform, on the side of which the ritual pottery containers used for its purification and safety are located in a recess. In the cave-reservoir are swarms of insects, such as bees, and the stagnant water of the reservoir, which is believed to be animated by the water spirit *nɔmmɔ*. This spirit is said to drown people when it gets disturbed[8]; thus a series of prohibitions were established as a means to ensure the safety of water collectors, as well as perhaps a means to politically control access to the water.

Today, the reservoir has been abandoned in favour of wells, access to which is free of danger and more convenient. Women mostly collect drinking water and water for cooking from the well located at the foot of the scree; they have to climb up and down the scree two times a day to fill up the compound's clay jars.

Conclusion

As they flow through the territory's atmosphere, the winds and rains as container substances bring fertilising elements and water to the land. But they also devastate the land, bring diseases, and enable evil entities to permeate the village boundaries, which always remain porous. As weather enfolds the place, it brings the sky and the earth and the inside and the outside of the village together in the same 'weatherscape', in which things remain fluid and are constantly being mixed.

The weather and the invisible world leave traces on the landscape that account for Dogon knowledge about the weather and thus their worldviews, which translate Dogon peoples' relationships to nature, society, and the invisible world. Often the villagers perceive rains and winds as a reaction by the invisible world to individuals' misbehavior or the dysfunction of society. Traces inscribed in the landscape by human presence, such as paths, furrows, and field boundaries, are washed away by the weather and are reinscribed season after season through human activities as a process of reforming the landscape and therefore reumanising it. Human-produced traces perceived to be polluting are erased through rituals in order to prepare the land to welcome rain and fertility.

Finally, Dogon practical and ritual knowledge about the weather is made and remade according to new climatic situations and Dogon adaptation to climate change. Therefore, their knowledge remains 'in-the-making' as the weather shapes and reshapes the landscape and social relations. Knowledge about the weather, which stands at the core of Dogon microcosmology, is recalled by the multiple traces of the weather. These traces, both ephemeral and permanent, are support for memory, yet they are also material evidence of droughts and floods and thus for fragile conditions of life.

7 The Compound: Fixing, Gathering, and Enclosing the Everyday

The notion of a *compound* (Dogon home) refers to a walled-in domestic space that contains multiple buildings and that is occupied by a family. In the Dogon community of Tiréli, which is virilocal, patrilineal, and polygynous, the term *gínna*[1] ('family') is used to describe a single built unit or a compound where the family of the lineage head resides. The term *gínna* and its multiple variations—commonly referred to in the Dogon and in French as *la concession* or *la famille* ('the family')—was defined by my sources as 'Within the walls, you find that there is a family that lives there. This is the place where we were born and that belongs to our ancestors'.[2]

The *gínna* is the place of the *wagem* (the ancestors)—that is, the main house or the first house of the lineage, which is also called the 'main family house' (Chapter 4). The *gínna dagi* is the 'little *gínna*', since it is formed from the beginning as the family extends. Finally, the *gínu* refers in its strictest sense to a compound that descends from the *gínna dagi* (Calame-Griaule 1968, 101–02; Paulme 1988, 48–49). The *gujɔ* is the smallest unit found, and it refers to the 'room' from which a compound generally grew.

In this chapter I examine the lived aspect of the Dogon compound within the perspective of life cycles. They concern not only the life cycle of people, as shown by Lane (1986, 1987, 1994) in his work on the spatialisation of Dogon genealogies, but also the life cycle or temporality of the Dogon 'home-scape'. The material life cycle of the home encompasses the Dogon's practice about and in the compound, such as women's activities, the abandonment of the compound, and finally the potential reuse of its ruins. I propose that the notion of the compound acquires its meaning from the activities and objects that this space-unit contains and from the particular network of interactions that the occupiers weave in their daily life in this, their home (Lane 1987). In other words, the compound gains its shape through people's daily shared, embodied, and material practice in the place. Although made and owned by men, the compound is defined as a female element, because it is used mostly by women. Although it stands as a place of intimacy and privacy, materialised through the high walls that enclose it, the compound remains relatively open and therefore public. Visitors frequently enter to greet the family or to catch up with the latest news.

The compound defines itself through a particular process of gathering people, activities, and resources, as well as boundary-making activities. It does so in the manner of an interactive, folded surface between the family that lives there and the outside world. I reveal aspects of this process through the depiction of activities within the place and therefore the buildings that make up the place, aspects such as fixing domestic elements that define people's roles and status, and some elements of modernisation of the habitat—revealed among the younger Dogon as a dreaming space, the boundaries of which expand through imagination. Finally, I look at the dimensions of the abandonment and then the potential reuse of the compound as means to replace the living compound within a life cycle of its own materiality. Hence, the compound stands as the social and cultural expression of microcosmology.

The Compound Enclosure: Protection Apparatus and Ontological Security

Similar to the boundaries of the territory, the compound's enclosure and openings are protective. In his monograph Weiss points out Haya of Kenya notions of 'encircling' and the importance of circular forms as means of establishing and protecting places and locales such as the house through binding rites (Weiss 1996, 40). Likewise, Dogon compounds in Tiréli are shielded by a series of magic (*doru*) elements that protect its internal content—notably from witchcraft and evil spirits, who intrude into the inhabited space.[3] Although these scourges always infiltrate and occupy public village places and the compound, their power and field of action are cancelled or reduced by the magic, depending on the efficacy of the artefacts.

The first protected elements of the compound are its enclosure and entrance(s). The walls of the compound enclosure and the rooms (that serve as shelter or bedrooms) are reinforced by a protection system that is diffused by a plant bulb or bulbs or in some places by specific plants (medicines), whose species is kept as a totemic secret. The bulbs are buried in the foundations of the compound. It is strictly forbidden, where two houses share a roof, to cross a neighbour's roof in order to enter his compound. This act would break the protection and is therefore perceived as an offence, since it metaphorically breaks social relationships between the two families. It is said that the protection field acts by having a fatal effect on the intruder. Specific acts of renewing the shield are operated through sacrifice. Similarly, stepping over someone's compound walls—even if they are damaged and reduced to rubble—is forbidden. The compound entrance is protected by a large wooden stick that is placed on the ground and covers the opening length. It constitutes a symbolic obstacle for night intruders. If a witch acts, the stick ensures this will not affect any families, because it protects the whole compound.

The entrance to the bedroom is also protected by magical items, which are placed inside the front door. According to Paulme, similar elements, called *nadulɔ*, are placed in the *dorí*, or vestibule that frames the compound entrances in some places. This talisman, composed of a cow's tail, an arrow, and a knife all tied together in baobab fibres and containing plant elements, is made to protect the house against the *já:bu* and *jinu*, which bring disease (Paulme 1988, 316–17). In a similar way, the body envelopes of men, women, and children are also protected by various amulets that are attached to specific body parts.

To protect the inside of the compound against these evil spirits, which are said to occupy the compound trees, a small clay pot used to cook sauce is hung in a tree. The nauseating smell of the dried sauce covering the internal lining of the pot repels evil beings from the compound. The water jar is protected against poisoning by a little bag of plant elements in the sand under the container. (The plant/medicinal content of the protections mentioned in this chapter cannot be disclosed.)

Finally, the hollowed joints of the compound walls are frequently stuffed with people's hair as way of preventing snakes, which are said to be or be sent off by a sorcerer, from penetrating the compound. If these protective features have been spoiled or made inefficient over time, the head of the family strengthens them through sacrifices. Thus, the existence of these 'encircling' symbolic boundaries reveal a constant ontological insecurity that is generated by unpredictable forces that coexist with the living or that enter their space.

Inside the Walls: Gendered Activities in Place

The enclosed unit of the compound comprises the courtyard, the granaries, and the room(s) as a single built unit serving as a bedroom. Given that the compound and its courtyard are partitioned into men's and women's places, the principle of gendered division is also applied to the built containers; they symbolise men's and women's activities as well as the distribution of their respective roles. As mentioned throughout, although the compound is built by and remains the property of men, it is defined as a female element, because most of the women's daily taskscapes (Ingold 2000, 195) occur in the home.[4] Women bring vitality to the home, as they maintain the place in good shape and keep it lively, and they feed the family. Women's domestic tasks are done in a systematic way through repetition and by following a practical logic of 'things that have to be done'. Their daily sequence of tasks includes collecting water from the well as soon as the sun rises, sweeping the compound, serving breakfast (very often the previous night's leftovers), processing millet spikes/washing clothes, washing the dishes, pounding and cooking, resting/weaving hair, bathing babies and the kids, and finally having a well-deserved night's sleep.

Introducing the Dogon Compound

The family that generously hosted me during my fieldwork in Tiréli extends to seven people in total: my host mother Bemu; her son Balugo (who is now the head of the family since his father died), and Akasom, Bemu's daughter and my younger host sister; Domu and Yasiwe, the elder sisters, left their children, Beca and Ogotêmmelu, under the household's care. It is common for the progeny of the family to 'give' their first child to the grandparents as a way of having him or her educated, as well as to provide assistance with daily tasks, such as drawing water from the well, as the grandparents get older.

The compound that occupies a large portion of the top of the scree comprises two parts. The first is for the family, where Bemu, Akasum, and the children stay. This place is dedicated to women and children. It extends into two apartments located behind, which used to be a guest house for friends, one of which I occupied. The ground floor constitutes Balugo's *gujɔ* (formerly his dead father's apartment). This space extends into a large terrace overhanging the public place and from which the village and the continuity of the Séno Gondo plain extend as far as the eye can see. The compound juxtaposes the grandfather's compound, now in ruins, which is used to keep some sheep and where compound sweepings are thrown. In this patrilineal society, the compound is transmitted from the father to his oldest son. When the oldest son marries, he is invited to build the first elements of his compound next to his father's, which he may later decide to take on as well when his father dies, by joining his own buildings to it. However, the son may just leave his father's compound, or part of it, to fall into ruin, as was the case with my host family. The house and fields are generally redistributed by the men of the family after the death of the patriarch. The compound's fence, or *gínu gonɔ jeŋe*, which is composed of a series of high walls of piled-up stones, is made up of the back walls of the bedroom and some of the granaries found in the courtyard (*gínu gonɔ*). The enclosure is interrupted at its northwest and southeast corners by an entrance and an exit (*gínu munú ãŋa* and *muna ãŋa go jin*) formed by wooden doors. In some compounds the entrance is made up of a corridor called a *dorí*.

The large family space is distributed on three levels. On the first one, as we turn to the left from the entrance, is the mother's room, called *gíni diye* (see next section). Next to this is the *yù: denwɛ*, or the 'millet house', which is used as an alternative to the millet granary, or *gúyɔ ana* (which is now a ruin in this compound). In between the two buildings, in a corner shadowed by a tree, stands the jar with drinking water. Opposite to the entrance that leads to Balugo's room, or *gujɔ*, stands a female granary in which seeds and condiments are stored.

On the first platform, at the corner of which a *neem* tree has been planted, is the *paná tori*, or pounding place. The *paná tori* is used for processing food resources with mortars, pestles, and the grounding stone (*yu naw*). Neighbouring women sometimes help one another by pounding together in a compound. This activity constitutes a daily helping-action that consolidates friendship networks. Similarly, pounding tools or even cooking utensils can be loaned among compounds. The place that frames this activity has been chosen for its specific qualities, which enable daily taskscapes (Ingold 2000, 195) to be performed successfully. The repetition of these tasks in the same place signals a sign of respect toward the millet, a source of life and staple resource of the Dogon, a vector of Dogon life that ensures life sustenance as well as good health. The repetition also symbolises the prosperity and stability of the family regarding food. In the villages of Kamba Sendé and Wedjé on the plateau, I was told that displacement of one of these cooking elements or moving the task to another place brings bad luck, and it may cause the eviction of a woman by a cowife. As such, these place-bound activities are defined by their relationships with millet and in particular its storing and consumption, on the basis of which space is designed.

Below this workplace lies the women's eating place. The location of the eating place always remains the same. Once a spacious and shady place has been defined, it is used daily, being replaced in its function only by the bedroom or the *tógu* when it rains. Here again, maintaining the fixity of eating places ensures good luck in relation to the food supply. Men, women, and children eat separately, on the *anã paná kayi* and *niaw paná kayi,* respectively, and this situation never changes. The place where large water jugs are found may also be used as a brewing area (*napu*) (Figure 7.1). Opposite to it, there is another female granary, or *guyɔ ya*, in which Bemu stores the condiments, the dishes, soap, knives, and other small tools, along with the food and clothes. Then comes the small space between the granary and the kitchen house, called *paná biri*, which is used to store firewood. The second entrance leads to an empty place, which used to be the grandparents' compound, now in ruins. Today, half the ruins are used as a communal rubbish dump, while the other half serves as a sheepfold. Depending on compound space and the size of the cattle, people may keep their donkey, few goats, sheep, and a plough ox in a corner of the compound at night. Chickens run freely in the compound and occupy a small chicken house at night, most often located near the compound entrance.

The first kitchen, which is open-air, *nipi goro*, is made with three stones and is used more than the second kitchen, which forms part of the compound enclosure and is covered and used mostly during the rainy season. Next to the

Figure 7.1   The cooking area is temporarily used for brewing.

second kitchen is a *tógu*, or shelter with a thatched millet straw roof, used as a resting place during the afternoon; this is followed by a millet granary (*guyɔ ya*). As we reach the ground level, we see a second room (*niniu girun*), occupied on market day by the uncle, next to a former kitchen, which was converted into a combined rubbish dump, shower, and latrines. (In general, the toilets, *bɔjɔ boji*, for men and for women, are located on the outside of the village, in the scree.) Finally, chatting and resting places for women (*din dɛ̃riye ji*) are located in shady places, such as under the compound trees (where women eat) or at the *tógu*, where women do their hair, spin cotton, or make clay pots. Men gather at the bottom of the scree.

My host family's compound contains three female granaries, or *gúyɔ ya*, and the ruins of the *gúyɔ ana*, or millet granary. Millet is now stored in a room smaller than a granary but large enough to be used for storing the cereal from generally small harvests. The male millet granary (*gúyɔ ana*) generally symbolises the economic activity and therefore the wealth of the family; as a male element representing a man's responsibility toward food supplies, it materialises his work strength, work capacity, and contribution to ensuring the continuity of the life of his family (Chapters 9 and 10). This responsibility is complemented by the women's tasks of processing, preparing, and feeding the family. Dogon compounds also have a *gúyɔ togu*, or patriarch's granary, which contains the family's altars and magic. The patriarch often rests in his *guyɔ togu*, which symbolises his age and authority, to keep an eye on the objects. Granaries constitute, through their attachment to people and their location within the compound, a material symbol that objectifies the presence and the roles of men and women.

The Compound Rooms: Storing and Nesting

The Dogon rooms, called *denw* or *gíni* (*diyɛ*), separately shelter women (with children) and men. As I have previously mentioned, the *gujɔ* designates a room for bachelors and/or the room from which a compound is generally constituted, although the term is now more often used for a young man's house. As the compound expands, the *gujɔ* is renamed *gíni*. In the case of a polygamous family, the cowives possess their own room. My host mother's room serves as a storing and sleeping place where she, her daughters, and her grandchildren sleep at night during both the cold dry season and the rainy season, while they use its roof (*dara*) for the same purpose the rest of the time. The rooftop of the building also acts as a container for dry spices, baobab leaves, millet, and sorghum. Her room, though relatively small, also serves as a storage facility in which all store their clothes, sizeable objects such as jars to cool down millet beer or store fresh water, cooking utensils, and some of their agricultural tools. The only piece of furniture found in the room is the built-in bed, made of stones and earth. Balugo's (the eldest son's) *gujɔ* serves as a sleeping area that he shares with his cousin Brama when the rain falls; otherwise they use the rooftop.

The door frames of the rooms function similarly to the *tógu na* shelter or even, as we shall see in Chapter 9, to the granary door; they are made in such a way as to canalize body movements—that is, to force people to bend down and enter the building slowly and thus calmly, as the Dogon put it. In this case, the room stands as a private place of harmony. As the uncle explained: 'Those who build a large room with a big entrance get it all wrong. People can enter directly and even see what's inside the room. . . . by bending, you leave the bad things out, and you bring the good things in with you'.[5] The 'bad things' concern any forms of aggressiveness, bad feelings, bad moods—even worries.

Harmony in the compound is also signified by the four walls of the house. Indeed, when the foundations of the house are designed, the head of the *gínna*, who allocates the plot of the land on which the house is to be built, makes benedictions in the direction of the four cardinal points. He takes a handful of earth, sand, or four little stones that he throws toward the four points. By doing this he invites in all the good things from nature that surround the new building place in the north, south, east, and west to come into the room. In some places this activity is accompanied by using a cow's tail to sprinkle water in the four cardinal points; thus God and the ancestors will favour the place and the people who live there—good things will come to the family. As stated by a builder, the gesture gives strength to the soil and to nature and offers a prayer to God to give the people good things. 'By praying to the north, south, east, and west, we invite good things to come to our place, and so we build in a peaceful place'.[6]

Today, the new *gujɔ* as well as modernisation of the existing compounds show different signs of well-being that do not necessarily concern the symbolism of the compound but rather the expansion, embellishment, and modernity of the habitat.

The Modernisation of the Gujɔ: Social Distinction and Prestige   In many places in the Dogon land, new buildings (*gujɔ*), not built in the traditional wet-mud style, are springing up, especially at the bottom of the scree. A *gujɔ* often belongs to one young man who hosts his friends until he decides to found a family. Or the *gujɔ* can be built by a group of young men who will live there when they get engaged. Although the latter form was more common in the past, today young men stay with their brothers and family and share a room, or they opt for the first type of *gujɔ*. These modern dwellings are built and occupied by the youth of the village, who earn cash in town with seasonal jobs, through trade in goods that they sell in shops or markets and as tourist guides. The size and overall style of these new *gujɔ* demonstrate a break compared with the traditional way of building and therefore conception of the compound.

As explained by a neighbour, the degree of modernisation of the house signals the head of the family's capacity to make money, to travel, and to bring ideas, style, and building materials, such as cement, to the village. Cement is frequently imported to the village and constitutes an important building element that is highly valued because of its resistance, as well as the connotation of being 'modern' Cement is a prestige item, often substituted by or mixed with 'Dogon cement' (*bo senŋe*), a form of red gravel used by those who cannot afford imported cement.

The door and windows of the modern homes are often made of tin and painted to embellish the habitat (Figure 7.2). The *gujɔ* is either left unenclosed or surrounded by a wall made of stones and covered with Dogon cement. When enclosed, the space of the compound is much larger than traditional compounds, especially for those who have built at the bottom of the scree. Furthermore, the *gujɔ* of today also possess a veranda, like the houses in towns, where the family can rest in the afternoon, drink tea, and chat. The signature of the owner of the building or the date of its construction, made with the metallic tops of soft drink bottles, is frequently put on the façade or on the doorstep. According to the youth of the village, a 'modern' *gujɔ* shows that 'you are successful in your life'; it constitutes a form of social distinction that also testifies to the improvement of the occupiers' quality of life and therefore of their well-being. Being creative also translates young Dogon men's concerns about the view that visitors such as tourists have of Dogon people and about making their habitat more welcoming.

Figure 7.2   This modern style *gujɔ* is made with stones extracted from the scree and Chinese cement. It displays large windows and a tin door.

The *gujɔ* testifies to its occupants' desires to separate from the traditional architecture of their parents' compound, which they often described as 'archaic' and impractical. In the same way, as young people convert to Islam, Catholicism, and Protestantism, they tend to detach from their family's annual ceremonies and ritual practices. Old people always complain that their children do not come to visit anymore, even if they live in the same quarter, or in some cases they complain that the daughters-in-law do not cook any more in their husband's family. The *gujɔ* objectifies a new lifestyle, values, and beliefs that break with traditional boundaries, allowing more personal development and individualism.

The Making of Young Men's Gujɔ as an Extraversion Process   Opposite a *gúyɔ togu*, which contains the family's shrines, access to which is strictly forbidden to women, is located the area of the *gujɔ* that is relatively spacious and colourful. The walls are covered with a thin layer of sand, which makes the inside brighter, and some posters of kung fu stars that Balugo bought at the market. These images of power depict kung fu movements being demonstrated by a Nigerian kung fu master whose persona is emphasised by depictions of fierce animals such as leopards. Some other parts of the walls are covered with old glossy pages of Western magazines that he collected from the tourists and a calendar from Sotelma (Malian telecommunications company). The air of the room is often filled with the smoke of cigarettes and Indian incense. The space contains a bed and some tables on which is displayed a collection of objects given to Balugo by tourists whom he took on tour. They range from plastic bottles, balloons, bottles of honey or alcohol, and packets of cigarettes to clothes and backpacks. Underneath the bed he keeps a box that contains a broken radio, mobile phone parts, and a battery charger that was given to him by tourists. These wait to be repaired and then potentially to be sold. The mobile-phone repair business was taking off in 2008, when I went back to visit the village, yet the use of mobile phones remains today limited to the dune and the top of the cliffs, where there is service. (Still, these days people do use their phones to watch films or take photographs as well as to listen to music.) The *gujɔ* place is often occupied by friends who come to drink tea, listen to music, play cards, and chat until late at night.

In the same way as the building materials imported from town and the modernisation of the architectural style of young men's houses, the material culture of young men[7] that accumulates in the *gujɔ* constitutes what Bayart calls a process of extraversion that he defines as 'espousing foreign cultural elements and putting them in the service of autochthonous objectives' (Bayart 2005, 71). Through the accumulation of wealth, young Dogon men display their capacity to access and achieve a town-like lifestyle through DVD players and television, radio and music. In contrast, in the *gujɔ* of the majority of the young men who have very little or no money, the room remains minimalist. The walls are often covered with a thin layer of sand or ochre mud, on which masks, figurines, and multiple symbols of Dogon culture are drawn with a piece of charcoal. The sorts of objects often found here are note pads and blank sheets of paper left by the tourists, flashlights and batteries, old mobile phones, clothes bought at a local market and carefully kept for special events, and cigarettes.

As described by the young men of the village, the *gujɔ* constitutes a space of freedom in which they chat and daydream about Bamako and the West, which they hear about from the tourists. Thus the *gujɔ* constitutes a form of detachment from family and traditional values, obligations, and responsibility toward family. Through these multiple collections of objects, the young men display the outside world in their homes. Young men often complain that they are stuck in the village because they have to cultivate the fields, which are the family's main resource. However, because the crops fail almost every year, they no longer see why they should carry on with this. But, because of their ties with the village, most young men do not have the means to explore the outside world. Thus, the boundaries of Tiréli are crossed only through their imagination, fed by the stories told by tourists, accounts of villagers who have made the trip to Bamako, West Africa, or to the West, and their collections of objects, which reinforce the idea of an outside world of cash, abundance, and leisure.

Young Dogon men gain prestige and respect among their peers for possessing knowledge about the outside of their boundaries. The lives of the young girls I met, however, are different. Girls do not have the luxury of dreaming; they have to serve the family. They have obligations that consist not only, as they do also for men, of providing millet and food or cash but also of ensuring the smooth functioning of the compound. From an early age they assist their mothers and grandmothers in daily life activities, such as collecting daily resources, cultivating, taking care of the children, processing foodstuff, cooking, cleaning, and washing.

Fixing Domestic Elements: Symbolism, Stability, and Prosperity

Initially, when newly occupied by a young couple, a compound is symbolically fixed by a series of elements. As recounted by Calame-Griaule (1954, 478, 1968, 101–02), the first of these is a bulb of $noɲo$[8] that is placed as a symbol of perpetual life in the kitchen walls, next to the stove. The bulb is always moist and is considered to ensure the continuity of family life. Although this practice was common in the past, I was told that today it is practised less and less. (I was told by Christians that they blessed their house and affixed a wooden cross on top of their door frame.) However, other elements such as the water jug and the stove, which are female elements, still symbolically fix gendered roles and ensure the continuity of the life of the compound. The bed and the $baga\ taɲu$ fork are two male elements that also represent the stability of the home.

The first two elements—the stove and the water jug—are, according to the rules, fixed once and for all by the woman. They signify the attachment of the woman to the place and to her work. Fixing the anvil in the village smithy, signifying the attachment of the blacksmith to the village and the activity of the blacksmith, expresses a similar idea. The fixing of such elements, which play a central role in the daily life of a family, materialises the stability and cohesion of the family. Through the act of fixing, a woman commits herself to engendering and maintaining life in the family (Lane 1987, 60). She is the only person who can move the three stones that make the stove or the water jug around, in order, for instance, to reconfigure her working site in a more practical way. However, if someone else, such as her mother-in-law or a cowife—each of whom has her own kitchen in the compound—breaks the stove or the water jug, or turns it on its side, this indicates the eviction of the first wife for good; such an action would constitute a sign of complete rejection by the family. In other words, if the elements that fix a woman's presence and objectify her contribution to the family's life are displaced, then so is the woman. As far as the stove and the water jugs are concerned, the act of fixing these elements is accomplished through pouring the first water into the jug or making the first fire with the wood of the $ponu$ tree[9] when the couple is newlywed. (The $ponu$'s uniquely scented wood is also burned while a woman is giving birth.) Finally, in relation to the fixing of the stove, fixing the water jug also signifies the acceptance of the woman in the family as well as the starting of life in a compound.

As a symbol of fixity, the stove also constitutes an element through which a wife symbolically affirms her entry into the family as a full member. By setting up the three stones that constitute the material support for the cooking pot, and by making the first fire, the newlywed spouse engages herself in metaphorically ensuring the continuity of that fire, that is to say, she assumes her role as wife. As already described, the stove is never moved by anyone other than the wife-owner, unless the couple get divorced. If this occurs, she leaves to set up a stove somewhere else. Thus the stove signifies the role of women in the compound and therefore the cooperation between men and women (Lane 1987, 59).

The flame of the fire specifically materialises the principles of family life. For instance, the kitchen walls, which are covered with thick layers of smoke, are never refreshed, because as they are a positive sign of life—an active occupation of the space (Chapter 8). The accumulation of smoke on the walls means that cooking pots are on the fire every day, and the activity of cooking signifies that there is a whole family to feed. Therefore, the smoke symbolises the family's output. It is said that the fire symbolises the woman as the compound's vitality, since she feeds the family. Furthermore, the fire and its index, smoke, connote the passing of time as well as the stability of daily life as composed by repeated and successive daily actions that maintain life. If a family is faced with extreme food scarcity, which constitutes a disruptive and therefore a negative form of disorder, the cooking pot is still placed on the fire but is filled with water in place of food. This common practice symbolically and psychologically helps to keep cooking activity going as part of the routine tasks. Because food scarcity strikes families unequally, leaving some with something to eat and others with nothing at all, a situation of complete cereal shortage, I was told, is akin to living in humiliation. Therefore, the absence of food (Chapter 11) is hidden by a smoking fire; fire and flame act as two symbols of continuity of life.

After use, the fire is generally covered with ashes, which keeps its embers going within the ashes until the next use. Putting out the fire abruptly with water brings bad luck on the family, because the fire materialises the continuity of life and food preparation that lie at the centre of all life concerns. Fire is often passed from one compound to another on a fragment of clay pot that holds some small sticks of millet spikes, which reanimate the fire. This passing on of fire also constitutes a symbolic act of maintaining good social relationships and solidarity with neighbours.

The elements that are fixed by men are generally the bed inside the *gujɔ* and the *baga taɲu*, which generally stands outside and consists of an upright wooden fork on which rests the eating bowl (*baɲá*) with the leftovers of the head of the family's meal. The stick holding the dish, symbolising food gathering and safe keeping, recalls men's role of providing food resources.

The Compound Ruins

When there are no descendants to occupy it, the compound is left to collapse into ruins. In Tiréli, the compound ruins located at the very top of the scree have been completely abandoned owing to the unevenness and impracticality of the topography (Chapter 4). However, the compounds located in the middle of the scree are still reused either for dwelling or other uses. The ruins function as a playground for the children, as dump pits, or as holding areas for domestic animals.

The ruins of a compound symbolise particular connotations of death and misfortune. In fact, people often say that 'those who used to occupy the place were unfortunate in their village life'. From my conversations with Dogon families about their perception of ruins, I came to realise that for them an abandoned compound is a place where life has stopped. Many explanations were provided for why a compound may have been abandoned. Migration and a need for emancipation through such as making cash to sustain the family were mentioned frequently. Epidemics and famine caused by recurring and interminable periods of drought or the devastation of harvests by locusts were also noted. In addition, the compound ruins as a patrilocal inheritance may cease to be transmitted for want of male descendants to take the compound. Finally, witchcraft is often cited as a life-long struggle that results in the dismantling of families by death or by taking people's souls away.

Compounds can, however, be rehabilitated by other male members of the family or even by someone outside the family, as long as the owner of the abandoned compound or ruins agrees. Alternatively, the chief of the village might allocate the place to an unrelated family if no original family member remains. Therefore, recovery can involve the abandoned building or parts of it, such as wooden beams and stones. The recycling procedure involves particular logics of inheritance and transmission and appropriation. As a rule, built materials cannot be taken away from a family to be used for someone else's home, since they objectify the labour and the prosperity of a family. In other words, mud walls, stones, and wooden poles circulate within a same kinship group. If not recovered, they are left to return to the soil. The compound site or the original building site (*gínu tɛru*) of the ruins (*gínu kòro*) remains the property of the ancestors. Hence, while designating the physicality of the place, the compound ruins also entail a principle of identity-making that concerns legitimisation of a family in the village through its ancestry affiliation.

Some people take stones from the patriarch's compound, which they then include in their own household structure in order to maintain their affiliation with the patriarch and their ancestors. Through this relatively uncommon practice, the built element, objectifying the memory of the ancestors, is physically integrated into the new house. The rock that stands in the courtyard of most compounds and on which the old men rest, or under which domestic objects are stored, is also subjected to the same inheritance and relatedness process. In fact, the rock is often blown up into pieces that are used to construct a new compound. There is always continuity between one house and another. For instance, when some men build a house, they place a stone in its foundation that belongs to the house of their ancestors, in order to ensure the continuity between the two houses and to maintain the ancestor affiliation.

As with the transmission of built material, reoccupation of an abandoned domestic site is in theory always carried out by the inheritor, usually the son or the brother of the deceased. However, some families might lease the site to people they know and trust. The first step of recovery consists of identifying the causes for desertion of the place. The cause can be linked to a curse, epidemics, absence of an heir, or migration. In general, the abandonment of a household constitutes a sign of pauperisation. In the second phase, a series of protection and purification rituals are undertaken before people begin to repair the compound. This act is generally carried out by someone who possesses the relevant knowledge of magic, as well as shrines to secure the site. The purification generally involves a series of incantations and fumigation that are undertaken to expel bad spirits or a curse. Third, the owner entrusts the place to a (male) friend or relative who will use it for about a year or two. His presence is thought to counter the ill effects of the compound. The temporary occupier is chosen for his mind's capacity to capture and neutralise the negative effects. He is often someone successful and with great self-confidence. Fourth, elements of the compound, such as the location and orientation of the bed located inside the house and the position of water jars in the courtyard, are generally changed. Making these changes to the site prevents the new family from experiencing the same fate as the previous owners. In short, although abandoned, the ruins of the compound can always be recovered through a particular process of appropriation and dwelling that operates through rites of 'decontamination' that objectify the ethos of the former owner's life trajectory.

Conclusion

This overview of the Dogon compound has shown a dwelling process through the daily uses and fixing of a series of gender elements that objectify men and women's roles in the compound. This site of action defines a particular form of containment and ontological security through gathering and boundary-making processes. This sense of ontological security transpires through symbolic practices of fixing people and activities into places through domestic elements or by containing people's behaviour through, for instance, architectural elements, such as small doorways, and finally by reinforcing a compound's boundaries with magic. The continuity, stability, and prosperity of life are maintained pragmatically through repeated and shared, embodied taskscapes (Ingold 2000, 195) that are allocated to fixed places in the compound, as well as through the gathering of resources. Finally, through abandonment and reuse of its ruins, the compound inscribes itself into a life cycle that defines and is defined through its materiality.

8 Domestic Waste: Doing and Undoing the Compound

The Materiality of Domestic Waste

The compounds of Teri-Ku Dama as the locus of daily activities also act as open-air containers in which multiple forms of waste[1] are sorted following local logic. Waste is transformed, recycled, or reused according to the degree of utility that is found in the materiality of the rubbish. Issues about waste in West Africa and in the Dogon region have been explored elsewhere (see, for example, Bouju & Quattara 2002; Bouju, Tinta, & Poudiougo 2004; Cissé 2007; Lane & Bedaux 2003). Here, I focus on cultural meanings of organic waste that are produced out of Dogon daily life practices that I contrast with other categories of waste that I have discussed in more detail elsewhere (Douny 2007a, b). I examine some of the multiple forms of rubbish in and around the Dogon compounds, which I conceive as being container devices for domestic matters. My overall objective is to show the implicit meaning objectified in both the materiality and the daily praxis of waste materials that people select and allocate to particular places and uses, or wash off or retain on their own bodies.

The first topic examined in this chapter concerns identification of emic categories of garbage, and the second investigates the daily dynamics of 'doing' and 'undoing' the household and by extension the body. I conceptualise Dogon perceptions and practices concerning waste materials in terms of a recycled microcosmology that consists of a complex of worldviews that encompass the life cycles of people and the environment through systematic conversions of domestic waste to which people attribute a new life. I suggest that the Dogon compound acts as an epistemological enclosure that contains life through the validation of certain formless and creative elements (Douglas 1966, 161).

The discarded material outside the compound is regarded as nothingness. However, this nothingness can always be brought back inside as long as a use is found in or for the matter. In addition, the waste inside the compound always ends up in the outside soil. Thus the compound enclosure remains permeable. In short, I attempt to explore the Dogon microcosmology, or more precisely their recycled cosmology, as objectified through the Dogon people's domestic waste and by focusing on the temporality and efficacy of its materiality as it is gathered or dumped outside the compound. In this view, rubbish becomes more complex than 'matter out of place' (Douglas 1966, 37).

Tidying Up the Conceptual Ground

As products of daily routines, jumbles of refuse function as cultural constructs (Douglas 1966). Their meanings change according to the context in which they are handled. Although this versatile domestic matter (waste) constitutes a form of disorder, processing it induces order. In other words, as Douglas suggests, dirt corrupts order as well as continually re-creating it (Douglas 1966, 35).

There are at least three distinctive processes by which the Dogon treat their domestic waste. In Western terms they are recycling, composting, and reuse. I define *recycling* as the reprocessing of plastic and metal waste that is turned into a new commodity. I use *composting* with reference to the transformation of organic matter. Composting is accelerated by the addition of liquids such as used water or urine. Finally, the concept of *reuse* refers to waste that is used more than once without being transformed or broken down.

In the West, *rubbish* is defined as useless and unwanted matter (Rathje & Murphy 1992; Strasser 1999). For the Dogon, this concept seems to apply only to elements that exist outside of domestic life. Nevertheless, outside refuse always has the potential to constitute a life resource. The notion of Dogon waste in the *tɔrɔ sɔ* is used here as part of a whole, or as a whole element, that does not *per se* have any use but that can potentially be physically or functionally turned into something else that is useful. Following one aspect of Thompson's argument (1979), Dogon waste is part of an ongoing process of creation of value from things within a particular context of poverty in which nothing is really thrown away. Thus, Dogon concept of rubbish, and consequently the notion of dirt, remains relative and ambivalent.

The Dogon of Tiréli employ a series of generic terms that enfold various waste materials within definitions that classify them according to their intrinsic properties or materiality. I came across local classifications of waste through my awkward, repeated participation in cleaning my host family's compound, as well as through management of my own waste. These activities were an interesting interactive and reflexive context that enabled me to locate myself within the native daily recycled microcosmology. Dogon people categorise waste through a conceptual ordering of daily life that allows them to set up and to maintain their sociocultural and symbolic boundaries. Apparently, through the naming of rubbish Dogon take control over the fuzzy reality of the matter. The local classification of refuse is as versatile as the daily practice that constantly redefines and generates new categories of waste with which new forms of worldviews are associated. In other words, categories of rubbish, even if they are solid, imply a certain fluidity. The flow of waste, both conceptual and physical, is made manifest though particular transformation processes. In one way or another, domestic waste is always in a state of becoming. Consequently, waste can easily move from one category to another.

Domestic waste was defined to me by the villagers as *nème* ('dirt'), including body dirt, and *lɔgo* ('detritus'), such as sweepings. Both terms indicate the substance and matter according to either a positive or a negative connotation, depending on the uses and meanings attributed to the waste. On the one hand, *nème* and *lɔgo mɔniu* refer to the repellent elements or awkward things that are in the way and are therefore rejected. On the other hand, *nème* and *lɔgo eju* refer to useful refuse that is recycled, reused, or composted; they are a by-product of activity and, therefore, signify life.

Retaining Waste and Dirt in the Home

In the Dogon, it is often said that the messier a household is, the better! In fact, the sayings *Áma gínu nèmeŋere* ('May [god] *Áma* make your house dirty') (Calame-Griaule 1968, 199) and *Áma gonte woun logujo* ('May [god] *Áma* make your courtyard very dirty') express the Dogon's wish for their houses to become increasingly 'dirty' over the years. Such idioms, which are declared at the founding of the house, wish long life and fertility to the inhabitants. The accumulation of dirt therefore communicates the capacity to feed people as well as to fulfil other needs.

I begin with what is, perhaps, the most aesthetic form of waste: smoke, the index of fire (Chapter 7). This form of waste, the smoke that fills the air of the compound daily when women are cooking or brewing, connotes the stability of life as time passes. Its significance as a sign of normality and stability is conveyed in the expression *Áma sɛbu ŋeoun noɲo* ('May god blacken the roof of your kitchen'). Fires are built daily, even in times of famine; thus pretending that the cooking pot is full constitutes a form of psychological resistance to the dismay of paucity (Chapter 7).

Fire, smoke, and their traces are indicative of the desire for prosperity. Similarly, the body traces left on the entrance wall to the compound are not so much dirt as signs of life. The many handprints, which darken over time, are made by inhabitants' repeated grasping of the entrance walls while entering and leaving the compound. Thus such marks (in Western views a form of dirt) are from body traces that are seen as a sign of life, because they are created by the daily passage of people—especially importantly of children. Hence, touching and impregnating the home with body dirt expresses life as opposed to death, which a clean place would signify. In fact, a compound without dirt indicates the precariousness of the lives of the people who occupy the place—spotlessness is lifelessness. Similarly, dried, smelly food residue stuck to cooking pots indicates the dynamism of the place, as does the accumulation of smoke. In this worldview, cooking utensils are left unwashed until next required, seen to represent a positive sign of domestic (dis)order. The women say that cleaning utensils straight after eating brings scarcity. Indeed, my host mother pointed out to me that washing utensils immediately causes the food that was eaten to leave the body. In other words, it brings hunger upon them. When the cooking pots are about to be used, they are soaked and scrubbed in a separate pot, and the grey water with food residue is given to sheep to drink.

The layers of dirt retained on people's skin and clothes also possess a positive connotation, since they are associated with labour and the intense and energetic physical work necessitated by the Dogon daily routine, called *wanaŋet* ('black work', meaning hard work), which refers to the capacity of a person to live by the sweat of one's brow. Furthermore, sweat accumulated on clothes used daily is perceived as a form of comfort as well as revitalisation of the person—a sense of reinforcement of the self. It is said that someone who is always clean is someone who is lazy (people with long nails are also considered to be lazy).

Finally, the layers of mud mixed with animal dung used to roughcast the house each year act as a second skin for the house (Chapter 9); thus dung is not wasted. All the forms of detritus convey a sense of activity, of everydayness and thus of preparation for the rainy season. (Scents create an ontological security that makes people feel at home.)

The Life Cycles of Millet

Millet plant is an important practical, economic, and symbolic element that serves multiple purposes and that requires a complex recycling process (Chapter 11). At the end of the harvests, millet straw is brought from the fields to the compound to feed the livestock. The remaining stalks are scattered in the compound, where they progressively turn into manured compost produced by people and domestic animals. Multiple layers of litter are almost a defining characteristic of many compounds' surfaces (Figure 8.1). These layers are predominantly composed of organic matter that includes animal dung[2] and the remains of millet, such as the stalks (*yù: bé:lu*), rachis, chaff, and some sweepings. They predominantly accumulate in an area of the home where animals are kept and in the latrines, in the period between the end of the harvest and the beginning of the agrarian cycle. After harvest time, the matured compost is taken to the fields to fertilise the soil and thus feed the crops. The crushing action of human feet on the straw compresses it and activates the process

Figure 8.1 Millet straw mixed with chaff and animal excrement scattered in the compound constitutes precious manured compost often qualified as 'gold'.

of decomposition. Additionally, the manured compost is constantly increased with fresh dung, urine (Sangaré et al. 2002), and large quantities of water, thus strengthening the rich fermenting matter.

In many places, *bìnugu* is generally found in the patriarch's compound and fields. This thick blend of manured compost that regenerates the fields also materialises the temporality of millet cereal and by extension, the environment that hosts it. In fact, incorporation into the soil of millet scraps, collected originally from the fields and constantly dampened, maintains the life cycle of the cereal. *Bìnugu* helps to develop the seed by providing fertiliser for subsequent young, growing millet plants. People often refer to the fields becoming 'clean', when a lack of vital substance in the soil causes the plants to weaken. This situation requires that *bìnugu* be spread over the fields.[3] Cleanness is associated with sterility, whereas dirt signifies productivity.

The second type of organic element[4] encountered in Dogon compounds, more specifically in the latrines, is called *yógo di(y)é* (*yógudiyé, yógo tí:, yógo tíé:*). It is often combined with the manured compost made from millet stalks. Although the villagers spread this matter on their millet fields, they also use it on their onion gardens. It is a precious fertiliser alongside the use of ashes and dried leaves. The term *yógo di(y)é* designates the chaff (husks), or *yógo* (the term *sé* was also employed), and the broken cores of the millet spikes (rachis) that appear in the form of small sticks (also called *ɛɲɛgiré*).

Millet chaff including the rachis is a by-product of pounding and wind-winnowing millet ears (Chapter 11) that may, in addition to millet stalks, be kept in the latrines. However, in some families, when it is dedicated for use in the onion fields, it is stored outside the compound in rock cavities or in the ruin of a house.

For the households in which this compost is kept moist by daily additions of domestic wastewater, the fermentation process of the *bìnugu* represents both a practical and a symbolic principle of fecundity. Indeed, I was told in many villages that a small clay pot called *mɛ kúnu tóroy*, containing the umbilical cord and the placenta of a newborn, is buried underneath millet compost that is kept in the shower or latrines.[5] By retaining moisture, the *bìnugu* maintains the principle of fertility of both the woman and the cereal.

Once the birth-matter has been enshrined, the new mother has to wash in the morning and in the evening for 35 days in the latrines of the menstruating women. Then, she has to disinter the pot. As described by Paulme, the contents are into thrown into a hole dedicated to this purpose that is watched over by the *lɜbɜ* priest, who protects the newborn child and the mother against evil spells (Paulme 1988, 436). The pot is then thrown into the latrines of the menstruating women, which is where contaminated calabashes and pots are discarded. According to Calame-Griaule (1968, 185–86), this particular rite is carried out in order to keep the placenta 'alive'.

Hence, the fertility of women is ensured symbolically through the connection made between the side-products of the womb and of the cereal. This connection is further emphasised by the use of the same metaphor to refer to sterile women (*gúnu*) and fields: both are said, metaphorically, to be 'dry'. The notion of 'dry' (*mà:*) also refers to the harsh conditions of life in the Dogon, such as poverty. Various linguistic expressions found in daily language make reference to this metaphoric use of *dryness*, such as when the Dogon refer to someone as living in a 'dry' place (the harsh, sterile, and barren conditions of the place). By extension, someone who is miserly has 'dry hands'; someone who is rude and/or who always makes problems has 'dry eyes'; someone with a 'dry mouth' *ãga mà:* is associated with those who never admit to being in the wrong. As reported by Calame-Griaule (1968, 185), *kíne mà: gabáy* ('dry heart') means careless, and *ku mà:* ('dry head') means whimsical. Unsurprisingly, someone with moist hands refers to someone with a lot of material means.

As mentioned earlier, ashes, called *únɔ*[6], which are the residue of firewood used in cooking and brewing activities, often complement millet waste in fertilisation. As noted by one of my sources, the Dogon concept of ashes follows the same particular pattern of birth, death, and rebirth followed by millet straw. In fact, after being revitalised by the flame of the fire, the dry, dead wood dies again as it is entirely consumed by the flames and thus reduced to ashes. This dead matter is then spread out on the fields to fortify them. The concept of the action of fire in the production of ashes involves not the destruction of the matter but its transformation.

Consequently, organic waste is defined in this instance as a tonic. It does not create life but it constitutes a substance that regenerates the life of earth. Added to the ashes, manured compost encourages germination of the seed, in the same way as water or urine activates the transformation of waste. The matter plays as significant a role in securing the prosperity of Dogon families as do the families' other fundamental economic (and for some of them ritual) preoccupations in relation to sustaining the stability, harmony, and continuity of life in their sparse environment. Hence, the practices and rituals surrounding organic matter provide considerable insight into the formation of local worldviews that bring together environmental and human life cycles. In other words, compost materialises, through refilling and transformation processes, temporalities regenerated through everyday practices and that are revived seasonally. (Note that in parts of the Dogon region, especially on the Séno Gondo plain, the lack of organic waste forces the use of expensive chemical fertilisers.)

Animal Remains in Domestic and Ritual Context

Another dominant living resource that exists alongside the multiple sources of waste materials that I have just described are domesticated animals. These provide flesh (food) and blood (sacrifice), skin (leather), and bones and excrement (compost and manure) that function in both quotidian and ritual life. Domesticated animals constitute a form of wealth and ontological security, since life and resources remain distinctly precarious. Domestic animals dedicated for daily consumption are generally butchered and sold in the market every five days on *dɔmbay* (the last day of the week). They also function as gifts—for instance, throughout the marriage process, as an exchange, or to repair the breaking of a prohibition as part of ritual sacrificial practice. The remains of domestic animals, whether used for a sacrifice in a compound or for domestic consumption, can be transformed and reused. Bones are generally scattered on the butchering site, where they are eaten by dogs, gathered and thrown in a field as fertiliser, or simply disappear into the soil. In some areas elderly women transform bones into powder that they rub on their fingers to spin cotton.

In the past, some cemeteries on the escarpment were dedicated to horses. However, I observed that on the plain, horses, alongside other animals such as dogs and cows, who died from natural causes but not epidemics, are disposed of in the fields in one particular location about 2 km away from Bankass, where they gradually rot in the open air and disappear into the ground. They are seen as a field fertiliser.

Animal remains, such as bones and horns, from sacrifices made in a compound where the meat is consumed by the men involved in the practice, may be kept or thrown on the fields later as fertiliser. The dry horns and skins may be reused by witnesses of the sacrifice to make or contain medicinal substances. Also, horns are affixed on the entrance or the inside walls of the house to protect the habitat against malevolent beings. In some compounds, horns and jaws are hung on the granary façade to account for the number of sacrifices that have occurred there over the years, thus signifying the extent of the people's animal contributions to sacrifices. In addition, the remains signify the privacy and danger of the ritual places.

Excluding Waste and Polluting Substances

I now examine some elements, called *nème*, that are considered to be negative. This term refers to repellent and useless domestic waste, such as faeces, sweepings from the compound floor, decomposing food remains, and plastics and other nonlocal elements, which are all allocated to the outside of the compound and are either progressively integrated into the soil or swept away by the wind. In some places, plastic and metallic pieces are reclaimed from outside the compound to make craft items for tourists. Body products and menstrual blood, however, which represent polluting and dangerous substances, are both excluded from the entire village.

Human Body Waste

Human excrement (*bɔdɔ*) and vomit (*gùrɔ*) are called *sãmu* ('bad smells that provoke disgust'). These bodily waste products are deposited in remote areas of the village. In Tiréli, local toilets are located at the top of the scree. Although body waste products are acknowledged as repulsive, they still signify life. For example, although children's faeces found in the courtyard are regarded with disgust, they are also seen as a sign of life manifested by the presence of children in the home. (The faeces are obviously always removed.). This is the same worldview that leads to the practice, as recounted by one of my sources, of not travelling for a few days after consuming sacrificial meat; it is believed that defecating in someone else's fields or village scatters the benefits of prayers. Indeed, the power of sacrificed meat (for example, from animals fed with medicines) partly remains in the faeces.

Menstrual blood, called *pùnu*, constitutes a rather complex polluting substance that detracts from the power of magic objects and taints water. It is therefore excluded from the compound and the village. The state of menstruating women makes them impure (*pùru*), a term that also applies to a particular state of dissemination of an individual's spiritual and vital forces, called *ɲama* (Calame-Griaule 1968, 229). In theory, menstruating women are not allowed to leave their temporary (for menstruating women) house enclosure to approach water points, nor are they allowed to use the common public toilet; they must stay in the house dedicated to them (*yápùnu gínu*). There, they cook for themselves with specific utensils that are restricted to the site because they are polluted. (Today, owing to religious conversion fewer and fewer women live in the house; however, it is still widely believed that the presence of menstruating women inside the compound affects the power of magic and shrines, which then need to be purified.)

In the past, once a woman's period terminated, she had to rub her body with oil extracted from the pit of the African tree grape (*Lannea microcarpa*), called *sá*, which stands as a symbol of fecundity. Women used it as a means to purify their bodies and therefore to recover their reproductive forces. *Sá* oil, considered to be a male substance, enabled women to regain their sexual power (Lane & Bedaux 2003, 86). As observed by Paul Lane in the escarpment village of Banani in the 1980s, if the village becomes polluted because a woman has left the *yápùnu gínu* house while menstruating, purification of the village is effected through removal of all the women's culinary materials. These are thrown into a place called *pùnulu diju*, where the utensils are left among the rocks and on which the clay pots are shattered. As part of the same cleansing, in each compound the water jars are emptied and left to dry in the sun in order to negate the soiling. (Emptying the water jars, called *lòy*, a term that also refers to the foetal envelope, could symbolically be associated with a form of purification of a woman's womb.) By discarding/breaking the polluted containers and utensils that contaminate the food and drink, villagers stop the pollution (Lane & Bedaux 2003, 87–88). Similarly, personal objects (for example, jewellery, cloths, hair pins) and cooking utensils (calabashes, pestles, and mortars) belonging to women who died—for instance, in pregnancy or while giving birth—are thrown outside the village on the cliffs, because they are seen as a form of pollution. In some of these places, one can find the wrappers of women who gave birth to stillborn babies. In the plain area near Bankass, people who died from cholera are buried individually in the ground; however, their clothes and belongings are buried together in a separate pit.

Sweepings and Nonorganic Matter

The Dogon of Tiréli call the useless trash that they expel from the compound *tɔro* and *lɔgo mɔniu* (Figure 8.2), sweepings that are thrown outside the compound or are sometimes thrown into the ruins (Chapter 7). Although the first, *tɔro*, is sometimes integrated into the compost because it is mostly organic, the second, *lɔgo mɔniu*, is thrown away. However, some families redefine *tɔ́ro* as *lɔgo mɔniu* by mixing their organic and nonorganic matter together.

Tɔro refers to inedible pieces of herbs and thorny branches that domestic animals leave behind, as well as incongruous things in people's food stocks such as little stones, sand, and rotten cereal kernels. As mentioned, *tɔro* also includes light sweepings, such as dust and tree leaves brought by the wind or by people. When cleaning the compound, women collect sweepings in a calabash with the aid of a small hand broom made of straw. The compound is

Figure 8.2 Useless matter composed of sweepings, pieces of plastic, and rags outside the compound

generally swept when eating, sitting, resting, and walking in the accumulated dirt become inconvenient for the occupiers. Domestic animals also clean up the place naturally, as they eat food remaining on the floor and on unwashed cooking pots.

The category *lɔgo mɔniu,* or waste that cannot be transformed, comprises potentially useless and irrecoverable, disparate items such as pieces of pots, pieces of cloth, torn up plastic bags, torn pages of school books, and pieces of shoes or of tin cans and other various metallic and plastic items. Belonging to this category of domestic waste are the weeds that grow and dry in the fissures of the walls and on the rooftop, which connote neglect and an absence of life. By extension, a field in which weeds largely colonise the ground and threaten development of plants conveys an idea of 'seediness'. Finally, the sweepings that clutter up public paths make people aware that this material did once serve a purpose. Sweepings are therefore a testimony to the dynamic of daily life, because they are produced by people or animals'

Discarded rags are among the sweepings, or *lɔgo mɔniu.* They constitute another form of waste that signifies a particular conception of the body and of life (Norris 2010). Ideas of longevity and prosperity of the body and of the individual are conveyed throughout the life cycle of cloth. Clothes that are falling apart are commonly referred to in the local language as *Áma sɛmɛlɛ daga* ('Make *Áma* leave this powerless rag out"—meaning outside the compound).

This idiom gives voice to the wish of the person wearing the rag that he/she lives a long and prosperous life. Once it cannot be worn, it has to be thrown away. Whereas the act of buying new clothes testifies to a financial investment made possible through work, discarding rags translates as a capacity to reject these useless elements that become unnecessary at some point. The rag that has accompanied a living body for a stretch of time reflects the body's longevity and also a need for renewal. Thus, regeneration of the individual is marked symbolically by the act of casting out the useless matter.

New clothes are always kept for events such as weddings and funerals during which people use them to manifest their personal success and ability to dress well. This situation is often described as *parader* or *l'art de la parade*, which means 'showing off with new gear'. During the Dogon New Year (occurring after the harvest during the cold, dry season, between mid-December and mid-January), people sing that those who do not have cotton (indigo and African wax-print clothes) can blame only the parents, who were not able to offer new clothes to their children who merited it. The practices associated with the renewal of the year represent a form of regeneration of the self that is made real through clothes and conceptual value of clothing. Wearing nice clothes daily is usually perceived as a form of claiming superiority and thus stirs up jealousy. Thus, after the event, people slip back into their everyday outfits. However, because of the great availability and diversity of clothing products bought in local towns or, more frequently, purchased in the escarpment markets, young people who can afford it revel in the art of displaying themselves in the latest fashion gear while they are working in the fields. Older people, however, wear the same clothes every day. As was pointed out by my assistant, the older people's attitude toward dirt that accumulates on their clothes references their daily labour. The dirt on clothes expresses the passage of time and provides psychological comfort offered by the smell and the decay of the fabric. In short, the everyday rags that people wear objectify the efficient, daily performance of the body. The value of the faded and shredded textile resides in its covering of soil, perspiration, oil, and dust, signifying people's engagement in daily life and labour. Furthermore, the rag contrasts with the longevity of the healthy body that wears it.

Changing clothes enables people to distance themselves corporally from their daily routine as well as to show the renewal of the self in public. It also testifies to the ability to overcome the everyday and its harsh conditions by buying and wearing new clothes. Thus rags can be seen as a form of biographical matter that can, in the wearing, define the body in contrasting ways as they constitute a form of matter that objectifies social dynamics and temporalities. Further, and perhaps, counterintuitively (to Western conceptions of the world), if thrown away, the rag reinforces the longevity of the body. Within this continuity, excessive use of fragranced soap and body lotions veils the everyday in the same way that excessive washing of clothes can be seen to mask the fact that they have been used. The value that the younger Dogon place on breaking out of the everyday can be seen in how they often spend the little money they have on bars of soap or, more stylishly and expensively, they choose packs of washing powder.

Wearing clothes redolent of the (bought) smell of freshness is associated locally with the ethos of modern town life, which is thought to appeal to 'clean' and 'attractive' people. The qualities of these imported modern products generate new perceptions of the self and of society in the young people's minds. As said by a 25-year-old villager: 'Poverty makes Dogon people unclean. When I cultivate crops in the plain, I don't have any means. So, I become dirty again'. By this, the young man means that he does not have the money to spend on soap and proper clothing, while he is busy working in the fields. He explains that he saves and spends his money buying Chinese medicines against malaria and drugs to give him energy. The daily hard and intensive cultivation work affects his physical condition and appearance. In contrast, after agricultural work, he spends most of his time in town, where he can find small jobs, wash as often as he can, and be presentable.

Finally, the *lɔgo mɔniu* litter that is thrown away from the compound encompasses multiple forms of medicine packets, batteries, envelopes, flip flop plastic shoes, elements that cannot be repaired, lids, bottle tops, and broken plastic containers of imported products that can no longer contain anything. These are produced locally but are brought into the village mainly by Westerners. This waste generates new forms of worldviews as the potential seen in the matter is creatively reused and recycled—that is, turned into new commodities. These can be used for domestic purposes, such as to scour cooking pots or even to carve clay pots or decorate masks with, for instance, empty blister-packs for medicines, as Polly Richards as shown in her research on Dogon masks (Richards 2003, 236). In many places in the Dogon area, this modern rubbish tends to be retrieved to manufacture small masquerade figurines and miniature vehicles to sell to tourists. In some villages, scraps of enameled pots are periodically collected by metal dealers who sell them in Bamako. Some of the dealers go down to Lome in Togo by truck where they can sell enamelware directly to foundries.

The Reuse of Foreign Waste

When kept in the granaries or in the house, the shiny tin cans of milk powder, coffee, sardines, and tomatoes are reused to store money, spices, and other things. They belong to a separate category of *nème*, seen as neither positive nor negative. This broad category includes items such as plastic mineral-water and shampoo bottles, body-cream pots, and film containers. It seems that the Dogon consider the container that remains after the consumption of a product to be an object in its own right. Indeed, the locals' (Dogon kids' in particular) constant and persistent pestering of any visitor for such containers can border on harassment. Plastic and glass bottles are, for instance, reused to store petrol, local beer, and millet cream.

Synthesis of Dogon Domestic Waste

As I have noted, the Dogon keep useful and meaningful body dirt, compost, and smoke on the body or in the household temporarily. In contrast to this, body waste products, decomposing matter, fragments of modern/Western rubbish, as well as sweepings, rags, soapy liquids, and, finally, menstrual blood, are all kept or removed to the outside of the compound. Dogon categories of waste are summarised in Figure 8.3, which shows how Dogon waste is dealt with through particular contextualised practices. I have demonstrated that certain outside matter, such as modern/Western, plastic, and/or metallic elements can often be retrieved to be turned into something else, as long as a particular use and meaning is attributed to it.

Dogon concepts of domestic waste enfold fluid categories that reveal complex modes of relating (Hawkins 2005, 7; Hawkins & Muecke 2003). In other words, the inside/outside conceptual ordering of the domestic framework materialises local worldviews that are variable and changeable, as the domestic matter takes on different meanings according to different individuals (Drackner 2005). The place to which, on the body or the inside/outside of the household, domestic waste is allocated is based on the materiality of that piece of waste. This place defines as tangible the qualities of the rubbish that determine its new potential/use. However, as I have shown, this dichotomist vision possesses a more complex dynamic. In fact, metallic and plastic things can always be reclaimed. Consequently, the porosity of the epistemic boundaries

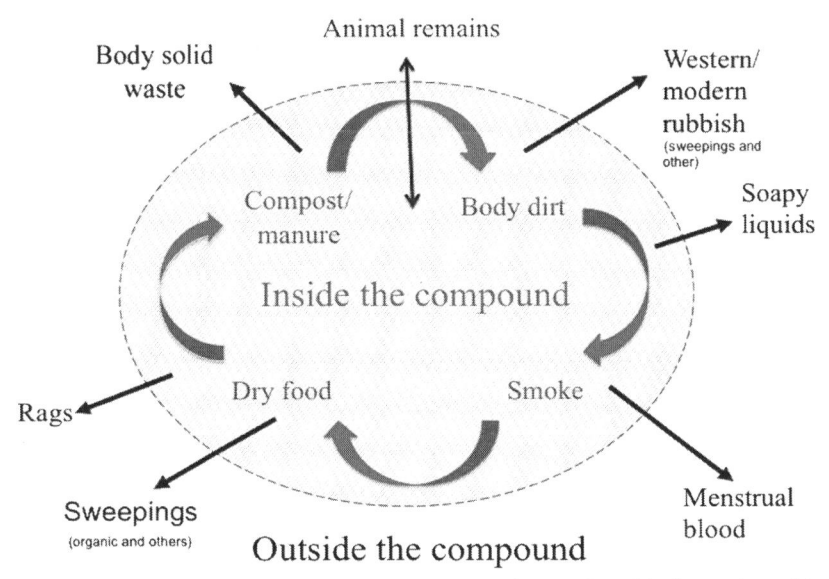

Figure 8.3 Diagram showing Dogon categories of waste found inside and outside the compound

of domestic waste indicates that 'Dogon dirt is a matter all over the place', that is always 'in' and 'out' of the household.

Through the multiple examples summarised in Figure 8.3, I propose that Dogon garbage materialises particular temporalities. In fact, it appears within the category of that which is temporarily retained, or temporarily refused. Hence, Dogon rubbish always remains in a temporary state of 'becoming' (Hawkins 2005). It is fundamentally generative and regenerative. The temporal and mutable characteristics of Dogon rubbish manifest themselves through the reuse, recycling, and composting of domestic matter. Any kind of rubbish that can potentially contribute to the renewal of people and places is seen as positive—that is, as a source of life.

Although for the Dogon rubbish and detritus represent disorder, each residual mark, smell, or piece of rubbish possesses a capacity that, when realised through action as an object of use becomes part of an order of things by which the Dogon cope with scarcity, either by containing that which is scarce, by symbolising the continuity of life, or by sustaining that life through the generation of new economic means—that is, objects they can trade. In fact, the detritus that remains after the consumption or use of imported or local products constitutes a form of wealth and thus a sign of prosperity. Through the multiple daily *cyclia* and *recyclia* of waste that operate according to the materiality of each piece, Dogon domestic waste takes part in what I call a recycled microcosmology. Always in the making (Barth 1987), this microcosmology of return embraces the life cycles of people and of the environment.

Conclusion

Dogon domestic waste as 'matter all over the place' operates according to its own local discipline based on the meanings attributed to it by people—that is, according to the potential/use found in the object's materiality. Dogon domestic waste objectifies particular temporalities and conceptions about the ways people relate to one another and engage in the world by containing and decontaining waste inside and outside the always permeable boundaries of the home and of the 'living' body.

9 Making an Earth Granary: Embedded and Embodied Technology

The earth granaries of the Dogon people stand as a prominent characteristic of their domestic landscape. Dogon granaries, warm beige-coloured containers, square in plan and crested with a conical thatch roof-hat, compose the compound's enclosure or stand independently within it. Each is built on a set of stone pillars or a rock, which adapt remarkably well to the uneven and steep topography of the Bandiagara escarpment scree. Dogon architecture is camouflaged within the surrounding landscape of the escarpment scree and, with their back walls facing the Séno Gondo plain, their granaries create a series of ramparts that functioned as a fortification against invasions (Lauber 1998). In fact, with their lofty stature, these storage facilities constitute a thick fence that conveys a sense of both impenetrability and intimacy, providing a structure of containment in a landscape of scarcity.

There are four types of granaries in the cliffs area, namely, *gúyɔ ana, gúyɔ ya, gúyɔ tógu,* and *aɲiːgúyɔ,* and they all belong to the head of the family.[1] As its name indicates, the *gúyɔ ya* is gendered female (*ya*), whereas the *gúyɔ ana* is gendered male (*ana*). Earth granaries distinguish themselves not only through their design but overall by the way they are compartmentalised and thus by what they contain.

In Tiréli, the male granary or *gúyɔ ana* (Figure 9.1), possesses a flat roof and a single compartment. It serves to store millet harvests (*Pennisetum spicatum*). The female granary (*gúyɔ ya*) (Figure 9.2), characterised by a round top, is allocated to women but is also used by men (Chapter 10). The *gúyɔ ya* (also called *yùːsa gúyɔ*) used by men generally possesses two (or three) compartments at the bottom (a matter of the owner's choice) and one at the top, which contain millet spikes, millet seeds, and the owner's belongings and ritual

Figure 9.1 The *gúyɔ ana*, or male granary, serves to store millet.

Figure 9.2 The *gúyɔ ya*, or female granary, is used by women or men.

paraphernalia. The female granaries that are used by women generally comprise three or four compartments at the bottom and two or three at the top (again according to the owner's choice) and hold the women's spices, pulses, cooking utensils, and personal effects, such as jewellery.

Two other granary forms, which are not gendered, can be observed in the Dogon compound. The *gúyɔ togu* ('shelter'), which possesses a square base and top and belongs to the patriarch, is made of two compartments, one of which contains the family shrines and ritual objects, while the other functions as a resting space. The second type of granary, called *aɲi: gúyɔ*, which is small and round at the base, has a conical top and generally contains the hibiscus harvest (*aɲi:*, or *Hibiscus Sabdariffa*).

The structure of all these storages is designed in relation to the nature of its contents, which have to do with men and women's domestic and ritual roles in crop, livestock, and food production. Dogon granaries are material metaphors that objectify people's relationships, roles and history, crops and fertility, and, by extension, the life cycle of the natural environment from which raw material such as wood, earth, and stones are extracted to build a home. Although there are exceptions to the rule, Dogon granaries are essentially built and roughcast by men during the hot dry season before the start of the agrarian cycle.

In this chapter, through a detailed examination of the manufacturing process of the body of a Dogon female granary[2] located at the top of escarpment scree in Teri-Ku Dama, I look at implicit forms of embodied daily practical worldviews that are embedded in the materiality of this domestic container and that manifest themselves through praxis. Furthermore, an examination of the building process enables an understanding of how Dogon men work with and think about earth materials and thus how they conceptualise the built environment through 'making' and through their body.

Here I concentrate on the building of the structure and roughcasting of the edifice, which require working with earth matter. Because it is made of earth, I suggest that the granary objectifies entangled life cycles of people and the natural environment (seasonality) as well as acting symbolically as a vector of life's continuity. I show that these cyclic temporalities transpire through systematic interplays that occur between the body of the builder and the earth matter that is being transformed and shaped. In other words, because it is entirely handmade, the granary as an embedded social technology (Sillar 2009) integrates body dynamics that are conveyed to its materiality. These concern the kinaesthetic and sensory experience of earth 'matter in-the-making'. Hence, I propose that relationships between the body and the granary being made are, primarily, beaten into shape through the haptic experience of matter in which the rhythmic movements of the bodies making the granary are incorporated, a process that Warnier describes as 'thinking through one's fingers' (Warnier 1999, quoting Mauss and Halbwachs). Finally, as a semishared participatory and socially embedded performance, the shaping of granaries connects multiple body dynamics of builders and apprentices who work synchronically to assure the stability of the building.

The Building Process of the *Gúyɔ Ya*: Embodied Practice and Embedded Temporalities

The making of earth containers occurs during the same period as the reactualisation of the village shrines (Douny 2011), which is a particular shifting moment through which Dogon villagers also prepare themselves to re-enter a new agricultural cycle that will demand of them a considerable amount of strength and vigilance. This liminal period is characterised by a unique euphoria caused by the reawakening that follows the dry season's long period of rest and the 'healing' of the split between those who cultivate onions and those who leave the village in a temporary exodus to work in the town. Their return (and therefore the social gathering of families before the first rain) enables the village community to re-engage and maintain social networks before the laborious and intense rainy season. This period of a few weeks also constitutes a time of doubt. Indeed, being socially and domestically recontained, people pass through this period with the hope that they will have plentiful rain and a good harvest—hoping that they will be able to fill the containers they have made.

When the fonio *Digitaria exilis* harvest approaches (fonio is harvested before millet), more granaries are constructed in the compound if necessary. People tend to delay this task because the harvests are completely unpredictable from one year to the next, especially if it is for the millet harvest, which is particularly liable to fail. Often the storage space remains half empty; the neglect or the abandonment of granaries indicates scarcity. The opposite can be observed in the plain area, where a row of up to 12 oversized millet granaries is more likely to be found than on the escarpment. This abundance symbolises the prosperity of a family that has many people to feed owing to successful harvests and the good quality of the owner's land. However, overexploitation of the soil and the drastic climate conditions are making this abundance less common.

From a technical point of view, as indicated by the shape of the earth granaries built by the Dogon in the Baye and Bankass area, materials and building techniques are inspired by termite mounds.[3] A blacksmith in the village of Ende explained that in remote times, Dogon people abandoned their initial habitats made of straw and started to build with earth by observing and experimenting with the shape, structure, and material of a termite mound, which remains predominantly cool; in fact, its hard materiality blocks light and heat. Termite mounds are also waterproof from all sides—the matter contains insect saliva, which acts as a powerful glue and possesses impressive waterproof qualities. It is said that termites collect pieces of straw and leaves that they incorporate into the earth that they dug from 2 m underground. Then, the earth is gathered on the ground and the walls are built up from the inside. In some areas of the Dogon region, granary builders may break the walls of the termite mounds and use them as a solid building compound that they add to wet mud and straw. Not long after the wall matter has been removed from the termite mounds, they mysteriously rise again, with fresh dark brown wall layers.

Wet Mud Preparation: The Materiality and the Symbolism of Earth Matter

As stated by Mauss and reemphasised by Pecquet, referring to earth that is the main component of the houses of the Lyela of Burkina Faso, matter is a 'living principle' and a 'living body' (Mauss 1974, 166; Pecquet 2004, 152). Pecquet describes Leyla's perception of *banco* as earth-based matter mixed with water as both a material and a power (Pecquet 2004, 157), a concept that exists across West Africa and that includes the Dogon, to whom earth matter is a material of power owing to its inherent capacity to bear and give life. As Prussin writes: 'it [earth] is a source of well-being, of prosperity, of fertility, and of the continuity of life' (1982, 204).

In Tiréli, as I observed, earth for building granaries is collected from a pond but is also often obtained from breaking and recycling old granary building materials, the earth of which is thoroughly pounded and dampened with large quantities of water that the children bring to the building site. They often help to knead the frothy mud (*lɔgɔ mán*), which is first reworked with the hands and then the feet, an activity that is called *lóːdo* or *lɔgɔ lòro*, before being restructured by hand by adding some fonio straw (*põ sɛmi*), which serves as a binding material (Figure 9.3).

All the dismantled components of the former granary are piled next to where the new one is being constructed. These include the pillar stones and all the wooden elements: the door and its frame, and the sticks that formed both the foundation grid and the supporting pillars of the upper compartment. The only new additions are water, millet and fonio straw, pot shards, and gravel, which are incorporated as a means of regenerating and consolidating the wet mud substance and structure. I observed that the matter, just as for clay pottery, is generally prepared long in advance and remoistened immediately before use. It is prepared and left covered on the construction site with the surplus fonio and some rags. It remains on the site for about four days and is dampened three times a day; the longer it matures the better. As mentioned, fonio straw is an important material used in the construction of the walls. It is needed to maintain the cohesion of the mud matter during construction and finally to increase the wall's resistance to rain (the fibres bind the mud).[4]

Many Dogon families observe a series of totemic prohibitions regarding the composition of the wet mud that they use in building work. For instance, in certain families, the totem bans the use of fonio straw in the wet-mud mix, and

Figure 9.3 Children help to mix the recycled walls of a granary that have been crushed and mixed with fonio straw and water.

therefore they use alternative materials. (The ban is due to the negative power of fonio, which would affect the contents of the granary.) Finally, throughout the preparation of the wet mud, the tactile character of the mud mix, which heavily smells of silt, is evaluated and adjusted for its softness before it is shaped into large dark balls of a sticky texture.

Building the Granary: Body Techniques and Rhythm

The building site was cleared of dirt before the granary foundation (*gǔyɔ té*) was set. Using millet straw, the mason indicated the dimensions of the building by transferring the measurements of an existing granary base to the new construction site. According to Calame-Griaule, a measurement known as *nùmɔ tà:nu* (the length of the forearm to the finger tips) is used to measure granaries (Calame-Griaule 1955, 485). The granary rests on a wooden gridlike form based on nine pillars of piled up stones called *tíbu tène*, which ensure its stability and prevents rain and pests from entering the building, imperilling its structure and damaging the granary content.[5]

The Building of the Granary Walls   Before starting the upward construction of the walls, called *kara* (also *béne*), the builder tested the texture of the mud by dropping and rolling it on a rock. Finally, he adjusted the matter by adding some water and fonio. When the matter was of the correct consistency, he placed the first wet mud ball on one corner of the platform, extending the matter with the flat of his hands toward the opposite corner and pressing it onto the wooden support. The wall's foundation was laid by moving round the outside of the structure and attaching a ball of mud to each previous one. This step was carried out with the help of the builder's children. Each layer, which included the divider for the internal compartments, called *káru*, was added in an anticlockwise fashion, terminating with the placement of the *áma* mud cones, which have the same shape as the shrine used in the magico-religious practice of the same name. These cones are made of small balls of wet mud that are slightly curved on the outside by being pressed in the palms of both hands and laterally folded in on themselves.

The *áma* cones ensure the consistency of the construction and design of the four corners (Figure 9.4). These technico-symbolic elements facilitate the repetition of the construction as the mud balls constituting the new wall section are attached directly to them. Hence, the *áma* determine the straightness of

Figure 9.4   Folded mud *áma* cones form granary corners and ensure the granary's consistency.

the granary walls. They also consolidate the building by forming its structure. Finally, they indicate the width of the walls required. Symbolically, the cones act as signs of continuity, on a practice-based level, each time the construction process is recommenced. As reference points they mark the evolution of the edifice. They also act as an expression of the wish to complete the building work on time, that is, before the first rains and thus the beginning of cultivation. Finally, the *áma* cones reinforce the idea of ensuring the longevity of the building, the abundance and permanence of its content, and, generally, the continuity of life. Similarly, a protection is secretly placed in one of the granary walls, generally right after the building of the foundation, to ensure long life of the edifice and protect it against thievery. The builder also prays to God to give him good health to be able to finish the work and to protect his family against famine.

Making granaries constitutes a practical learning process that often turns into a game for the children, who help by bringing water and mud to the site as well as by kneading and mixing. Knowledge is passed traditionally from the father or grandfather to his sons and/or grandsons. This process operates fundamentally through systematic exposure, observations, and through the reproduction of gestures, although people passing by are always welcome to give advice and suggestions about the construction. Although the young men of the village might have some knowledge of construction, most of them no longer possess detailed knowledge of the practice. In the past, everybody was able to make his own granary; now, it is basically a matter for experts. People were more self-fulfilled and autonomous in the past. These days, if a man has the money, he is more likely to pay a builder to construct his granaries and/or his house. The same steps[6] are observed from one course to another as well as from one builder to another. (Although the first 40 cm of the walls are made from the outside, the rest of the construction—for greater ease—is undertaken from the inside with the same motion.) The ball of mud is attached to the *áma* corner with two hands (Figure 9.5, top). The builder pinches this ball with his fingertips to facilitate the fixing of the next line. He stretches the mud toward him with both hands by applying some downward pressure in order to fix it on the existing portion of wall (Figure 9.5, bottom).

With the palms of his hands, he presses down to attach it better to the wall,[7] and simultaneously he flattens the matter by increasing its height. Finally, he flattens the outside of the walls with the flat of his hand and his forearm, a movement called *diadiu* (Figure 9.6). In this way he increases the height of the walls, proportions the matter, and ensures that it adheres properly to the existing wall structure by smoothing the mud of the wall with his hand.

The matter has to be distributed equally in order to make the edifice stable. The builder evaluates the width of the walls with his hands by palpating the matter. The divider walls, which are about 8 cm wide, are made with a similar technique, except that the top of the wall is flattened each time with the hand.

Figure 9.5 The mud is carefully fixed on the *áma* corner.

Figure 9.6 The outside portion of wall is flattened with the palm of the hand and the forearm.

Three forces are applied to the matter: horizontally to stretch it along, vertically downward to attach it, and vertically upward to raise the wall height. The portion of the wall thus extended is about 15–20 cm tall. A circular, centrifugal dynamic is also applied to the building as the builder operates from the inside—which is the case for most daily activities, such as potting and pounding. However, when the builder is helped by his brother, as is the case in our example, the sense/direction of this building can become completely random. Although it is commonly advised to keep the same sense/direction in order to frame the building within a continuous logic, variations occur from one builder to another, depending on the builder's views on such matters. This use of body technique in building is often determined by a personal economy of gesture, comfort, and ease of movement, since the building work occurs under particular climatic and time constraints.

While the first 80 cm of the walls are made from the outside, the rest of the construction (for greater ease) is undertaken from the inside with the same motion. The slightly curved walls are sprinkled regularly with water. (It is believed that a rigid construction would make the building collapse quickly.) The compartment walls are always made after finishing the wall course. The layers of mud can be observed on the surface of the finished walls, which sometimes show the traces of the builder's fingertips, which are thus bodily indentations as part of the matter. About halfway through the construction, the opening[8] of the granary is designed, and it will be closed by a small wooden door (*áŋa diyɛ* [*áŋa dará*]), a recycled part of the former granary. (The Dogon granaries are well known for their highly decorated wooden doors and locks [Bilot et al. 2003], which are valued by antiquarians and tourists.)

Building the Granary Head   When the construction has reached about 1.7 m tall, the walls are folded progressively inward. The builder confers the shell shape to it by tilting the *áma* cones standing at each corner. This step, called *gúyɔ kú: yɔnɔ*, literally means 'to fold the head'; it requires a great deal of precision to prevent the earth material from collapsing under the pressure of rain in the years to come. Thus, here again the *áma* constitutes the structure of the granary top. As the shell takes shape, no more *áma* cones are added, and the wall 'gathers' to form a small opening (*áŋa*, 'the mouth') in which the builder stands. As I observed, the builder increased the wall of the vault by applying a ball of wet mud to the existing surface and by extending it with the flattened palms of his hands, which were placed inside and outside the wall. Finally, as he leaned over the construction, the builder smoothed the surface with his right hand, keeping his left hand on the underside in order to stabilise the wall. As the builder brought the wet mud toward himself as a means to extend the walls, he became progressively self-enclosed within the construction, as is shown in Figure 9.7. As the opening becomes very small, the builder gets down inside the

Figure 9.7 Building the granary's vault—bringing the matter toward the body.

construction and carries on with the building from the inside in order to make the opening as small as possible. (The top of the granary is often compared to a pot owing to its round shape and the technique of extending the wall to form a small opening.)

When the final phase of building the granary—called *kú: màrun* ('to form the head'; that is, by hand)—is accomplished, the granary reaches a height of about 3 m from its base to the top of its shell, which is not perfectly round. All of the granary's dimensions are calculated so as to contain the 'height of a person'—what is called *igɛ:ru para*. The closing of the structure's opening is done by placing either a small clay pot or an *áma* cone into the hole (Figure 9.8). The *áma*, which is inverted (if compared to the áma shrine, which has the same shape) (Chapter 3), is used in this way only for female granaries serving to store

Figure 9.8 The granary shell is closed with an *áma* that is inserted in the hole at the top of the granary.

millet. According to one source, the inverted *áma* constitutes a highly symbolic device that is more than just a practical device to close the female granary top and protect its contents from the rain; in addition, it acts as a phallic element that ensures the permanence of the granary cereals. It also represents the fertility of the field and of the people. Thus the process of inverting the cone brings together the life cycle of the fields, of humans, and of the granary, made of earth. The *áma* corners reflect the society's fundamental preoccupation with the continuity of life in a particularly harsh environment (Douny 2011).

When the final *áma* element is inserted in the granary top, the builder normally spreads a cream (*púno*) made of ashes (*únɔ*) diluted with some water over the top of the granary. This act of inauguration usually signifies the pleasure of having a brand new granary; some people smear a libation of millet cream on top of the granary as a means of wishing for a successful harvest and a full granary.[9] This kind of libation—with or without millet—is also performed right after the millet harvest to thank God for what the granary owner has obtained as well as to ask for more the following year. And thus the builder signals that the container is now ready to be used.[10] This symbolic gesture is a way of showing and legitimising the seriousness and the labour of the builder. Furthermore, for the Dogon, earth matter 'becomes empowered' by being mixed or associated with organic components and substances. The inauguration of the granary signifies the renewal of the life of the compound and, by analogy, of the fields. Hence, the intention behind the pouring of millet substances (as in the cream poured on top of the construction) is to ensure symbolically the longevity, prosperity, and fertility of the granary's contents, as well as the fields and human life (Blier 1983, 1987; Prussin 1999, 424–33).

(As an aside: When finished,[11] the female granary whose construction I observed was not perfectly straight [Figure 9.9]. Indeed, the top shell showed a curve that indicated a lack of dexterity on the part of the builder. When I returned to the site a year later, the granary top had not survived the rain.)

The Roughcasting and Repairing Phase

Roughcasting/plastering (*lɔgɔ páru*) constitutes a repeated stage of the operational sequence of granary building/rebuilding. As part of its material life cycle, roughcasting consists of a process of renewing the edifice as well as, by extension, the built environment, as in the case of the house. By being performed right before the rainy season, it protects the habitat elements; as a builder stated: 'The *lɔgɔ* is like an ointment that you apply to your skin to protect it'. The repair entails the roughcasting (Figure 9.10) of the external wall surface (known as *táru*) that is carried out by adding a layer of wet mud and so thickening the existing surfaces and filling in cracks.

The wet mud is the same as the mud used for roughcasting the outside walls of the house (*gindɔgɔ táru*), which is done to consolidate and protect them.

Figure 9.9   Overview of the asymmetrical granary

However, for granaries, fonio straw may be added. The mud that is collected from the pond (*waɲu*) is very black and gives a cemented aspect once it has covered and dried on the granary surface. Most of the time, cow or donkey dung, or, alternatively, ground African grape skins (*Lannea microcarpa*), are added to the wet mud, which is first left to rot in a jar a period of three weeks and sometimes up to a year. Because of their high concentration of potash, donkey faeces added to the earth mix activate its decomposition process (*ɔmɔgu*) as well as strengthen the matter via a waterproofing function. Once mixed by hand, a ball of gluey, smelly wet mud is thrown on the outside wall of the granary, for roughcasting. Then it is smoothed out with the flattened palm of a hand. When the wall is covered with new mud, it is sprinkled with some water and smoothed again.

Building with Earth as a Gathering of Temporalities

The seasonal praxis surrounding building an earth granary that is described as a sequence of embedded tasks schematised in the *chaîne opératoire* (Figure 9.11), appears as unified chunks of tasks, generated by body movements

Figure 9.10 Roughcasting the granary by applying smooth layers of fresh mud

and the tactile experience of matter, that occur daily before the rainy season. Therefore, because the sequential process of manufacturing, repairing and recycling a female granary represents a series of choices and constraints (Lemonier 1993) that deny temporal linearity, the operational sequence is a gathering idiom—that is to say, a gathering of raw material, bodily dynamics, and tasks into an object that is 'in the making' and that is intended for subsequent use. The *chaîne opératoire* as a visual narrative reconstructing the entire operation makes it possible to apprehend time as a dimension materialised in domestic form and corporeal expression. Time is articulated by multiple temporalities that imply segmented daily human tasks of a relative *durée*. These tasks are synchronised and repeated day after day with the same constancy, and therefore they aggregate into cycles, which are, in turn, determined by the seasons and, most specifically, by the life cycle of the unbuilt-on environment such as the fields. In short, time encompasses human life cycles.

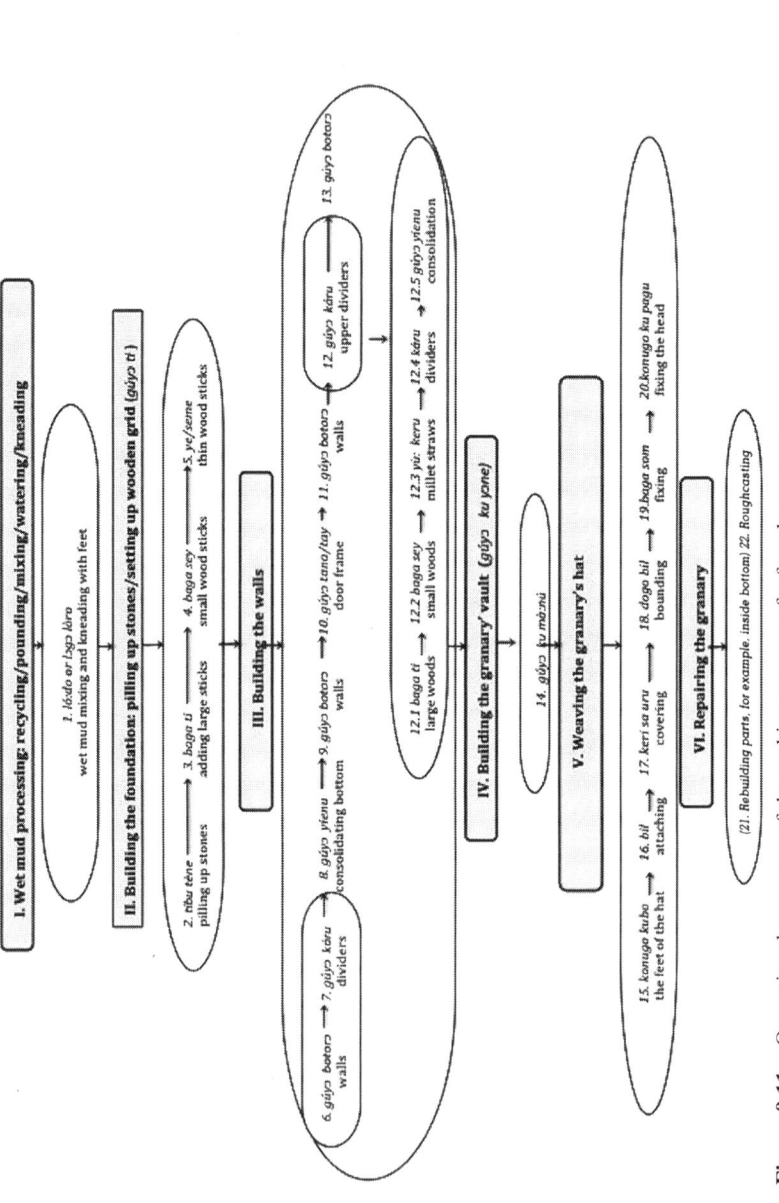

Figure 9.11 Operational sequence of the making process of a female granary

Body Dynamic, Senses of Materiality and the Transformation of Earth Matter

As shown in the previous section, the manufacture of a granary is performed with a particular intensity, body tension, and coordinated dynamics that are based on a corporeal adaptation to the matter—because this matter is exclusively worked with the body as a tool. The body/container relationship stands within a triple dynamic that forms the bodily experience of the matter (Figure 9.12). This dynamic encompasses the body axis and tilt, the body rhythm applied to the matter while it is being shaped, and finally the movement of the hands, including the haptic experience of earth.

Although the first metre of the granary is built from the outside, three-quarters of the construction is performed from the inside. The body kinetic is applied to the matter with an always similar, continuous centripetal force that maintains the construction. This is done through hand movements combined with the motion of the body within the granary structure. Hence, the container objectifies the body dynamic through major recurrent circular motions. The task requires the body to balance on its own axis, providing through this requirement an equilibrium between the builder's body and the container being built. As the granary is being built, the body becomes contained within the material forms, and the builder becomes almost trapped in the final stages of construction. During the shaping of the female granary, the body embodies, as

Figure 9.12　Tactile experience of mud

well as is embodied by, the edifice. It adapts to the matter as the matter adapts to the body.

The building process facilitates, with astonishing regularity, the replication of movements and technique for the first part of the edifice. A great homogeneity of construction is observable through the movements. The walls are built up until they form a shell, which completely encloses the builder. Breath, heartbeats, and exhaustion alleviated by songs convey a particular rhythm that enables the builder to shape the matter. However, the top of the granary remains asymmetrical. According to the builder I observed, although his technical knowledge was good, he miscalculated the proportions and the quantity of matter—and he was hurried by the premature start of the rainy season. Perhaps his efforts to finish the work in haste caused his miscalculation.

The making process operates through a particular sensory and kinetic experience of earth matter or sensed observation of matter, which is required to effect the metamorphosis and resistance of the matter. In fact, it is predominantly the olfactory experience of earth, occurring in the mixing and kneading of fermented wet mud, and its tactile qualities that provide indications of the adjustments required to be able to build with it. In addition, because wall portions are added at different times of the day, the manufacturing process can also be seen through a series of dry beige and progressively wetter, and thus darker, brown layers. The stripes' shades indicate if the wall is dry enough to be continued. The evaluation of earth matter through its tactile experience is a process that Warnier (1999, quoting Mauss and Halbwachs) describes as 'thinking through one's fingers'. The hand movements animated by the builder's internal body rhythms—which guide breaths, heartbeats, songs, and whistling—leave fingerprints that appear on the granary walls and thus materialise the builder's body rhythm.

This is also reflected in the overall geometry of the construction. In fact, the assembled mud balls that are pulled downward, stretched lengthwise, pulled upward, and then smoothed with the fingers and the palms of the hands to become the walls are not apparent on the surface. As it is turned into balls, the mud is gently pressed to test its level of moisture and consistency. Furthermore, it is worked onto the entire wall structure with actions that attempt to cause it to be straight for the first part of the building and curved at the top, where it forms the building's roof shell. Here, the rectangular parallelepiped and dome geometry of the granary result only from the pressure of the hands and fingers on the matter and not from any preexisting technical structure or particular tools.

Consequently, granary making requires an acute sense of detail, great practical expertise, and a complete understanding of all the chemistry and mechanisms involved in the transformation of the earth. Knowing thus becomes experiencing. Making granaries, as a gendered form of habitus, constitutes itself through repeated, shared daily praxis (Bourdieu 1990). It results from a long-term learning process rather than through exclusive cognitive exposure.

In other words, the activity remains a fully sensorial and kinetic operation in which the whole phenomenology of the container, expressed in terms of colour, texture, smell, and geometry, stands at the core of the shaping process. Hence, the sense of proportion and the replication of more or less the same measurements are achieved through a tactile experience of the matter. Building a granary involves knowing exactly where and how the matter has to be balanced, the weak points of the containers, and the texture of the matter to be prepared. Mimesis and learning through the emulation of the matter constitute the two principles of the making of earth containers.

Containment, Gathering Processes, and Cyclic Temporalities

The materiality of granaries objectifies a double gathering process that, on the one hand, comprises the weaving of social networks through daily practical performances that constitute both a learning/teaching process, as well as a form of entertainment, while, on the other hand, it comprises the collection and retention of natural resources in the home that create or re-create a containing environment. Through building, the builder appropriates and re-materialises the landscape from which the earth, stone, and wood are extracted. These two forms of gathering define a particular form of material containment that generates local conceptions of the body, of nature, and of society and that constitute a local microcosmology.

First, making and repairing earth containers is a form of a social construction of everyday life. Manufactured within a participatory mode of performance, containers act as a social gathering principle in which young apprentices, relatives, friends, and neighbours take part by advising and/or practising, as well as by being entertained. In the case of major building work, such as building granaries and repairing or roughcasting old *gínna* compounds (family houses), the collective task reinstalls family networks. Participation in this building work, often followed by the cultivation of the family fields, constitutes an act of identity that reunites and consolidates relationships between people. In short, the making of these containers, which benefit the whole family and are symbolically owned by the ancestors, still reinforces the sense of community through a shared agency in a society that is becoming more and more individualistic.

Second, the collection of material from the surrounding environment, such as clay, gravel, scree stones, pond mud, wood, straw, and tree fibres, constitutes a process of gathering local resources that creates or re-creates a domestic environment that exists inside the landscape from which the items are gathered. *Gathering* implies a dual process of de-containing and re-containing the landscape—that is, an emptying and subsequent rematerialising of it through making earth containers. In other words, the materiality of these containers, as well as other locally made forms, materialises the whole landscape as Dogon granaries are made of earthly substances that are reshaped 'from within'.

Furthermore, digging up the ground, extracting or even breaking the rocks, and collecting the stones to build a compound constitute an appropriation of the place that becomes complete through the making of containers. The granaries insertion within the landscape devises a series of domestic and social boundaries through which ordinary people relate to one another. Working with the environment's materials, and therefore experiencing its materiality, generates a particular sense of attachment to the place. In this sense, knowing and embodying its intrinsic properties through repeated sensory and kinetic experience as well as through its exploitation characterise the Dogon act of dwelling. Within this perspective, retention and circulation of container material strictly within one family is another form of social and resource gathering that functions here as a form of heritage, prosperity, and continuity of life.

Conclusion

Through this examination of the building process of a Dogon female earth granary, I have shown that the granary, as a socially embedded technology, objectifies particular embodied daily and seasonal worldviews. These views are made manifest on the level of technical, material, and bodily praxis. The making of this earth container objectifies a form of body containment that highlights the local conceptions of both nature and the body as the edifice is being shaped through movement inside and outside the material form of the granary. The *chaîne opératoire* proposed in this chapter has revealed interwoven cyclic temporalities that have been conceptualised in terms of a gathering process. This gathering process encompasses both the life cycles of people and of nature as being materialised in a recycled earth container, the matter of which constitutes a highly symbolic element of the continuity of life and its renewal. Therefore, the granary, by objectifying the temporality of the landscape through its substance and materials, constitutes a form of ontological security that provides some reference points in space and time, which stand at the conjuncture of the environmental and the human life cycles. The manufacturing process of an earth granary defines a cosmology in the making (Barth 1987) that is a process of perpetual re-creating of the domestic environment that contains people and that conveys a sense of regeneration in tandem with the renewal of activity, environment, self, and society. Thus, making containers at that particular moment of the year reinitiates a whole process of containment that is completed for the granaries during the harvest period when they are filled.

10 Pandora's Granary: Material Practices of Concealment

This chapter explores the form of containment that transpires from the material practices of storing in a Dogon granary. I use an examination of the *gúyɔ ya*, one of the four Dogon granary types (Chapter 9), with a focus on men's and women's daily uses of this female granary. Although this examination exposes local concepts of gender, I do not discuss them in depth in relation to the domestic sphere. My primary interest lies in the material practice or process of storing millet in this particular gendered object, which reveals itself to be a form of concealment that acts as a mechanism for coping with the stresses of daily life, such as food shortages.

I show that the body movements about 'filling' and 'emptying' and so required to access the granary enable to highlight a particular mode of concealment. It is undertaken by men in order to hide the contents from the view of the women. Thus, body techniques of concealment are a means for the owner of the granary to maintain the privacy of its powerful contents. From within a broader perspective, I demonstrate that the material form itself acts as a conceptual interface between the individual, the society, and the drastic environment. It materialises a cosmology of scarcity that refers to local world-views, to attitudes toward life's stresses and, in particular, to the precarious conditions of the crops. I argue that the bodily and material practice of storing in granaries and, therefore of concealment, reveals men's attitudes toward women in a particular context of necessity.

Concealment as a Material Practice

The crops failed the September I arrived—the rain was delayed across most of the region, and there had been insufficient harvests the previous year. Granaries were consequently reported, and commonly assumed, to be empty. Food shortages struck families and villages unequally—on the one hand, rain falls sparsely in the Dogon area, and, on the other, the quality and amount of the crop harvested also depend on the quality and quantity of the seeds, the fertility of soil, and the fertiliser owned by the families. Consequently, almost no family harvests the same amount as the next one. However, the Dogon people's practices assume that the harvest will be bad every year and for everyone. Scarcity is expressed as hunger (*giyɛ*), as the absence of millet that is assumed or pretended to be there. Hence the act of concealing foodstuff comprises two dimensions. First, although the type of content of Dogon granaries is known to men and women, the quantity remains unknown, except by the owners: that is the husbands or patriarchs. Second, although concealment, as both bodily expressed and encapsulated in the material form of the granary, creates doubt about the quantity and thus may prevent theft, it also causes psychological stress. In other words, the sealed granary generates assumptions and questions about what it does or does not contain.

The everyday 'doing' and 'undoing' of granaries, or the use and non-use of granaries, translate into action(s) masking the scarcity of millet, which disappears rapidly. Thus, the desperate need for full containers reflects local conceptions of life and death. From within this perspective, I propose that these material forms stand as solid metaphors for the real live bodies whose stomachs also often remain empty because constant shortage of food.

The Dogon idea of concealment is embedded in the local term *kínɛ*, which is frequently used to signify 'something that is being hidden inside of something' (Calame-Griaule 1968, 159). In a similar way, the term *bóduru* means to keep things for oneself. As a practice, concealment stands as a boundary marker that defines the gathering of hidden resources. Through an examination of the management of granaries, I look at concealment as a practice of setting things apart, as well as of distancing people from one another. As I have previously suggested, concealment as an embodied practice of things and knowledge discloses social and gender relationships between the individual self and society as well as between men and women. Concealment generates status and power; it is an authoritative process of ownership and of access that is enacted everyday. In other words, concealment contributes to the formation of domestic boundaries through a practice of retaining, maintaining, and hiding both things and knowledge in the granary.

As a mode of containment concealment takes its own form, which is objectified in the materiality of the female granary being full or empty. The process of storing in Dogon-earth containers that embody a form of concealment is developed here using the metaphor of Pandora's box as a means to expose Dogon worldviews. In other words, I suggest that concealing foodstuffs within this particular context of scarcity prescribes a cosmology of hope. I propose that the ambivalent Dogon *gúyɔ ya* (also called *yù:sa gúyɔ* when used by men), which symbolises life when full and death when empty, constitutes a threat for women if ever opened by them. Hence, the mechanism and philosophy behind Pandora's box allow me to think about the object-container within a context of absence, because the building objectifies the fears and hopes of Dogon men and women. The granary is banned for women, because it retains powerful ritual objects or conceals an absence of life resources. In addition, the granary contains high-quality millet grains from selected spikes that will be sown (*yù:sa*). Women's access to this millet for cooking would tragically jeopardize the survival of the family. While the ritual objects can cause death, the absence of foodstuffs can lead to psychological breakdown at the thought of there being nothing left to eat. In this respect, the Dogon granary as a Pandora's box tells us much about gender relationships and worldviews. Although its opening by women would reveal the identity and the quantity of its content, thus possibly releasing fear and despair into the compound from this 'Pandora's granary', hopes for a better future always remain at the bottom, with the millet seeds that the granary preserves.

Men's and Women's Uses of the Female Granary

The *gúyɔ ya* granary constitutes a domestic technology that is divided in such a way as to meet the storage requirements of men and women. Although the number of compartments of the *gúyɔ ya* for a woman is based on her own decision, most of these edifices comprise an average of four divisions in the bottom and two at the top. The more a granary is compartmentalised, the more difficult it becomes to store things unless the plan is for the granary to hold various and relatively small secondary harvests such as hibiscus, groundnuts, and beans. The compartments generally indicate what they are meant to contain. (A cross-compound study of granaries would be interesting to examine, diachronically, Dogon food habits and consumption patterns as well as to evaluate the availability or disappearance of certain plant and cereal species. In the same way, granary ruins can tell us something about periods of drought.)

A compound that includes a large number of granaries tells us things about the size of the family, which, for instance, is likely to be a polygamous family with many mouths to feed. In this case, the granary symbolises wealth and success in life, while absence of a granary or granaries indicates the opposite. Sometimes, the neglect of granaries reveals a lack of millet, which can be alternatively stored instead in hermetically sealed polypropylene woven rice bags in the house. The female granaries used by the women of the family remain intact and are repaired seasonally but are abandoned if the owner is deceased. The *gúyɔ ya*, used by a man to store millet and his personal objects, generally comprises a minimum of two compartments at the bottom and one or two at the top.

The granary's location in the compound usually says something about its ownership. Those that stand in a corner of a compound, or relatively far away from the main areas occupied by women and children, are generally those of men. The granaries located near the kitchen belong to women. However, men's and women's granaries can be distributed randomly, which usually occurs if the size of the compound does not allow the distribution just described.

As mentioned, the *gúyɔ ya* granary is female but can be used by either men or women (with different compartment systems). However, the granary remains exclusive property of the men because they built it. (Women are strictly forbidden to access the men's granaries.) These intimate storage spaces are part of people's lives; they are used by men and women, young and old and are places where, for the most part, men and women organise their lives independently from each other. The granary stands as a space where men and women curate their responsibilities toward the family through a specific content that concerns exclusively and independently either men or women.

Women's *Gúyɔ Ya*: Food, Personal, and Domestic Objects

Theoretically, a man can always access his wife's granary since the compound and so the granaries remain his property. As was often claimed by men, the *gúyɔ ya* of women contained far less than theirs: women do not own anything (according to the men)! Some granaries contain various plastic boxes, buckets, cooking utensils, and pulses. Once opened, the granary of my host mother liberates smells of dried pulses, desiccated food remains from unwashed containers, spices, and sand that once preserved beans; the slightest movement causes dust to rise and fill the air inside the granary. It is particularly stuffy, and the warmth and emptiness of the building creates an atmosphere of inactivity and desolation. By way of contrast, the neighbour's *gúyɔ ya* hosts numerous things, such as cotton cloth or indigo dyed cloth (whose chemical dye has a particular smell reminiscent of gasoline), cotton batting for spinning packed into a basket, a smelly, goat-leather belt, remaining food, and, finally, a bouquet of spices, herbs, and onions blended with Chinese camphor body cream. These scented elements are hung on wooden bars and accumulate in the bottom of the compartments.

In the bottom compartment, women often store their harvest, which mostly consists of groundnuts, hibiscus, baobab leaves, and beans, all of which can be sold on the markets. For instance, grilled peanuts are sold in small plastic bags as a delicacy, and they can also be pressed to make oil. The dried flowers of the red hibiscus are boiled, filtered, and turned into a juice called *dableni*.

Cotton is spun and then sold to be woven by men. The women's income is spent on spices, cooking utensils, cloth, jewellery, body cream, and soap.

Finally, the space located under the granary between the pillars, called *gúyɔ bɔlɔ* ('under the granary'), is also used as a storage space. Technically speaking, it exists to minimise the heat inside the granary since the space remains relatively cool and airy. This is where the chickens shelter during hot afternoons. Large pieces of broken containers, broken knives, and metal tools such as axes are kept under the granary where they are out of reach of the children.

Gúyɔ Ya for Men: Millet Harvests, Seeds, and Magic

The men's *gúyɔ ya*, also called *yùːsa gúyɔ*, is generally used to store millet spikes that serve for domestic consumption. The *gúyɔ ya* is also used to pre-serve high-quality millet spikes, the grains of which are destined to be sown and are kept in leather bags in the granary until the fall of the first rain. Furthermore, the *gúyɔ ya* may also be used to store high-quality millet spikes used for brewing or libation during family rituals. Finally, the granary hosts its owner's ritual and magic objects that are stuffed between the millet spikes. Old men, such as the patriarch, keep their sacred objects in the *gúyɔ togu* which is divided into two compartments. The aim of these objects is to protect the owner and his families, to defeat enemies, or to bring luck. I was told that the earth structure of the container acts as a shell that encapsulates and retains the aggression and powerful effect of its ritual contents.

The functioning of these artefacts are kept secret. I am mostly concerned here with how these objects relate to the granary container. To my understand-ing, amulets, medicines, altars, and sorcery materials are intimately attached to the granary owner and constitute a heritage. They are prepared, curated, and managed by the owner in order to serve his own needs, such as to overcome malevolent entities and his own fears. These artefacts are generally adapted to suit the person who owns them; they may, for instance, protect the granary contents. As described by an elder, these objects act as a bridge between the visible world of humans and the invisible world of the dead and the spirits and therefore enable access to particular forces and knowledge that empower the individual. Although the objects function as powerful entities, their effect takes place only from the moment the objects become activated through sacri-ficial practice and incantations or prayers.

Preserving the secret mechanism(s) of these objects is of vital importance to their owner. Thus, it is the management of these multiple amulets and altars—that is, the knowledge and practices required to use them—that also must be kept secret. In other words, because the practice of maintaining, activating, and/or using the artefacts involves particular knowledge, language, and gestures, the nature of the secrecy concerns the 'way things are done'. The artefact use comprises particular materials, recipes, and procedures that are retained by the owner. However, my source indicated that if a witch seizes the objects, the thief can identify what the owner is protecting himself from and can thus bring him down. The role of the earth granary as an architectural container can be seen in the management of the internal contents. It consists of a way to contain and keep things secret—that is, to keep control of the objects' power. Similarly, on a collective level, the ɔmɔlɔ protections of the village are buried in the ground while the mud cone that stands at the surface simply indicates the presence of an object underground. Burying these artefacts in soil constitutes another means of concealing knowledge about them.

The *gúyɔ ya* granary, and similarly, the *gúyɔ ana* and *gúyɔ togu*, can be seen to 'outline' its own physical boundaries of concealment. In fact, as can be observed in some compounds, the edifice is surrounded by stones that warn women, children, and visitors from approaching. The same sort of enclosing mechanism is found around sacred sites such as the foot of specific trees. As proposed by Nooter, secrecy boundaries can be of three kinds: 'those that spatially separate people; those that socially delineate gender, age and class; and those that spiritually divide and bridge the living and the dead. These are porous, shifting and complex' (1993, 141).

While the Dogon female granary distances men and women by creating individual spaces for privacy, the male granary allows the men to constitute or empower the self through objects; these they manage as their personal belongings that they accumulate in the granary. As an envelope the granary reinforces the secrecy of the content through containment and concealment. In other words, sequestration of the objects makes them more powerful, since they remain unrevealed and unreachable—and the container discourages people from approaching them.

The *Gúyɔ Ya* Millet Reservoir: Symbolism and Embodied Concealment

As proposed by Prussin, the granary 'as a storage container . . . is not only a metaphor for physical well-being but a receptacle for the spiritual source of life, a symbol for the continuity of life and the future, receptacle for the grain that will guarantee life's sustenance from [one] harvest to another' (1999, 426). New or renewed granaries, as well as their number, testify to success in life. They express the family composition—the number of people to feed—and wealth (fertile fields that provide large harvests). They also reflect hard work, technical knowledge and skills in building, and, crucially, the management of food resources. To borrow again from Prussin: 'granaries stand as a metaphor for prosperity and fertility; the form of these extended dome-shaped mounds evokes a gender association' (1999, 427).

In her detailed examination of West African architecture and following Lebeuf (1961), Prussin reports analogies between the roundness of the material form, its content and pregnant women:

> A full granary is a pregnant granary. And to be sure, [a] clay pot containing the seeds for the next year's planting is often sealed and buried deep within its womb-like interior (Lebeuf). The granary's form, its taut, close-to-bursting walls recalling the tight skin of pregnant woman close to term, is only one of its feminine attributes. (1999, 427)

Thus the symbolic explanation tells us that the top of the granary, being round, refers to a pregnant woman's womb. Hence, by giving this shape to the building, the fecundity of the granary is symbolically materialised, since the womb symbolises fertility and therefore life (Chapter 9).

In Tiréli, the top of the granary, like clay pots, 'looks a bit like a woman'. Villagers always say so with an expression of amusement on their faces, but they would never tell me why a container resembles a woman's shape or a woman a container. The shape of the granary's top might suggest the roundness of women as underlined by Calame-Griaule (1968, 168). For Griaule, while the 'genderedness' of the object could be explained by its respective male or female uses, it was the storing practices in their relations to the geometry of the building, along with the analogous comparing of the edifice to the shape of a woman's body, that may have caused him to view Dogon granaries as anthropomorphised (Griaule 1966, 29 in French version). According to Griaule, the granary (generally) appears in the Dogon cosmology as a civilising element that came down to Earth as an ark in immemorial times. In this claim, which was never confirmed to me by the villagers, Griaule specifies that the granary is also symbolically located in men's collarbones, where, according to his source, Ogotemmêli, all spiritual principles reside. As mentioned in Chapter 9, I was told that the granary is built so as to fit a human body standing up. This conveys an idea of body scale rather than straight anthropomorphism as proposed by Griaule.

On a practical level, my sources told me that the round top enables an individual to stand up in a granary and therefore to better manage his belongings. The *gúyɔ ana*, which is also used as a container for millet, possesses a flat roof that facilitates the storing of millet spikes. As we shall see, they are laid out in a particular way in order to preserve them and to enable their extraction later in such as way not to break them. Therefore, the container frames and stabilises its content. Originally, the two types of granary shape and name served simply to distinguish which gender used which container. However, the female granary is also used by men to store their belongings and to conserve millet spikes, as well as high-quality millet spikes and seeds. According to my sources, this is a strategy to confuse potential thieves or witches.

Although the architecture of the granary has been planned so as to prevent damage to its contents, the inside is sometimes also symbolically protected. In fact, at the approach of the rainy season, men offer a libation of millet to the granaries as a means of ensuring future abundant millet harvests. The following words are used: *áma bá: gò mu* ('may God [Ama] give good harvests') and *áma bá: gɔye tɛmɔ̃* ('may Ama make us see the next harvest' or 'may the food give longevity to people'). The same process is carried out for the *daba* hoe that is used to break open the earth during the sowing process; the libation is undertaken as a means to foster good work.

Other protection practices also serve more purely technical ends: cold ashes can be spread at the bottom of the edifice in order to preserve millet against parasites. It also protects sorghum and sesame. (Millet possesses its own protective envelope. Each millet grain is contained in a sheath, and the sheaths are tightly packed on a stem.) Other pests, such as mice, are eradicated by smoking out the granary with chilies that are burned off in a small clay pot that rests on three stones (to avoid burning down the edifice) and that is placed at the bottom of the granary. Then, if necessary, this step is repeated by fumigating with the pulp of the calabash fruit. The two fumigations are particularly powerful and were used in the past to kill enemies; both, and in particular the calabash pulp, cause the lungs to burst.

Harvesting and Filling Up the Body of the Container

Storing millet when the harvest is abundant is a collective endeavour. After regular and accurate evaluations of the state of the crops, the head of the family starts cutting the ears and packing them on carts. (I was told that the task is generally carried out by men, although I saw women helping.) As the harvest failed for certain families, notably mine, the spikes were pounded in the fields (instead of the village). The grain was brought back in large polypropylene woven rice bags to be stored in men's *gúyɔ ya* and/or in the men's room. As mentioned, the quality of the harvest varies significantly from one family's fields to another's and from one village to another. Consequently, some areas have more favourable harvests than others. Similarly, the quality of the soil varies from one place to another.

Generally speaking, collecting, transporting, and filling a granary are taskscapes (Ingold 2000, 195) that are always done by close family members who trust one another. Under no circumstances can a stranger come and help. According to my source, people always hide what they have obtained to avoid jealousy and to prevent people from stealing. Hence, each family has a different schedule to collect crops in their fields, and families avoid providing details about their harvests.

Once the cereal has been brought back to the compound, it may be left to dry on the roof of the house. After a couple of days, once the spikes are dry enough, they are stored in the granary. As far as the storing process is concerned, the millet ears are first packed against the far back wall of the granary; then, the front space is filled up. The granary contains up to four columns of millet ears in the two bottom compartments. The person standing outside the granary passes the ears to the second person, who stands inside and stacks them. Millet ears are placed in layers and in staggered rows as a means to stabilise the packed content. This tight and compact arrangement also serves to prevent rodents getting inside the rows. If the millet ears are well stacked in the granary, the cereal can last for up to seven years. Once the compartment is filled to a certain point, the person standing inside comes out of the granary, and the two people carry on filling it from the outside. They stop once they reach the level of the door. Thus each compartment is filled up, one after the other.

As indicated, millet is never thrown into the granary but is carefully organised in order to favour its conservation; it is said that the millet would 'run away' if it is not handled with care. The cereal must be treated with respect.

Emptying the Granary: Embodied Practice of Concealment

The opening of the millet granary usually must be authorised by the oldest man of the compound, who is responsible for magically protecting the granary and thus the sacrifices. Every morning, the patriarch or one of his sons opens the granary where millet is stacked and removes the necessary millet spikes, which are then processed into food by his wife (Chapter 11). For a large family of between 15 and 20 people, the head of the family removes one large basket[1] (Figure 10.1), with about four handfuls of spikes for making lunch and three handfuls for the evening meal. Once the spikes are pounded, the grain obtained is stored until it is time to pound it. Sometimes, a larger quantity of millet is processed to brew millet beer. Hence, women have the task of processing and cooking the cereal but do not have control over the quantities they cook and the stock of millet.

One of the first things one notices when a granary is opened is the sound of the wooden door grinding on its hinges. The second noticeable thing is the warm, soft, and dusty smell. In addition to the daily granary openings, every week, depending on the family's consumption, some husbands open the millet granary to extract the spikes and give them to their wives for pounding in order to free the grains from the spikes (Chapter 11). This generally large quantity of grain that will be consumed over several days is usually kept in the *gúyɔya*. However, nowadays the grain taken weekly may be stored in a Chinese rice bag that is kept in the house.

It is difficult to generalise about the storing process since variations can be observed clearly from a compound to another. In fact, I have rarely observed millet ears being pounded daily; it requires a lot of work and therefore considerable time. I have observed that in some of the families who migrate to the plain to cultivate, the remainder of the harvest still left in May is pounded before the start of temporary exodus.

Figure 10.1 A quantity of millet is taken from the granary and given to women for pounding. (photo by Salif Sawadogo)

The movements and the positioning of the body in order to empty the granary are the same as for filling it. As the spikes are taken out, a cavity in the packed rows of millet is created. From there, the body can be positioned to better access the rest of the interior of the container. The extraction of millet from the granary is a relatively acrobatic procedure. First the man stands on a wooden stick fixed to the structure that helps him to reach the opening. Then, he grasps the door frame with his hands, lifting his body up all at once. Relying on the strength in his arms, he brings his head inside (Figure 10.2); then, after his torso is completely inside the building, his legs stick horizontally out of it (Figure 10.3).

He then lifts his legs slightly to give him balance before he folds them, placing his knees on the door frame. Finally, he stands up inside, on the dividers of the granary, and gets into the upper compartment (Figure 10.4). The container is built to fit the body of a person and allow him to reach its contents.

Figure 10.2 Starting to enter the female granary

Figure 10.3 The torso is inside the granary.

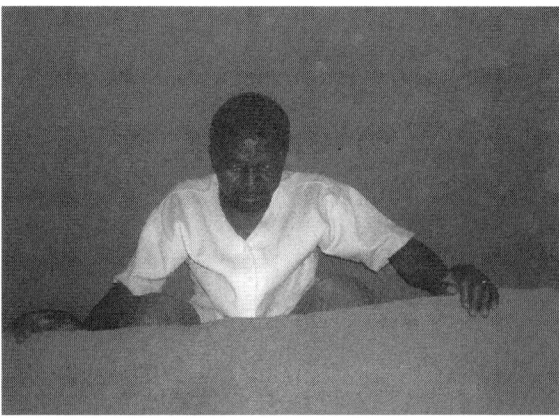

Figure 10.4 Jumping (top) into and landing in (bottom) the upper compartment

Inside the granary, the cereal surrounds the body in order to facilitate its collection while remaining unseen from the outside. There is indeed no chance to glimpse anything through the opening from the outside since the body blocks this. Because the granary openings are small, they discourage entry; access to the structure remains difficult, as it requires considerable effort, suppleness, and time. This arrangement dissuades people from stealing, since thieves will in theory not have the time to take things without being caught. Also, it is impossible to hide in the granary for a long time without becoming dehydrated, as the small, dark space remains hot.

As mentioned, the granary's particular configuration enables the owner to keep the inside private—to maintain it as well as to reinforce the concealment of its content. It also defines gender distinctions through the management of hidden properties. By canalizing the path of movement and limiting of bodily access, the *gúyɔ ya* granary as a closed structure controls the expression of both the authority of the content as well as of its owner.

As specified by one of my sources, the movements required to get in and out of the granary as well as to grab the spikes are done slowly and with care. They are dictated by the granary design and define attitudes of respect toward the precious content, as well as toward the harmony of the compound's life. As I have shown in Chapter 5, the same design and control of behaviour can be observed in the architecture of the house. In fact, the small size of the door is meant to keep the inside private as well as to frame behaviour—that is, to ensure that people enter the house with a calm attitude or, in one villager's words, to 'bring the good feelings in and leave the bad ones out'. Unlike the compound's round open space and its entrance vestibule, which engage social interactions and create semipublic places, the narrow granary entrance and its dark, packed, and stuffy inside space and atmosphere enable the space to be kept private and thus maintain and reinforce concealment.

The Porous Container: Thievery, Witchcraft, and Dilapidation

Men maintain their control over the family unit by managing scarcity and the anxiety associated with perceptions of an empty granary. Concealing also prevents undue waste of scarce resources and impedes witchcraft and stealing. As a neighbour told me: 'If my neighbour sees that I've got millet and he hasn't any left, he is going to have to resort to witchcraft because of jealousy'.[2] According to him, witches act out of jealousy and necessity and kill 'successful' people in order to split families up. A man who possesses many resources and is known to be a hard-working cultivator stands a good chance of becoming a victim of rivalries and of theft. Theft occurs mainly in periods of extreme scarcity.

Women's access to the granary is forbidden by men. They are said by men to be particularly prone to wasting food. The neighbour just mentioned, in the presence of male friends openly told me that 'if women were to access a granary, the building is certain to be emptied quickly.[3] They would take all the millet to sell on the market. Also, they often prepare too much food and waste it'.[4]

The wasteful character of a woman is read by men according to the way she walks. As an elder explained: 'If you see a woman walking with the tip of her feet opened, she is a wastrel. But a woman walking with the feet toward the inside, she is surely a saver'.[5] Similarly, a woman wearing a wrapper that is folded on the left side is considered as an 'easy', unstable, and unreliable woman. According to men, a woman's character is thus embodied. Women are generally described as irresponsible, lazy, disorganised, and bad managers. Consequently, women are never allowed to know about the content of the cereal granary.

Men and women work on two different temporalities and economies. In fact, men define themselves as saving for the long term and looking out for their future while women are seen as spending on a daily basis or as saving only the very minimum that will be squandered in the market anyway. Women's cash is also spent on large amounts of millet destined to be brewed and rapidly distributed in return for cash in the market. According to the men, most women do not calculate benefits and losses. Consequently, they are seen by men as ending up wasting their time and energy in brewing without making any profit. Yet, men are always happy to drink their beer and not pay if they can.

Nevertheless, according to the women, the female task of brewing as is necessary to maintain social networks. Selling and sharing beer constitutes a leisure time activity for them, one of those rare times when they can enjoy themselves instead of struggling through their routine. In other words, women need to brew in order to be socially active and generally visible in the village.

Another attitude that is commonly picked on by the men concerns the spendthrift character of young women. They say that women spend all the money on unimportant items such as cloth, jewellery, soap, and body cream for themselves and for their children, whom they often spoil. But, as explained by a group of women friends of mine, it is crucial for them to stay dignified by wearing decent clothes and taking care of their skin even when food is scarce. Hence, they put on their jewellery and do their hair no matter if they are rich or poor. While talking about men's and women's respective roles in finding food, my elder host sister would categorically tell me that it is the responsibility of her husband to find millet. Hence, what she earns is spent on spices, cooking utensils, and things that are strictly for her. If a husband is not fulfilling his task, shame falls on him. As she said: 'People don't like being looked at as poor. If a man mismanages his family, the wife leaves. Then he is on his own, unhappy, his reputation will be ruined with others, because you know people talk about it'.[6]

In some compounds the management of food resources and therefore of millet is also carried out by women. In fact, women are increasingly taking the initiative when it comes to finding food. They create associations in which they discuss financial matters and try to develop strategies to cope with food shortages. Similarly, in the touristy area of the Dogon region, multiple NGOs and organisations have set up programmes to support Dogon women, or *plans d'appui aux femmes Dogon*, that provide micro credits to Dogon women to start their own businesses (for example, selling food, condiments, charcoal) as well as to manage the production and selling of craft items such as indigo cloth. Therefore, these women 'entrepreneurs' make money for their own expenses as well as to sustain the family. They carry on with their domestic tasks and they also contribute food while, as they say in a joking tone, men are wandering around in the village, chatting and drinking tea.

So, as mentioned, the existence and amount of cereal in the granaries is concealed by men. In their discourse and practice, they use concealment to impede witchcraft and theft as well as to prevent gambling, waste, and psychological distress/breakdown among women. Because it is women who process and prepare food, women can always guess the state of food resources. Thus whether or not a shortage is perceived by the women depends on the men's entrepreneurial strategies of dealing with shortage before it is discovered by the women; it is up to the men to develop strategies to find millet. According to the men, the extent of the granaries' contents are kept 'silent', in order to avoid a general state of panic in the women, which can lead to a psychological distress on the women's side of the compound and women's refusal to keep up with the daily taskscapes, such as supplying the compound with water.

Issues about food stocks and their scarcity are never inquired into or discussed by men and women; men and women carry out their own tasks on their sides of the compound without taking over each other's 'business'. Help occurs through the complementarity of their roles as individuals, not in terms of sharing each other's duties or taking on what another could not do. However, as we have seen, some Dogon women are taking personal initiatives in order to cope with food shortages. Hence, it seems that concealment consists of a means for men to maintain their control over the family unit—to maintain their authority, role, and power, which, increasingly, could easily be taken over by the women through their own initiatives and strategies.

Conclusion

I have shown that the structure of the female *gúyɔ ya* regulates behaviour and restricts access to foodstuffs as well as defining gender relationships and their boundaries in the compound. The symbolism attached to the granary converges toward principles of fertility of the cereal and, by analogy, of the women. The prosperity of the families manifests itself through the round structure of the building that also references a woman's womb. The Dogon granary, as a structure for containing food and property, controls and frames bodily movement and behaviour as a means to conceal and thus manage its content. The daily practices of the gendered container reveals particular ways of concealing men's property from women as well as from other people.

While my examination has focused on such practices in the particular context of a food shortage, the amount of cereal stored in the granaries is, necessarily, hidden from women. This is done to prevent women from being wasteful if the granary is full or to keep them from suffering fear, anxiety, and breakdown if the granaries are empty. The granaries' design prevents thievery from outside the compound or by women, who, according to the men, could easily spend the contents or gossip about it to a neighbour, which could attract thieves. As I have shown, the material practice of concealing constitutes a means by which the men can maintain their control over the women as well as their power within the compound.

As an emblematic domestic feature, the female granary represents men's and women's roles, status, and, metaphorically, their own bodies. I have proposed that this built element objectifies, in its own materiality, cosmological principles that relate to society and to relationships between men and women and the environment. The material practice of concealment reveals a particular form of containment that is about gathering, protecting, and bounding life inside the earth container. In a similar way, when empty the granary limits and conceals fears about scarcity and therefore death. The female earth granary is a Pandora's box that functions as a control device designed by men and objectifies a cosmology of scarcity that encompasses men's and women's perceptions about food as well as about each other. When open, the full container expresses life. However, when empty, it expresses poverty, fear, and death.

11 A Microcosmology in a Millet Grain: Cooking Techniques and Eating Habits

In Tiréli, as in many places in the Dogon region and in Mali, Dogon alimentation relies primarily on millet.[1] Rice dishes accompanied with an oily and salty sauce are perceived as prestigious; however, affording it on a daily basis remains too expensive for most families.[2] Although they struggle to obtain food, Dogon families always insist on sharing it with foreigners, because for them hospitality is a tradition that is also a form of pride. In this chapter, I propose a reading of Dogon microcosmology as being objectified in a millet grain and with worldviews shared by people in one bowl. As shown by Douglas, in her essay 'Deciphering a Meal' (1972), the content and ritual of a mealtime scrutinised from a structuralist approach can reveal implicit meanings about a society's beliefs, prohibitions, taboos, and taste. Douglas proposes that cultural meanings about a meal are found in a sequence of meals—that is, 'in a system of repeated analogies. Each meal carries something of the meaning of the other meals; each meal is a structured social event which structures others in its own image', (Douglas 1972, 69).

From a different perspective, I look at Dogon microcosmology as it is manifested through the sequence of production and consumption of a millet-based meal called *sagujá* (consumption of meat remains occasional). I focus on the expression of Dogon daily and practical worldviews as they reveal themselves through both routinised body dynamics or embodied practices and gendered discourses on millet—a staple crop that stands at the core of Dogon's daily and ritual life. By taking into account a whole sequence of technological operations that encompasses the processing and transformation of millet through cooking, and finally eating the dish, I highlight some of the cultural significance and thus the symbolic meanings attached to millet, as well as people's perceptions of social relations. In this respect, I also show some of the ways by which Dogon families cope through food practice with the recurring and common sub-Saharan predicament of scarcity.

The Dogon Cultural Significance of Millet

Millet (*Pennisetum spicatum*), called *yù:*, is a staple crop that is widely cultivated throughout West Africa. It is known for its exceptional nutritional properties, as it is high in protein and energy, which people need to accomplish their intense daily routine. Moreover, millet possesses a remarkable adaptability to adverse soils, and when the crops do not fail owing to a shortage of rain, it represents a form of food security. Other cereals, such as sorghum (*Sorghum bicolor*) and *fonio* (*Digitaria exilis*) exist, but they seem to be far less cultivated by the villagers of Tiréli.

According to Griaule (1965), the Dogon's intricate corpus of myths reveals that sorghum, fonio, and millet play a central role in the Dogon's cosmogenesis. For instance, the Dogon believe that fonio is the image of an atom from which the world derived. The grain burst, and the world spread and is conceived as being animated by a spiral movement (also in Calame-Griaule 1965, 228). Fonio, as the 'infinite small', functions as a reservoir or 'a granary', from which all elements of the world are generated (Griaule 1968, 472, 474). Sorghum, fonio, millet, and also rice are associated by the Dogon of Sangha with stars: *ɛmɛ ya tólo* (the star of the female sorghum), which is known in the West as Sirius C; *yù: tólo*, or the star of millet (unidentified by Griaule); and *ara tólo* (the star of rice, unidentified by Griaule)—both of which revolve around Venus, called *yazu* (the morning star). Last, *pɔ̃ tólo*, or the star of fonio (*Digitaria exilis*), is known by the Dogon as Sirius B. In Griaule's work, which has been contradicted by van Beek (1991), the stars of sorghum and fonio are said to be the satellites (celestial orbiting bodies) of Sirius (*sigi tólo*), and they are located in the *Canis Major* (Dog Star) constellation (Griaule 1965, 468–76).

Dogon views on cereal as part of the great scheme of the cosmos might be interpreted a material metaphor that may express the cultural significance of cereals in Dogon life. For instance, the Dogon's social, economic, and religious life revolves around millet's production, distribution, and consumption, and its absence leads to the fragmentation of the society (Bouju 1984; Jolly 1995, 253). Furthermore, naming stars after millet and fonio could constitute a way of appropriating the night sky, which, for instance, helps to orient travellers and hunters at night and to remind them of agrarian tasks and the calendar, as well as many rituals and ceremonies associated with them.

Dogon people describe millet as well as granaries as a symbol of 'life'. Women explain that before they marry, their parents always try to find out whether the family of the future groom possesses many granaries and therefore whether there is normally something to eat. It is said that the men who possess more than four millet granaries marry the most beautiful women of the Dogon region! Thus, millet remains one of the main concerns of Dogon people, as it rules many aspects of their ritual, social or daily life in their compound. Furthermore, the cereal is seen as a symbol of the culture and identity[3] of the Dogon; as they say in Tiréli: 'Millet is the food of the Dogon. It makes us strong. Without it we cannot work well'.[4]

Millet that is seen as a product of hard and intensive labour is grown on the ancestors' land. Cultivation techniques perpetuated over centuries is a form of heritage. Shared as a meal and drunk collectively as beer, millet constitutes an element of social cohesion and fraternity (Jolly 2004, 15) .The brew not only creates social networks, it also brings together the life cycles of the people with that of the fields, in both ritual and daily life, as a form of linkage and regeneration of the individual, as well as of society. When offered in the form of libations to the God *Áma* or to the ancestors, the cereal functions as a meat offering by acting as a bridge between the supernatural world and the world of humans. Because of its life force, the cereal possesses a particular power with its own ritual consequences. Finally, I was told that millet is considered to be gendered. Millet spikes, seen as a phallic element, are cultivated by men (although in most places women cultivate for their husbands), and they are preserved in the men's granary (Chapter 10). The grain as a whole is a female element, since it is processed and cooked by women. Millet grain, as support-ing life, also carries fertility symbolism. However, millet seed is the property of men and is safely conserved in a leather bag or sealed clay jar in the female granary called *gúyɔ ya*, which is owned by men.

The Multiple Uses of Millet: From the Stalk to the Grain

The multiple parts of the millet plant—stalk, with or without its roots, leaves, spike (or ear), and grains—are all used and recycled in a systematic and inter-esting way (Figure 11.1). As has been mentioned several times, millet plants that are collected from the fields[5] constitute important practical, economic, and symbolic elements that serve multiple purposes.

First, the tender stalks with leaves are used as reserve fodder for the cattle during the hot dry season. Second, the more resistant stalks, including their roots, are used in making houses, such as the roof of the men's house (*tógu na*). Beyond the technical qualities of the dry stalks that keep the inside of the *tógu na* dark and cool, the stalk objectifies particular worldviews. For example, as a participative activity shared by the men of the village, the roof of the *tógu na* that is remade after damage is subjected to a principle of recycling. It is made of new and recycled stalks while the damaged ones are turned into a condiment, as explained shortly. Beyond protecting a structure, the roof con-stitutes a gathering element; it involves the whole community of Tiréli as well

Figure 11.1 Material extracted from millet plants

as relatives from the surrounding villages, who bring bundles from their own fields to contribute to the refreshing of this 'common' roof. Hence, social networks are regenerated in the same way as the roof.

Third, millet stalks can be burned and turned into a condiment called ɛ. The ashes are filtered through cold water in a pierced clay pot called ɛ: tɛguru. Then the collected bitter yellowish substance, ɛ: di, is used in the preparation of a dish (ɛ: já) made from millet ground on a stone. According to Paulme (1988, 335), the stalks used in the preparation of ɛ: já function as a salt substitute. This ɛ: 'dead' substance is also used to heal wounds or to neutralise evil spells and poisoned food. Indeed, it is said that the victims of witchcraft, if fatally afflicted, can be brought back to life by the ɛ, which as a dead substance, counteracts death.

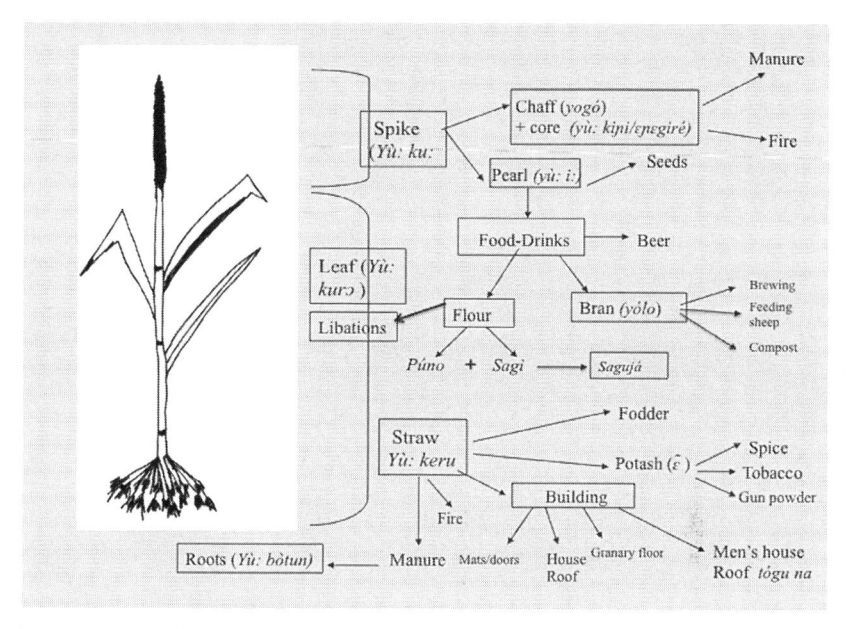

Figure 11.2   Millet parts and uses

After the harvest, the millet stalks that remain in the field are collected and then layered on the compound surface to decompose into manure to fertilise the crops. In Chapter 8 I discussed the use of organic waste and in particular the production of *bìnugu* as a thick blend of compost that regenerates the fields of millet and that may include millet chaff (*yógo*) and broken rachis (*ɛɲɛgiré*) extracted from millet spikes through pounding and winnowing. These organic materials form a good millet-based fertiliser for millet as well as onion fields. Hence, this manured compost, which brings together environmental and human life cycles, plays a significant a role in securing the prosperity of Dogon families. Manured compost is a fundamental economic preoccupation that the Dogon have in relation to sustaining the stability and continuity of life in their scarce environment. Dogon's full exploitation of resources also transpires, as shown, through the extensive uses and recycling of every single part of millet stalk and its spike (Figure 11.2).

Processing Millet Spikes

Processing millet spikes (ears) consists of pounding them, enabling the breaking off the rachis (core) and bracts and releasing millet grains that have developed from clusters of fascicules that are packed on the spike (Figure 11.3). Therefore, pounding millet spikes and winnowing (the second step of the processing of spikes) allows the removal of dry organic matter or chaff.

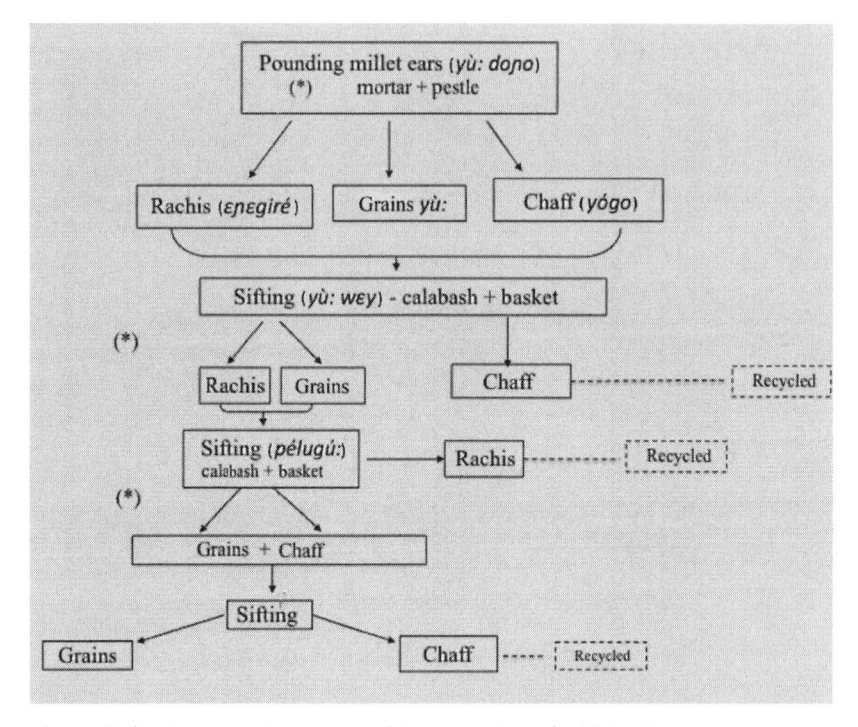

Figure 11.3 Operational sequence of the processing of millet spikes

Millet spikes are first collected in a large wooden mortar (*kú[y]nà: nà*) in which they are pounded (*yù: doɲo*). Generally, this collective task (formed by repeated sequences of synchronous poundings) takes place at the top of the scree or in spacious, airy, or breezy places within inhabited areas of the village, because millet chaff (thin dry bracts or scales enclosing mature grains) causes skin and eye irritations. As Lane has observed, the pounding occurs toward the outside limit of the village in order not to attract to the village the malevolent spirits that are responsible for various diseases and afflictions (1987, 56). Then, the broken-down spikes are placed in a large calabash that is energetically shaken with both hands through a movement called *pélugó: (pélugú:)*. Once the chaff and grains have been detached from the rachis of the millet spikes, the grains are pounded again and then sifted from a calabash into a basket, a wind-winnowing technique called *yù: wɛyi* (Figure 11.4). The combined tasks of pounding and winnowing are repeated up to four times as a means to properly remove the grains from their casings (*yógo*).

Processing 20 kg of millet spikes, which serves for preparing daily meals for one week, requires good body strength and endurance; the task can last for a minimum of two hours when done by two or three women. Pounding distorts women's hands and causes calloused palms and fingers and considerable pain

Figure 11.4 Sifting millet—*yù: wɛyi*

in the back and in the neck. The pain can be temporarily alleviated through singing, to maintain endurance and motivation. The quantities of cereals to be processed are determined by men, who, as mentioned earlier, claim that women would squander the cereal by cooking too much, selling it, or making too much beer with it, if they had full access to the millet granaries.

Processing Millet Grains

There are two ways of processing the millet grain: pounding and grinding. Both techniques are used in the making of the *sagujá* dish[6] also known as a form of *tô*. In general, these techniques determine the texture of the flour and the taste of the millet dishes. Symbolically speaking, while pounding keeps millet 'alive', grounding 'kills' it (Calame-Griaule 1965, 248; Cartry 1987, 173 footnote 32; Jolly 2004, 126). Millet is mainly found in the form of a cream called *púno*, as a soft paste called *ɛ:já*, whereby millet is ground on a stone and cooked with potash, or more often as a harder paste called *sagujá*, served with a baobab-leaves sauce. Because the daily menu is planned in reference to men's management of cereal stocks, the women more frequently prepare millet cream for lunch time and millet cake base (*sagujá*) in the evening. Cooking *sagujá* or even *ɛːjá* twice a day would rapidly lead to an empty granary before the next harvest, so it is often alternated with millet cream (*púno*). Millet beer is also widely consumed in the village. Deep fried millet pancakes are sold in the streets of the village and on the market, but are usually consumed during celebrations.

Processing Place and Technology

Processing millet occurs in the *paná tori*, or pounding place, where the mortars and pestles are kept. Pounding constitutes a learning process as well as a daily helping-action that consolidates friendship networks between women. The utensils for pounding and cooking can be loaned from one compound to another. Repetition of these tasks in the same place, in the pounding place, is a sign of respect toward millet and food in general, and, as the women say, it brings good luck to the families.

Processing food and cooking it require very resistant utensils, such as heavy mortars *kú(y)nàː* and pestles *kú(y)nàː í* ('the child of the mortar') and a small grinding stone called *yùː nà íː*. Pounding, which enables the shucking of millet grains, always occurs late morning and late afternoon. At these times, the sound of the heavy pestles hitting the bottom cavity of the wooden mortar creates a particular daily life music and therefore an atmosphere that is generated by women's body dynamics. The sounds of pestles hitting wooden mortars that emanate from within the compound walls echo along the face of the cliff that stands behind the village and acts as a speaker (depending on the wind). To some extent, these sounds that occur twice a day and then are amplified by the rock serve as timekeepers for people working or travelling nearby; they know that lunch or dinner is being prepared and that soon they can stop working. Women generally evaluate the time of pounding according to the intensity of daylight and heat—for instance, when the day's heat decreases, that announces the end of the day and meal time. Finally, pounding at night is prohibited, because it attracts evil spirits, shows disrespect to the ancestors, and overall would be difficult in the dark.

Pounding Millet Grains: Body Techniques and Learning Process

The pounding of millet grains (*yùː pèdu*) consists of shelling the grains by breaking them off and removing the bran—the thin, scaly external envelope (*yóro* or *yólo*). Pounding, called *yùː toru* (*tólu*), aims to pulverise the grain's hard and translucent center (*sagi*). Thus these processes produce the *púno* or *sagi* millet flour that are both used in the making of *sagujá*.

Body dynamics and techniques determine the quality and texture of the flour and therefore its flavour. When millet grains are carelessly processed (pounded, sieved, and ground)—for instance, too quickly—the flour contains tiny fragments of *sagi* that cause stomach pain, men complain. In other villages I was told that the men discouraged their wives and daughters from having millet ground mechanically, using the village mill, because the resulting millet does not taste good, a large amount of *sagi* remains in the flour,[7] and women have to pay to use this technology. It does, however, saves them considerable energy and time.

Successful pounding requires much practice to keep synchronous coordination of movements. Pounding movements in general involve lifting up the arm and the inclination of the body axis (forward) simultaneously with the blow of the pestle in the mortar, then lifting up the arm again. Pounding is done with both hands and by alternating hands for a short while so as to relieve exhaustion (Figure 11.5). The task is sustained through songs but also by clicking fingers on the edge of the handle (a gesture and sound called *karú*)

Figure 11.5 Pounding techniques

that is located in the middle of the pestle. Women also throw the pestle in the air and clap their hands before catching it as a means to reenergise the body. The women each place one foot slightly against the bottom of the mortar as a means of stabilising it.

I determined that it requires between forty-five minutes and one hour to pound 3 kg of millet. While the pounding is generally done by two or a maximum of three women, individual body rhythm responds to the other(s) by mimicking the gestures, in the case of an apprentice, but overall by listening to each other's sounds. Girls rapidly learn to pound millet from the age of six and may be able to pound like an adult from the age of 10. Hence, women spontaneously create a particular choreography and soundtrack for cooking, the daily rhythm of which is felt by the child that a woman may carry on her back, lulling it to sleep.

Interruption: Breaking a Pestle

Pounding of millet can go wrong. For instance, pestles inevitably weaken over years of systematic daily pounding that put pressure on the wood, which can crack. Pestles (and mortars) that are carved by blacksmiths in *pèlu* wood (*Khaya senegalensis*), which possesses great strength and hardness, wear down after about 10 years at the level of the handle.

One night as three young women were pounding millet, one of them broke the pestle at the level of the handle. In a state of panic, the young lady was immediately taken to a neighbouring village where she had to make a sacrifice. This ritual, which is performed in accordance with the laws of the ancestors (*atɛmu*), aims at counteracting the negative effect of breaking a pestle that is caused by either the breaking of a prohibition or the disregard of traditional values or bad social behaviour. She brought with her half of the pestle, four millet spikes (Figure 11.6), four straws of a broom, four fruits of a tree (unknown) and 200 francs to give to an elder (her cousin), who is in charge of restoring the situation by moving the spikes and straws around the young woman's body, in what is called *godiu diaramu*, ('sweep off bad things'). Breaking the tools brings bad luck, such as a disruption in food stock and fertility. The other half of the broken pestle was thrown away outside the compound.

Pounding, Wind Winnowing, Sieving, and Grinding

In my host family, an average 3½ kg of millet were pounded daily for making two meals (cream and paste) and for seven adults and two children (Figure 11.7). First, dry millet[8] is placed in the mortar with about 50 cl of water and is pounded until the grains are cracked. Then, they are removed and dried for about 10 minutes in a calabash, then sifted by using two calabashes. This technique of winnowing (*yù: wɛyi*) enables the separation of millet flour, including *sagi* from the bran, that are contained in a *koro sí* calabash by letting

Figure 11.6 While being used to process millet grains, the pounder broke at the level of the handle.

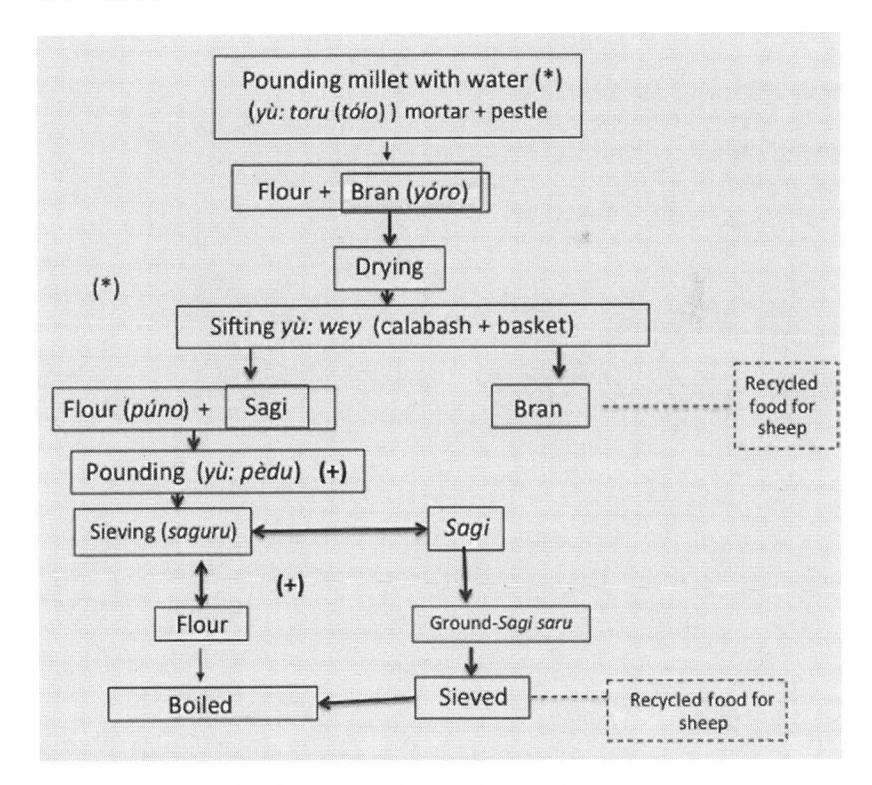

Figure 11.7 Operational sequence of processing millet grains

the product to fall from a height into a *kódu pílu* calabash placed below on the ground. The latter calabash collects the heavier particles while the millet bran (*yólo/yóro*), the lighter component, is blown to the side. (The bran is generally mixed with water and fed to the sheep.) The flour is pounded a second time as a means to reduce the amount of *sagi* in it. Then, it is sieved (*saguru*) in order to separate the white millet powder (*púno*). Any remaining sieved-out *sagi* is ground on a stone placed on the ground in the compound, an action called *sagi saru*, in order to reduce it into powder. The remaining *sagi* is either given to the sheep or boiled before the flour, as it is harder.

As mentioned earlier, processing millet grains through repeated daily poundings has a negative effect on a woman's back, neck, and skull; it generates pain and headaches, although the women maintain a good body position, keeping their backs straight and not bending excessively over the mortar. The force is thus provided by the arms. In addition, the palm of the hand is marked by callused tissue, and, as pointed out by an old woman, the women's fingers and hands become deformed over time.

Cooking and Eating: Scarcity in a Bowl

An aluminium cooking pot, which has largely replaced the clay cooking pot, is placed on the fire and filled up with water. Sometimes, tamarind is added as a means to flavour millet cake, to facilitate its digestion, and as a food preservative. As a symbol of fixity and cohesion, the fireplace is made out of three stones constituting an element through which a newlywed spouse symbolically affirms her status and role[9] of engendering and maintaining life in the family (Lane 1987, 60).[10] The *sagi*, or rough flour, is boiled first. Then the *púno* is added on top of it. The cooking pot is then covered and left to cook for about 45 minutes. At the same time, the sauce (*ɔrɔ nínɛ*) is being prepared on one side of the fireplace in a small clay pot with a large opening and filled up with water. A large quantity of baobab-leaves powder is sieved and then added to the boiling water. For those who can afford it, some salt, powdered dry fish (*ídu*), some glutamate cubes or crystals, three or four small mashed onions and some oil can be added. The traditional supplement or alternative to these condiments is *kãwã*, which enhances the flavour and viscosity of the sauce.[11] *Kãwã* is made of fermented hibiscus seeds (*Hibiscus sabdariffa*) and has a strong pungent smell, called *ilɛ:* ('ripe' or 'cooked'), that refers to death (Calame-Griaule 1996, 81). However, *kãwã* is perceived as a living element because it is obtained through fermentation. *Kãwã* possesses many vitamins and minerals and is said to cure mouth and stomach ulcers, strengthen teeth, and restore intestinal flora. A more expensive variety of *kãwã* is called *sumbala*. It is obtained from alkaline fermentation of the African locust bean (*Parkia biglobosa*), or néré tree, which is found mostly in the South of Mali and is also imported from Burkina Faso. This nutritious condiment is also protein-rich and contains vitamins and minerals. Hence, *kãwã* and *sumbala* as fermented matter are perceived as living, because they bring benefits to the body as they revitalise, energise, and heal it. Finally, these condiments thicken the sauce and give a slimy texture to it that is said to facilitate the ingestion and digestion of millet cake, which is heavy and compact and if eaten alone can cause constipation. (This illness is considered by the Dogon as severe, owing to the fact that it is believed to lower sexual energy and fertility and overall to weaken the body. It is said to cause the rapid development of dormant malaria, transmitted to humans by a female *Anopheles* mosquito.)

In the cooking pot, as the millet dough is rapidly setting up and its colour is turning light green, it is energetically mixed by use of a *pàlukile*, a long wooden spatula. As the dough gets thicker, more compact, and heavier, it becomes very difficult for the cook to stir it. Then, the homogenous and sticky dough is scraped out of the cooking pot using a fragment of calabash (*kɛbɛlɛ*). Finally, the dough is shaped by hand in a traditional wooden bowl (*baɲá*), which is often substituted with plastic or enamel containers,[12] to form a bumpy compact loaf that is hollowed in the middle, where the gluey and smelly dark-green baobab leaf sauce (*ɔrɔ níŋɛ*) is poured (Figure 11.8). While this high-carbohydrate *sagujá* dish is served with a protein-rich sauce,[13] its exclusive daily consumption does not remedy people's vitamin and mineral deficiencies. (Cooking is a particularly arduous task that requires considerable physical strength to process and mix up dough but also to lift up heavy cooking tools. In addition, women's exposure to the smoke of the firewood damages their sight and lungs, and the heat of the mid-day sun, added to that of the fire, makes the task even more exhausting.)

Figure 11.8   Filling up containers with food

Women always try food first to check the seasoning—that is, *dà: nɛmu* ('to taste food')—and meals are prepared twice a day: at lunch time, around 13.00 (the *ága kentègu,*'that squished a drop in the liver') and in the evening around 20.00 (*digɛ paná* or 'food of the night') (Dieterlen & Calame-Griaule 1960, 78). There is normally no breakfast, but sometimes the leftovers are eaten. The few remains are dried on the roof top of the house in a calabash. Then they are recycled by being pounded and reduced to a powder to be recooked and served as an occasional breakfast (*dià: ogu yomu*).

The location of the eating place always remains the same. Once a spacious and shady place has been defined, it is used daily. Maintaining a fixed place ensures good luck in relation to the food supply.[14] Children, women, and men eat separately, since men and women do not have the same activities and schedule. When people are waiting for late comers, food that is cooling down is protected by a small fragment of millet stalk that is dropped in the container as a means to symbolically prevent curious spirits from reaching and so spoiling its contents (also done in transporting and storing food and drinks without a lid). Men also say that the proximity of women reduces, or might completely damage, the power of the amulets and/or protections that the men wear, as well as the medicinal and magical protective substances that they ingest to protect themselves against witchcraft.

The round container that is placed on the ground is visually divided into wedges by the people sitting around it. Each person has his or her own part to eat. No one can eat someone else's portion of food; this is impolite. Those who are still hungry must wait until everybody has finished and then eat any remaining food.

Before starting to eat, people wash their hands and wrists in a large tin can of water that is passed around by holding the can with both hands. This gesture is a sign of respect toward the receiver of the can and also prevents from spilling water. And I was told that presenting a container with both hands signifies social cohesion. The gesture symbolises the complementarity and necessary cooperation between individuals (and families) who are represented by the fingers and thus the hands. Food is always eaten with the right hand; the left is used for cleaning oneself or blowing one's nose, and eating with it would be a sign of disrespect toward millet, the ancestors, and the woman who prepared the millet. Participants recite a ritual expression (*Áma iriye ule monɔ̃*, meaning 'may this food given by God Ama bring us health and energy') before eating while touching the edge of the bowl with the left hand to stabilise it and preparing to eat the millet cake with the right hand. Often, a piece of food is symbolically taken out of the bowl and thrown at the four cardinal points or simply on the ground for the ancestors.

The lump of millet cake is held in the palm of the hand and gently kneaded to cool it down. This tactile experience fulfills anticipation, as the cake's texture is sensed by the skin of the hand before being chewed in the mouth. Once swallowed, the hard millet paste quickly fills up the stomach and prevents hunger (*giyɛ*) all day long, until the next meal. God is thanked (*Áma bilarpo*) and entreated (*Áma yogo u*, 'may God Ama give us food tomorrow'). In addition to gathering around the same bowl of food, and eating with one's hands in the same pot, social and kinship relations among eaters develop and are strengthened through saliva's exchange. When dipping into the bowl of food, the fingers impregnate the communal food with the saliva that coats them. The food imbued with saliva is then ingested by everyone. Through the ingestion of this 'shared' body substance, the 'outside' other is incorporated into the individual, a social process that is described as 'being and remaining together'.

Before washing their right hand in clear water, people peel off the dry deposit of food left on the palm of the right hand by rubbing it on the left hand. Again, this gesture also constitutes a symbolic act that signifies the complementarity and usefulness of both hands as the left hand is said to be fed by the right. It expresses the wish for harmony in a society that is symbolised by the two hands while the individual is represented by the fingers.

Techniques and Strategies of Concealing Hunger

In a context of food shortage, devising strategies to find millet remains the task of men. While most families have to rely on their cereal banks, others stave off hunger by selling their harvests. In fact, reserves of millet—which for most people is all they have—are sold at high prices as the price of millet shoots up during periods of hunger. As millet stocks decrease, the price increases to 17,500[15] CFA and in some places can reach 21,000 CFA. Therefore, shortages generate a particular a form of economy. Those who do not have the money to buy millet save every grain.

An extreme shortage occurs when the granaries are completely empty and the man is unable to sustain his family. Such a situation is, as mentioned earlier, kept hidden from others. Women pretend to have something to cook by setting up a fire, and children hunt lizards. The smoke coming from the household is seen as a sign of 'normality', showing the neighbours that there is something to eat. Although most villagers are in the same situation, scarcity is still hidden within the compound enclosure, and it is not talked about for reasons of dignity. In the same way, by keeping a fire going, women attempt to cope psychologically with the drastic situation.

When food is scarce, the quantity served per meal is reduced to the minimum, and many subterfuges are applied by the cook to hide scarcity and to maintain her dignity. For instance, the millet cake that is presented as a round loaf in a wooden bowl is hollowed to the maximum in the middle to contain as much baobab sauce as possible. The millet cake is always shaped and presented, as a container, in such a way as to disguise the lack of millet paste. In this respect, the container acts as a camouflage. Finally, millet cream is made out of double the usual quantity of water and with very little millet powder; thus the taste and texture of the liquid signify the lack of resources. In the village of Kani Kombole, during times of famine the grains of baobab fruit (*Adansonia digitata*) served to make a thick paste (*ādāŋa*) that eased hunger.[16] The grains are roasted, ground, and cooked in the same way as millet and finally mixed with some oil extracted from these grains. People claim that two or three handfuls of this paste suffice to overcome hunger for about 40 days.

Note that, as in many parts of Africa, Dogon people associate a fat and fleshy body, said to be 'well-fed', with health and wealth, whereas a skinny body represents 'poverty'.

Understanding Scarcity through a Processing, Cooking, and Eating Sequence

The operational sequence of the production and consumption of a millet-based meal (*sagujá*) (Figure 11.9) enables us to highlight some of the Dogon worldviews about scarcity, specifically in relation to food. These views defines people's relationships, beliefs, and attitudes toward society, toward millet in general, and thus to nature in a context of food shortage.

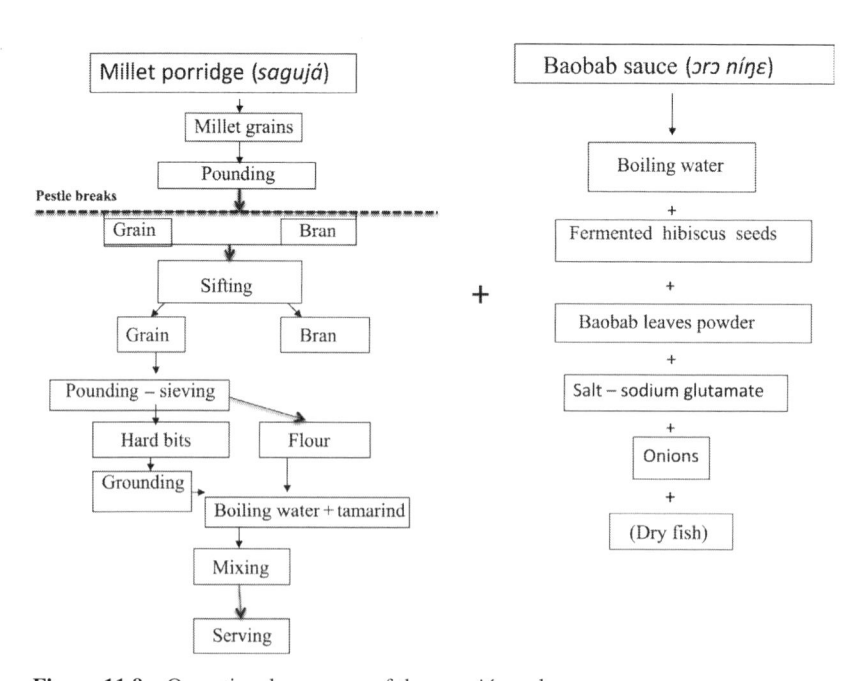

Figure 11.9 Operational sequence of the *sagujá* meal

First, the extensive use or recycling of every single part of millet is part of a process that exploits food resources to the maximum; it translates a particular economy of matter: nothing is lost, all is used and reused with care. Second, the routine processing of millet spikes and grains and then its cooking highlight the considerable physical endurance, synchronicity of movements, strength of women, and accuracy of movements that enfold technical knowledge about body techniques, women's understanding of the matter and its transformation, and finally the timing and care that women exercise during processing.

As mentioned earlier, bodily techniques and steady rhythm are necessary to produce the meal successfully. And beyond women's will to feed their families with good and tasty food, their fear of wasting cereal and spoiling a meal occupies them constantly, especially in a context of scarcity. Although a broken pestle, as described earlier, does not entirely affect the preparation of the meal (except maybe on a timing level), it does have a psychological effect in terms of fears about the discontinuity of one's life.

Third, millet consumption and eating habits regarding cereal unmask strategies developed by women to cope with scarcity on the plate as well as the recycling of everyday remains of food that are processed and cooked again. Here again, these enable the family to cope psychologically with food shortages. Hence, the operational sequence shows daily temporalities as a repetition of tasks operated through systematic accurate and efficacious body movements, or action on matter. First, these actions aim to obtain edible millet flour and paste with no remaining shaft that could endanger health; second, they avoid spoiling food during preparation; and third, they serve to hide scarcity throughout the process. Finally, sharing a daily routine that strengthens networks of solidarity among women and can also fill the void of scarcity with activity.

Conclusion

Men and women consume the same dish resulting from their intensive daily labour and therefore experience the same microcosmology of scarcity. However, they do not share the same bowl, since they eat separately, and therefore they do not necessarily share the same worldviews, because men and women have different agendas. I have shown that millet objectifies a particular space-time continuum from which their microcosmology develops through the transformation of millet as a living matter—Dogon microcosmology being 'in the making', here, although cooking reflects a process of containment. Millet grain as a containing metaphor concerns how Dogon people perceive, embody, and finally enact scarcity in their everyday life. Moreover, millet as a container substance (Lakoff and Johnson 1980) bears and transmits life as well as shaping the outside and inside of the body. In other words, millet engenders the body as the body engenders food through its own dynamic.

12 Cosmological Matters: Toward a Philosophy of Containment

Environmental conditions in the Sahel in conjunction with human factors leading to a severe degradation of the land have long affected life resources in the Dogon region—such as millet, which too often remains scarce if not unattainable. In addition to localised flash floods, long periods of drought followed by delayed, irregular, and insufficient rainfall brought by the West African Monsoon frequently prevent crop development. Hence, hidden behind its dramatic natural and cultural aesthetics, the Dogon landscape of the village of Tiréli in the *tɔrɔ sɔ* region enfolds a dimension of absence—of water, of fertile soil, of millet (the production of which characterises the Dogon people's self-subsistence economy).

My account has examined the Dogon's microcosmology, or ways of living in a twenty-first-century landscape of scarcity through containment. In this context, Dogon cosmological matters unsurprisingly revolve around millet, water, and earth, which bind the Dogon to their ancestors, the spiritual world, and the land and thus the natural environment, on which the Dogon people depend almost completely.

Cosmological Matter

Matter is the 'stuff' by which things and therefore the world 'come-into-being' and so exist. The conditions of life in the harsh Dogon environment rest on the sufficiency, efficacy, and intrinsic properties of matter made of water, earth, and millet, which are perceived by the Dogon as living and active and which characterise the materiality of the Dogon landscape of Tiréli.

My main focus has been to highlight the Dogon's implicit forms of practical worldviews that are expressed through Dogon men and women's shared daily and seasonal embodied practices about the landscape's matter and that imply particular techniques of transformation that form a heritage. These Dogon daily practices, usages, and customs (*dɔgɔ sɔ*) are framed by a long-standing animist system of worldviews (*ɔmɔlɔ*) that rules the social and political dimensions of the Dogon community of Tiréli and that is, however, being challenged by new practical worldviews, in a society that is becoming increasingly individualistic.

I have suggested that the traditional *ɔmɔlɔ* system as a social memory that is forged by the laws of the ancestors (*atɛmu*) is furnished by a broader West Africa or Mande symbolic reservoir and is altered by Dogon daily practical worldviews. Hence, Dogon worldviews gather into a microcosmology that is 'in-the-making' (Barth 1987). According to this perspective, the concept of cosmology has enabled me to circumscribe the Dogon's ways of making sense of their world—that is, their ways of knowing (Barth 1987, 2000) and thus of making themselves at home in a landscape of scarcity. This microcosmology, which is objectified in the materiality of the Dogon cultural landscape, emerges from the Dogon's long-term engagement in this landscape of scarcity, which I have conceptualised as a container.

Dogon microcosmology reveals itself through ongoing pragmatic and symbolic material practices or systematic 'makings' and 'doings' of the landscape of scarcity, through a sensorimotor and in particular tactile experience of matter. Hence, Dogon microcosmology is grounded in people's daily life experiences of the materiality of their landscape. Dogon's life cycles are brought into the life cycle of the environment, and they are expressed through local concepts of fertility (that is, living matter made of earth and water and processes such as fermentation) and so about regeneration of life in more general terms. In other words, technical transformation about recycling, kneading, fermenting, pounding, and grinding matter, as it appears in the multiple embedded *chaîne opératoires*, articulates symbolic processes and notions about the regeneration of life that thereby denies linear temporality and so conjures up death. While death is denied through transformative processes involving fermentation and recycling of matter, materials are reenergised and made even more efficacious as they are being given a second life. According to this perspective, earth shrines are revitalised at the turn of the rainy season through plastering with earth and sacrifice, a ritual act that enables nature and the surrounding society to be reinstated (Chapter 4). Similarly, soil is refertilised by addition of organic manure, provided by a fermentation process through recycling, to encourage millet seeds to germinate (Chapter 7), and food is fortified by addition of fermented substances.

Containers

I have grounded my analysis of the Dogon people's ways of living in a twenty-first-century world, on an examination of material forms of containers, including the landscape and the built environment, as a means of exploring cultural knowledge that is not verbalised but fundamentally embodied. Containers constitute an active and reflexive ground for shared agencies, a cosmological template with which to think about the world as well as to make oneself in the world. Material and symbolic forms of containers as unifying principles and interfaces that retain and release living matter are means by which people order and structure their world and their human/nature interactions through their everyday life practices. Containers are multiple material means by which people are encircling, containing, and thus gathering things and matter around and for themselves. I have proposed that these material and metaphorical forms of containers frame Dogon's conceptions about space and time as much as they define a paradigm about a philosophy of containment through practices of containing.

Containers create particular locales in which people inhabit the world and via this process define their world through an inside/outside dialectic (Warnier 2006). I have envisaged Dogon containers as a self-contained model locally defined through a centripetal, anthropocentric, and an inside/outside spatial logic. For instance, Tiréli's territory is composed of the village or 'inside', which is surrounded by the bush, an 'outside'. It functions as a 'life-giving reservoir' (van Beek & Banga 1992) from which people extract their daily means of subsistence (Chapter 5). Both areas (the inside and the outside) are protected by a series of shrines, which at the same time define the boundaries of the territory (Chapter 3). These are spatial divisions of the landscape, as well as temporal ones, since they separate the cultural world of the living from nature as well as from the supernatural world.

The atmosphere as a container substance (Lakoff & Jonhnon 1980) that provides the basis for the weather to occur enfolds the outside and inside of the territory that contains the village and the compounds that contain the granaries, a bowl of food, and the human body. From this perspective, the Dogon world and their microcosmology are metaphorically comparable to a stack of fragile and scaled calabashes, often seen in Dogon compounds, in which the largest one contains a series of smaller ones, all containing living matter. Thus, the Dogon 'lived' world can also be defined as a metonym, being holistic rather than individual. The idea of the whole being greater than the sum of the parts constitutes and frames this particular Dogon sense of containment and therefore of ontological security that is reinforced by the living materiality of container forms and of their contents.

The Dogon landscape, village, and compounds form enclosed surfaces of interaction between the individuals and their outside world, and these surfaces are culturally inscribed. The cultivated bush constitutes a surface of inscription that gets written on by, among other things, people's footprints (Ingold 2004), through people's daily crossing and seasonal taskscapes (Ingold 2000). The materiality of the landscape is therefore constantly marked and shaped by movement of people and of things, as well as by the weather, which leaves traces on the landscape's surface. The dynamics of movement manifest themselves through the motion of the body—that is, through daily activities such as collecting foodstuff in the bush, cultivating, walking, planning the land, and, on a domestic level, building a compound, gathering and dissociating domestic waste, making or storing food in a granary. The act of daily walking through the land and the village (Chapter 4) constitutes an act of appropriating the place, as well as attributing new configurations to the place, such as, canalizing tourism, which constitutes an economy that is increasingly important to the Dogon.

Containment

I have suggested that a philosophy of containment acts as a definition through Dogon processes of building and dwelling (Heidegger 1971 in Ingold 2000, 172–88) in container forms. In other words, containment refers to modes of living, dwelling, and therefore the act of containing oneself in the world through building, fixing, binding, and enclosing. These dimensions have been explored through an examination of the diachronic constitution of the territory of Tiréli as well as of the daily 'making' of the Dogon compound. Boundaries generate a particular sense of attachment to the world and create an ontological security (Giddens 1991) in a scarce environment. In fact, the ontology of the milieu essentially brings into perspective a recurrent fundamental instability that is generated not only by food shortages, long periods of drought, and an ongoing process of desertification but also by precarious health, past and present invasions, witchcraft, and the souls of the dead and evil spirits. These calamities are symbolically kept at bay by a protection system that surrounds the territory.

We can thus view a philosophy of containment as a gathering process. This process generates a sense of cohesion, collectedness, and togetherness that is achieved through ritual reactivation(s) of the territory's shrines and during the *búlu* celebration that manifests the renewal of the land and of the social network (Chapter 2). This gathering process also transpires in the collective embodied practice of building someone's granary, repairing the men's house, and cultivating, gardening, and pounding onions and millet, all of which strengthen networks of solidarity and lineages. For instance, harvesting and processing millet collectively within one family and then consuming the cereal from one same bowl convey a sense of unity. Social and kinship relations are strengthened through collective seasonal and daily embodied tasks about millet, which, as a form of heritage, is grown on the ancestors' land. Containment as ruled by the Dogon traditional ɔmɔlɔ system acts as controlling behaviour through moral and societal values that aim at appeasing tensions, preventing outbursts, and containing anger in order to avoid a state of war. Similarly, the built features, such as granaries, are made with small openings that frame men's and women's attitudes toward each other's behaviour and so foster secrecy. Furthermore, containment principles are found in the materiality of the landscape and of the compound as containing devices but also in the matter and material elements that they gather inside them. As an example, the material practices of concealment in a female granary was revealed (Chapter 10) as a particular form of containment that is about gathering, protecting, and enclosing life inside the earth container.

The same containment principle was shown to be at work through my examination of the collection and curation of rubbish inside the compound (Chapter 8). Finally, resources such as the recycled earth of old granaries and ruins stand as a form heritage that is gathered and retained, to be transmitted within a family. In fact, recycling materials enables the symbolic 'building up of oneself and one's family', that is, enlarging one's compound to make it prosperous. Recycling is undertaken, along with the earth material of the walls that already bear the labour of the relative who shaped the original granary, with components such as beams and stones that are now being transferred to a new granary. Therefore, the construction material of a granary is kept within a single family nucleus—it is never passed to an outsider, since this would transmit the prosperity to someone else. Hence, the materials of domestic containers are retained within a family even if the containers stand as ruins.

Movement and Fixity

The shaping of the materiality of the landscape also occurs through modernisation, seasonal migrations, and religious conversion, all of which are forms of movement that are transforming Dogon society and worldviews. The dynamics at work here are characterised by a process of extraversion that defines the adoption of external cultural elements to achieve local goals (Bayart 2005). Notably, this extraversion process was shown through the planning of the built environment of Tiréli and the modernisation of the compounds that now extend at the foot of the scree and indicate a progressive expansion of the material boundaries of the village. I have shown that the dwelling and building process of Tiréli occurs through a dialectic between movement and fixity that concerns the foundation of the village, and the enclosing of the landscape as well as of the compound. The act of fixing is both symbolic, as in the case of the magical protection of the compound, and pragmatic, for instance, through the repeated and shared embodied tasks that are allocated to fixed places in the compound, which create continuity, stability, and prosperity in life. The acts of building on the scree and fixing the built elements and the land through shrines constitute another form of inscription that defines and maps out the land. I have suggested that the shrines materialise Dogon cultural identities—that is, the history of Dogon migration, settlement of the escarpment, and the enclosing and protection of space.

Finally, the weather (Chapter 6) shapes and therefore attributes particular configurations to the landscape as rains and winds dramatically affect it. The violent wind and the rain erode the land, break trees, and destroy the built environment, yet they also fertilise the land by bringing and enriching organic materials and nutrients. The weather and its permanent or ephemeral traces help to define the landscape.

Porous Boundaries

I have examined Dogon containers by looking at the dynamics of movement that are applied to these material forms and that define them. Movement, generated from the inside and the outside of the container, acts as a dialectic through which the Dogon material world and therefore worldviews are formed. Dogon containers remain permeable and reversible, through my explication of the multiple forms of movements involved in their making and doing. The porosity of Dogon boundaries, as seen through an examination of how domestic waste exists inside and outside the compound and constantly flows between the two spaces, causes the inside of the container to become its outside and vice and versa. For instance, the waste collected in the home is brought (and in some instances returned) to the field to fertilise the soil. Thus, through the flow of waste, the life cycles of people and of the environment become intertwined in one same *recycled* cosmology.

The boundaries of the Dogon village are remade through acts of building, expanding new horizons of life. Ritual expert knowledge about shrines is lost through time, leading to new forms of meanings and practice. Ritual objects forming a heritage are plundered and sold to antiquity dealers and tourists, threatening existential practice such as rain-making with extinction. For young people, leaving tradition through, for instance, religious conversion, is both a spiritual and physical move out of Dogon rural life, traditional system, and the cosmology of scarcity. Finally, boundaries are also permeable in the sense of the flow of materials and substances in and out through either destructive or propitious rains and winds or the loss of millet to thievery or spoilage of resources when a granary door is opened.

Existing boundaries expand, and new ones may be created, keeping the Dogon village and its reality at the centre. A Dogon microcosmology through boundary making and gathering processes describes a particular form of containment—that is, creates an ontological security in a particularly harsh environment in which scarcity of the means of subsistence is the norm. Hence, through an account of the forms of Dogon containers, I have proposed the development of a philosophy of containment that concerns ways of 'being-at-home in a world container' through the embodied experience of the materiality of the world as a container that is shaped and reshaped internally and externally.

Closure and Openings

In the light of the villagers' daily making and doing of containers, that is, of the territory on the one hand and of the compound and its elements on the other, implicit forms of practical worldviews have revealed themselves through people's embodied practice of these material forms. I have suggested that these meanings are the basis of a Dogon microcosmology that therefore brings together people and the environment into one container. This Dogon relational and changeable microcosmology as an agency defines itself through modernisation, the movements of things and of people, and therefore daily embedded histories and events that reproduce on the long *durée*. Dogon of Tiréli's microcosmology develops, adapts, and adjusts to new, changing situations through making/unmaking/remaking and thus doing/undoing/redoing physical, social, symbolic, and political boundaries that always remain porous. While boundaries aim at retaining 'life', matter is inevitably lost in their making and doing process. Yet, permeability that engenders loss is at the same time an essential condition for Dogon microcosmology to persist and so to allow movement to regenerate life within containers. Loss may explain Dogon needs for systematically strengthening boundaries and strategies and for creating an ontological security. In that sense, containment enables people to achieve well-being that is an attempt to bring a village into unity and keep a sense of continuity in a landscape of scarcity. Therefore, in my conclusion, containment stands as a unifying principle that provides a sense of continuity and consistency and that brings the Dogon of Tiréli into unity, as a means of reestablishing order and providing situatedness in a landscape of scarcity.

In 2012, the Dogon were facing recurring floods as well as new political and territorial challenges. In addition, the porosity of the boundaries of the immense surface of the State of Mali and decades of governmental laxness of security have allowed infiltration by groups of Jihadis and drugs and arms dealers. And the fall of Gaddafi's regime provoked the return of Touareg fighters to Mali and thus an influx of heavy weapons. These occurrences have resulted in occupation by armed groups and the setting up of politically unrecognised yet violently experienced new, superimposed, and movable boundaries. Their design was based on Islamist colonisation, which claims motivation by a form of Islamic law (sharia), and the weakness of an Azawad independent state self-proclaimed by a small proportion of ethnic Touaregs.

The Islamists were claiming ownership of the territories of the North and still threaten today to destabilise the entire Sahel region, already profoundly destabilised by famines, epidemics, and a harsh climate. Hence, beyond Dogon boundaries there were even more uncertainty and scarcity, as northern Mali was being progressively taken over by armed Islamist groups.

In 2013, in a 'post-crisis' and progressive rebuilt context after the collapse of 20 years of democracy in Mali, the sense of 'Dogon-ness' is expressed through its sense of belonging to the State of Mali as 'one and indivisible', being overall 'free' and 'secular'. As the containment structure provided by the state has vanished, old conflicts about land ownership, rights, and tenure have resurfaced in the lawless Dogon region, leading to ethnic conflicts between the Dogon and the Peul and among the Dogon. New security borders marked by series of checkpoints have been set up by the Malian army on the main axis linking the Dogon region to the former Islamist bastions, forcing Dogon people to move 'in' and 'out' of the region in new unprecedented ways. While MINUSMA (United Nations Multidimensional Integrated Stabilization Mission in Mali) troops flow through the Dogon region to achieve their peace-making mission, weapons and drugs are brought in and sold on the black market. Because of the absence of Malian security forces and justice processes, thieves ransack people's homes. The long-delayed rain made people flee the villages in search of work and gold in the neighbouring countries. In the meantime, some 350,000 refugees are awaiting political stability to come back to their homeland.

In the Dogon region, the absence of rain, of the state, of tourists has generated a climax of total uncertainty and paranoia about hidden Islamists' presence in the territory. Dogon people, who are suspicious by nature, live in fear within their own village boundaries. Consequently, history as a cosmological matter that in a Dogon view may always repeat itself, is forcing the people to think in new ways and act beyond their own boundaries while containment as history in the 'in-the-making' raises new ontological questions. In the light of these historical events, some of which I experienced in 2012 and 2013, some new questions may be posed such as: Where and how did Dogon containment come from? Would the people's current extensive need for protection stem from the Dogon being historically an agriculturally specialised people and not warriors, or from their lack of centralised political power, or of being geographically situated at the crossroads of multiple people's histories? When might containment have happened? And what caused it?

These are just a few questions that may lead to a broader understanding of Dogon microcosmologies as ontologies that are not just the Dogon ways of living but overall ways of being in the twenty-first-century world. I shall leave them open for now.

Appendix A Dogon's Identity: From Immutability to Cultural Diversities

While 'Dogon', as a self-naming term means 'those who know "shame" but who are free and possess a sense of honour' (Bouju 1995a, 333), the Dogon of the plateau and of the cliffs are called by the Fulani *haabe* ('pagan'). The Fulani also name the Dogon of the plain *kaado*, which the Dogon often view as pejorative; first, this term implies that the Dogon are 'people who easily lose their temper when provoked', referring to the Dogon's recourse to black magic while resisting Fulani raids and therefore Islam before colonial times. It also implies that the Dogon are 'sharp and brave', in reference to their hard-working nature.

Within these ethnonyms, each Dogon village possesses a single family name that signifies aspects of the members' identity, relating to historical events, behaviour and personality traits, economic activities, and ways of living (Chapter 4).

Dogon have close geographical and historical ties with, for instance, the Songhai (Hombori and Douentza areas), the Fulani (Bandiagara plateau), the Mossi and Samogo in the bay region, and the Marka-Dafing south of the Séno plain and cliffs (Sokura, Tanga). Malinke and Fulani languages exert strong influences on the Dogon language. In the same vein, as Goody observes, Islam has affected Dogon culture in the long term and their animism system in particular (Goody 1971, 456–57).

Finally, in addition to four ceramic traditions that were identified across the Dogon region (Mayor 2011, 11), the Dogon possess some seventeen languages: *donno-sɔ, mombo, tɔmmɔ sɔ, tomo-kan, bondum-dom, dogulu-dom, tiranige-diga, naa-dama, tɔrɔ sɔ, baageri-me, korandabo, jamsay-tegu, ampari-kora, teɲu-kan, yanda-dom, oru yille,* and *naa-dama* (Hochstetler, Durieux, & Durieux-Boon 2004, 11–12). These also have internal divisions (Hochstetler, Durieux, & Durieux-Boon 2004) and variations (Douyon 2010) and include an unclassified language called *Àna tiɲa* (Blench & Dendo 2005). Whether the Dogon languages known as an isolated group of Niger-Congo (Williamson & Blench 2000) are Gur or Mande is, however, still debated (Hochstetler, Durieux, & Durieux-Boon 2004). Hence, the diversity of Dogon culture may be attributed to Dogon encountering and culturally mixing with established local groups, commercial and cultural influences, imported religions such as Islam, French colonisation, technology, and thus modernism and tourism (Ciarcia 1998, 103). Dieterlen mentions that some Dogon possess a Soninke origin—such as the Drame or Darambe people of the village of Arou, where the Hogon or Dogon's spiritual chief for those stemming from Arou ancestors resides in a sanctuary (Dieterlen 1982, 78). Finally, the seasonal and temporary migrations of the Àna Yana Dogo—that is, 'those who travel far away' (Petit 1995)—to Ivory Coast, Ghana, and Guinea Conakry in the search for work (Dougnon 2007) should be taken into consideration.

Appendix B   Dogon Mande Origin through Oral History

According to oral history, the Dogon locate their origin in the Mande (see, for instance, Bouju 1995b). The Mande is defined as part of a vast coherent 'ideological system' (Mayor et al. 2005, 31) and is said to be the West African 'cradle of humanity'—a region from which people, knowledge, and religion scattered all over West Africa (de Ganay 1995, 38–41), encompassing some 44 ethnic communities of West Africa (de Ganay 1995, 14, Dieterlen 1957). The Dogon situate their origin in the village of Dogoro, in Manden Kaba, near Bamako. This I gathered through interviews in Kani Kombolé, Walia, and Sokura between January and September 2011. Marka-Dafing interviewees of the Sokura area claim the same origin as the Dogon (Douny 2013).

Around the end of the twelfth century, the Dogon, formed of three families—the Dyon, the Ono, and the Arou (said to be part of the Malinke group)—left the Mande, refusing Islamic conversion (Dieterlen 1982, 9). In the version collected by Dieterlen (1941), a fourth family, the Domno, is mentioned, which migrated to the plain area; however, my sources did not recall this. They migrated to the towns of Ségou and Djenné before arriving in Kani Na, of which only ruins remain, near Kani Kombolé, where they settled temporarily. Other versions about the Dogon migration exist (Desplagnes 1907; Huet 1994; Petit 1998). The three ancestor groups then separated and progressively migrated toward the plain, the plateau, and the escarpment, where they settled down. The details of this series of migrations, during which the descendants of these four families founded the present Dogon villages, were not recounted to me but are related in detail by Dieterlen (1941).

As far as the migration-line history of the people of Tiréli is concerned, I was told that they originate from an ancestor called *Aru* (Arou), who founded the present-day political site of Arou; his descendants then divided to found their own villages. All of my sources agreed to define Arou as a site and a sanctuary rather than a village. By using this translated term they indicate the importance of Arou's shrine, which literally constitutes and defines the place of power from which the protection of Arou's Dogon communities is managed and which is occupied by only two families. In addition to his role of authoritatively representing the his people, the *Hogon* (the spiritual chief) is responsible for calling the rain. He also assumes the legal function of ultimately settling conflicts, mostly between villages. Thus Arou, as symbolised by its shrine, represents and centralises political and religious power.

The versions of the Dogon migration story that I collected from the Saye people of both Tiréli and Pèguè provide a concise story that forms a straightforward migratory schema. In contrast, the versions collected by Dieterlen show, in a notably detailed way, the great complexity of the migration process, as based on the ramification, multiplication, and separation of the descendants of the three ancestor families. Moreover, the tales collected from the 1930s based on mythical elements indicate the desertion of certain villages because of invasion and their subsequent reoccupation. They also give accounts of the great complexity of the migration process and multiple occupations of the escarpment. Although these stories provide interesting accounts of Dogon migration, they still await verification, and Dogon voltaic (Volta basin) origin should also be taken into account.

Appendix C Dogon Exoticism: From Ancient Egypt to Outer Space

Griaule's work has had a very wide influence on the development of tourism and the popularity of images of Dogon exoticism amplified by Western and non-Western media, with, for instance, 75,000 websites dedicated to the Dogon in 2003 (Bedaux & van der Waals 2003, 7), as a result of which the Dogon undoubtedly gained prominence. Over time the Dogon have used their cosmogony as a means to promote and to legitimise their cultural identity—for example, through writings (Dolo 2001; Guindo & Kansaye 2000) and as a tourism marketing tool. Popular written accounts often categorised as pseudoarchaeology offer questionable interpretations of Griaule's work by establishing unfounded connections between the Dogon and an alien civilization (Temple 1976). Finally, African scholars such as Cheick Anta Diop (1974) have strived to demonstrate the Dogon's origins and cultural influences in Ancient Egypt, an argument supported by Dogon intellectuals and Dogon people involved in the tourism industry and that also feeds the imagination of outsiders.

Appendix D Challenging Griaule's Work: A Brief Overview of Dogon Studies

Criticisms regarding Griaule's field methods and the multiple contradictory interpretations and inconsistencies in his colossal thesis abound, making his ambitious work questionable, as many scholars have demonstrated (for instance, see Apter 2005; Ciarcia 1998; Clifford 1988; Doquet 1999; Douglas 1967; Lettens 1971; van Beek 1991, 2004). Long-term ethnoarchaeological projects and anthropological research in the Dogon region also have challenged Griaule's work. For instance, Bedaux's considerable work on the Tellem culture, Gallay's extensive research on Dogon ceramics, Lane's study of the Dogon built environment, and more recently Huyscomb and Mayor's interdisciplinary Ounjougou project have uncovered fundamental aspects of Dogon history, settlements, and identity. In anthropology, a series of monographs based on thorough fieldwork break away from traditional 'Griaulised' views of the Dogon by rightly emphasising Dogon cultural diversities and dynamics, in the lens of everyday life practice and ritual performance—for example, Paulme's (1988) descriptive study of Dogon social organisation; Teme's detailed examination of the political and ritual control of the land in the *tɔrɔ sɔ* area (1997); Doquet's (1999) extensive work on Dogon masks, tourism, and cultural patrimony; Bouju's (1984) ethnography on the Dogon's socioeconomic life concerning the production of millet; and Jolly's (2004) monumental research on Dogon millet beer. Furthermore, van Beek's critical work explores Dogon *tɔrɔ sɔ* culture, including that of Tiréli, with a particular focus on Dogon religious life (2003a), tourism (2003b, 2005b), and aspects of agricultural practices (1993 and 1992, with Banga).

Appendix E Methodology's Development: Doing Fieldwork in the Dogon Region (Pre-Malian Crisis, 2012)

The methodology I developed takes into account the specificity and reality of conducting fieldwork in the Dogon region, which was problematic at the time I did my main research. Owing to massive levels of tourism and the effects of scientific research on indigenous daily life (in many places but, one hopes, not in all), the systematic use of ethnographic tools such as the interview and, by extension, the collection of open discourse was ineffective if used to the exclusion of other methods. My experience was that information is biased and largely coloured by Griaule's ethnographic statements, compiled into symbolic stereotypes that serve to substantiate the authenticity and the uniqueness of traditional Dogon culture and therefore often to acknowledge and assert local identity (also noted by Doquet 1999, 207–41).

Moreover, conducting interviews in the area of the Bandiagara escarpment often led initially to local attitudes of suspicion, reticence, deliberate modifications of information, and even to lies and jokes. Therefore, for the core of this research I chose to examine Dogon life mainly through my systematic participation in and observation of Dogon everyday and ritual life over 17 months, including an agrarian cycle. Parents and children were very kind and patient in showing me how to make and do things. I framed my participant observations within two methodological threads: praxeology (phenomenology oriented) and the operational sequence (*chaîne opératoire*). I collected practical forms of knowledge mostly from my shared daily experience of working with men and women of between 20 and 45 (it is difficult to know people's exact ages). These people were able to technically describe their daily tasks and their experience of things, which I could then contrast with mine, as part of my learning process.

Yet, the villagers were not able to provide explanations as to 'why things are the way they are'. As they say: 'We have learned that [practice/technique] from our parents, who themselves have learned that from their parents', and so on. Therefore, toward the end of my fieldwork and during subsequent trips I employed semistructured interviews, to gain greater depth of knowledge about the Dogon's daily and ritual practice. I collected more detailed explanations from my long-term sources, with whom I also double checked my observations and interpretations. I informally interviewed highly skilled older people, as well as knowledgeable men and women older than 45 and many elders of the village.

For more specific queries about land shrines, the weather, aspects of the tradition and beliefs systems, and also symbolic meanings attached to actions and material forms, I relied on the knowledge of ritual specialists and the blacksmiths. I was able to contrast the results of my research in Tiréli with some observations and semistructured interviews that I conducted in other villages across the Dogon region during multiple short trips. Finally, for this research I was guided and assisted by two Dogon villagers who helped me greatly with the language.

Appendix F The Tale of the Foundation of Tiréli

Taken together, stories about the foundation of the village and the foundation of its built features and land shrines are material and cultural elements that very often serve to legitimise Dogon identity as well as their ownership and control of land. Tracing the history of human displacement enables us to understand the idea of belonging to the place and the Dogon sense of attachment to the land. The physical appropriation and the Dogon people's logic of dwelling lead to the formation of contiguous boundaries that generate local ontologies of containment. With this account, I present aspects of Dogon migration history and especially of the foundation of Tiréli. I use the tale as it was told to me by the elders of Teri-Ku. However, I assume that multiple versions exist in both districts of the village and are reinvented over time by various storytellers. These multiple versions may also support the village's district politics.

The origin story states that one of Aru's sons, Argo, left the Mande to settle along the escarpment and found the village of Pèguè. Because of a conflict with his clan, his son Enẽ decided to leave the village and searched for a new place to establish his home. According to Dieterlen (1941), the ancestor Aru (Arou) and his sons moved along the escarpment, where the sons founded their own villages, including Tiréli and Pèguè, separately while Aru went farther north to found the site of Arou, named after him. The occupation of the escarpment and the plateau areas by the Aru clan continued with the subdivision of these groups.

However, Dieterlen's version of the Dogon migration process indicates that the villages of Tiréli and Pèguè were founded before the site of Arou. As Dieterlen indicates, the village of Pèguè must have been abandoned following an invasion, a frequent occurrence at that time, and would have been reconstructed recently—around the middle of the nineteenth century—by some of the Arou people (1941, 49). By extrapolation, the people from Pèguè who originated from Arou and the descendants of the Aru ancestor (the Argo family) would have settled subsequently in Tiréli. One hypothesis holds that this village was in turn abandoned by Aru, forced to leave because of an incursion.

The elders of Tiréli/Teri-Ku recount that their village was founded by two brothers Enẽ and Ko-u. The first was a hunter, the second a cultivator. Enẽ, the older of the two, arrived first. He was hunting in a place with abundant game, where his dog found a water reservoir. Moreover, the area included a large area of cultivable land. Given the discovery of these three resources, the hunter Enẽ decided to settle down there. After clearing a place at the top of the scree, he built a shelter, or *tógu,* under one of the prominent flat rocks from which comes the name of the place, Tawara, and its derivation, Tatara (known as such today and the name of the first district of Tiréli). Therefore, the name refers to the geomorphological characteristics of the site, which consists of massive rocks. *Tawara* refers to the flat rocks used as a vantage point, notably for hunting and on top of which the first *tógu na,* or men's house, was constructed. The name means 'to be fixed against the rocks or scree' ('I stick to the cliff').

Since Enẽ had not been heard from for some while, his younger brother, a cultivator, went searching for him and found him well settled. He decided to join him. Together they progressively cleared the site of the scree by cutting down the trees and the bush. This action was subsequently used as a name for the village of Tiréli. The place where Ko-u established his own *tógu,* a couple of metres up from his brother's settlement, was named Teri-Ku (known as such today), which means 'upper cleared place' or 'at the head of'. The brothers fixed the *lɔbɔ* shrine of the ancestors, as a safeguard for life, on a promontory on top of the scree as a means of protecting themselves from wild life, supernatural beings, and enemies.

My sources defined the *lɔbɔ* as the most important element of the village. It symbolises the acquisition and 'possession' of the place, by the two ancestors, for the foundation of Tiréli, as well its cohesion. In due course, Enẽ and Ko-u returned to Pèguè to collect their families and bring them to their new place. After a while, however, part of site was occupied by another group, allegedly by the Kor family. This family belonged to a subgroup descending from the Ɔno clan, who came from the plain but were renamed locally and became known as the Ongoeba. The Kor family came to settle in Tiréli after their clan was massacred by a neighbouring plains clan called the Duna; the survivors of this massacre had had to disperse across the plain. One of their factions, the Kor family, instead moved along the escarpment scree and found refuge in Enẽ's Tiréli. However, their coexistence quickly came to an end, because the Ongoeba were constantly stealing food from the Enẽ and Ko-u families.

A conflict between the two clans (Ɔno [Ongoeba] and Aru) broke out and led to the expulsion of the Ongoeba. The name the two founders gave to their families, Sáy (known today as Saye), derives from this event. The term *sáy* literally refers to the act of 'cutting something from its roots' or 'cutting off and knocking something over'—that is, 'to chase someone away'. This term also means bright and clever, with a lot of instinct or feeling (Calame-Griaule 1968, 238). As the place became safer, clusters of families from Pèguè joined them and organised themselves into a village. Thus, the *gínu múnɔ* shrine was fixed on the Tawara flat rock to protect the houses and the inhabitants, and much later they built the men's *tógu na,* followed by the *yápùnu gínu* (menstruating women's house) and, finally, the *binu gínu*. (Opinions differ about the time of the discovery of the actual site of village of Tiréli by the two brothers; the highest parts of the cliffs and its caves may have been still occupied by Tellem people, who would have then either been killed or chased away by the Dogon or integrated into their community.)

As the families grew, they occupied the other places on the scree, and the present-day districts of Tiréli took shape. At that time Ko-u settled in the place called Teri-Ku. This name has been kept today to designate the three subdistricts of Dama, Sábo, and Komangua. However, Ko-u decided to move his shelter farther down and named the site Dama, which means 'to push', as in 'pushing his house down on the scree'. Another meaning of Dama was given as 'I have cut a part of me to give it to you'.

At that time, people cultivated at the top of the scree because of Fulani slave raiders, forcing Ko-u to divide his field and to distribute parts of it to his brothers so that they could cultivate. One of his sons then created the district of Sábo and decided to build his *gujɔ* next to an African tree grape (*Lannea microcarpa*) with branches so frail that they threatened to break when people climbed it to pick the fruits. Those who named the site took this anecdote into account, naming the site Sáboy (today known as Sábo), a reference to the fragile *sá* tree.

Then the third subdistrict of Teri-Ku, Komangua, was created. This name also refers to the geomorphology of the place, which is characterised by sparse hollowed rocks (*kómo* or *kómu*). This place served as a temporary habitat for the people of Dama, who had decided to move in because of a lack of space in their former district. Thus, the term *kómo āga* ('the mouth of the hole') indicates a tunnel that was used as a shelter in case of threat.

As far as Tatara is concerned, it gave birth to Gujoguru, which refers to the *gujɔ,* or house (literally a room that is the property of the young man and from which he will develop his compound), of one of Enɛ̃'s sons, who left the family to start his own compound from this room. Finally, a last district, called Sodanga, was founded, which is today also the name of the district that includes the subdistricts of Tatara, Gujoguru, and Sodanga. The name comes from *sòmò–tanga*, 'to jump over the water fall to build my house'.

Political tensions exist between the districts of Teri-Ku and Sodanga. For some people, Sodanga, as a subdistrict, was built recently and is a separate political entity that does not contribute to village affairs. The tensions make it difficult at times to deal with the question of the village structure, since it triggers political protest and claims to the chief's position; thus potential sources of conflict are silenced, and the foundation of Teri-Ku's districts of Dama and Komangua are attributed to one of the two brothers, Ko-u, whereas the other three, of which Sodanga is composed (Tatara, Gujoguru, and Sodanga), are said to have originated from Enɛ̃.

Notes

Transcription Notes

1. Accent marks and vowels as proposed by Jolly (1995, IV).
2. As described and used by Polly Richards (2003, 8).

Chapter 1

1. The language called *Jamsay tegu* is also spoken in Tiréli, since they have relatives living the plain. *Jamsay tegu* means 'the language of peace', recognised as the oldest Dogon language; it is used as a vehicular language. The name was given by Fulani cattle herders, and it serves as a form of greeting (Calame-Griaule 1956, 64).
2. Their language *Bomu tegu* meaning 'language of the oafs' in reference to their character perceived by them as 'rustic' (Calame-Griaule 1956, 65).
3. For more details about the history of famines see Jolly 1995, 81–82.
4. See Jolly's history of the Dogon region for more details (Jolly 1995, 77–80).
5. The concept of materiality has received increasing attention over the years in the fields of archaeology and social anthropology (Knappett 2012, 188). See, for instance, the work of Graves-Brown (2000); Tilley (2004); Miller (2005); Meskell (2005); (Ingold 2012) to name but a few.
6. This Dogon term probably comes from Arabic *aduna*.
7. In this book I explore dimensions of water mostly through analysis of Dogon conceptions of rain.

Chapter 2

1. This claim appears in everyday life conversation and in 50 interviews (Dogon interviewees) conducted between 2003 and 2011 in the course of two different research projects. The main places of enquiry on the subject were Bandiagara, Tintam, Kambe Sendé Sangha, Tiréli, Endé Walia, Kani-Kombolé, Segué, Tanga, Bankass, and Baye.
2. Although in some places I draw on a series of commonalities that I observed over the past 10 years about the material practice of the Dogon of the *tɔrɔ sɔ* area and in other areas.
3. I observed that aspects of the villagers' practical knowledge—for instance, about the weather, building granaries, cooking, and waste recycling—are found in other areas in the *tɔrɔ sɔ* and the Dogon region and beyond—in *tɔrɔ sɔ* villages (Kamba,

Sangha) and the *dono-sɔ* of the Plateau (Pelou), the *teɲu-kan* area of the plain (Bankass, Koro), and the *dono-sɔ* of the cliffs (Kani-Bonzon, Teli, Nombori).

4. In my view, foreign religions (Islam, Christianity) often constitute the tip of the iceberg and at the same time *ɔmɔlɔ* tradition (*atɛmu*) is its submerged part. Dogon people acknowledge the tradition as a fundamental dimension of their identity that pervades many aspects of their daily and ritual life. Catholic, Protestant, and Islamic practices are said to be embedded into the tradition.

5. See Abramson & Holbraad (2012) for recent developments of the concept in anthropology.

6. I retain the concept of *cosmogony* for Griaule's usage and to refer to an elaborate corpus of creation myths that Griaule collected and interpreted. As a common understanding, today, these myths are assimilated in Dogon cosmology. In general, the term designates Dogon knowledge about the cosmos as they are found in Griaule, Dieterlen, and their followers' holistic work on Dogon culture and that is based on the Dogon cosmogony.

7. One of the main approaches to worldview in the social sciences lies in the work of Kearney, who defines it as a 'culturally organized systems of knowledge' (Kearney 1975, 248) that serves ideology and hegemony (Kearney 1984).

Chapter 3

1. I provide details about rituals concerning the village shrines in two publications (2009, 2011). Therefore, here I concentrate on the spatial division and structure of containment of the Dogon village territory.

2. By following part of van Binsbergen's definition (1981, 101 cited in Colson 1997, 47), I consider shrines as fixed, observable, and localised devices that are the focus of ritual and thus religious activities. In contrast, I propose that 'altar' refers to a portable or removable device (for instance, placed back inside a shed after being used for ritual purpose or repair) that is used in a similar way as shrines. Yet, Dogon altars, also called *áma*, shaped as cones of mud, figurines, or as gatherings of artefacts in a particular place, serve individuals' purposes (those of the linage in particular) and to protect a family or clan against malevolent entities and evil people (van Beek 2003b, 96).

3. This concept is also found in the *Bambara* tongue, which might indicate its possible borrowing by the Dogon people; it means 'life', 'spirit', or 'character' (Calame-Griaule 1968, 205–06).

4. Erratum: in two previous publications (2009, 2011) I misspelled the term and used *kerugue*.

5. The issue about the purity, impurity mechanism was developed by Dieterlen (1947); Paulme describes Dogon rites of purifications (1940), and these works are discussed by Liberski (1989). The purification of the lands through particular rites involving various forms of sacrifices is developed by Jolly (2004) and Bouju (1984, 1995). In Chapter 5, following Teme's (1997) thesis, I show some of the rites of purification of the land that are crucial for enabling the rain to fall and thus to fertilise the land.

6. The village of Tiréli possesses a shrine that protects Dogon men going to war. In addition to a myriad of magico-religious protections for the body—for instance, amulets—sacrifices are made at that shrine when the villagers are becoming involved in conflicts, for instance, in past slavery raids, World War II, and in the context of village armed conflicts regarding land disputes.

Chapter 4

1. Beyond an impression of homogeneity, the village architecture and in particular this of the foot of the scree, shows many new architectural styles and forms. The architectural diversity of Dogon villages and their spatial layout are partly determined by the geomorphology of the village sites (Lauber 1998; Schijns 2009). Although Dogon compounds are built and spatially organised in a similar way, they really differ in their style and shape (Lauber 1998; Schijns 2009).
2. It can be argued that this holds as well for the other districts and maybe for the other villages of the escarpment.
3. As I determined in many villages of the escarpment, it seems that the foundation of Dogon villages follows a similar narrative and elements.
4. *Oné inɛkan pu: ku: in bé dénu dɛnɛju inɛkan pu: anga i: in bé dɛnɛjé gínu.*
5. *Dédé ɲuwa lé gírun daŋutinu ina daran wɛ bɛrɛ iwa kɔrɔ gà kiré mu anrunŋé pu: doɲu suŋa.*
6. This was said in French: *çà c'est pour les gens d'avant.*

Chapter 5

1. In his work Bedaux exposes a third type of dwelling of the Tolloy, which predates the Tellem. The villagers referred only to the Tellem.
2. The Peul (Fulani, Fulfulde) are a widespread pastoral ethnic group that also lives on Dogon land.
3. Referring to the villages of the Plateau (*dono-sɔ*), Bouju mentions a *gidu* land shrine that is seen as an 'obstacle' (Bouju 1995a, 363).
4. Because of space restrictions, I do not discuss complex agricultural techniques in this volume.
5. In his thesis Jolly provides a detailed and complete description of fields, crops, and naming (Jolly 1995, 115).
6. Because of space restrictions, in this book I do not explore the aspects of Dogon cattle and other domesticated animals.
7. *Sorghum vulgaris*
8. Unidentified species
9. In June 2012 a deadly intercommunity conflict erupted in the Dinangourou area, in the village of Sari, that led to the death of around 30 Peuls and the destruction of 21 houses by Dogon.
10. *Tamarinus indica*
11. *Adansonia digitata*
12. *Ceiba pentandra*

Chapter 6

1. For instance, *jinu* live in the trees. *Yéban* (Griaule 1994, 153) are chtonic spirits that are associated with certain features of the landscape, such as rocks or dunes. They coexist with humans and help them to do good or evil. In van Beek's classification of spirits, *jinu* roam and inhabit the areas outside the village; in search of body parts, they attack people and newborn babies. *Yéban* are described by the author as the *yenew*, which reside inside the village and are sometimes found under granaries (van Beek 1992, 51–52).
2. The Sahel and thus the Sahelian condition is described as 'the dry bush' (*ɔru mà:*).
3. Dogon cultivators follow a traditional calendar. The Dogon week counts five days (*júgu*), and a year is divided into 11 lunar months of 26 to 28 days—depending on

observations of the cycle of the moon; the cloudy sky of the rainy season may hide the moon and cause a delay of a day or two in the counting.

Dogon people recognise three seasons: rainy, cold-dry, and hot-dry. Yet they include two more periods in their season calendar: the sowing period and the harvest period. These agrarian activities and thus the Dogon calendar are considerably disrupted owing to climate change. The Dogon year and calculation of the agrarian cycle start with the first big rain (May/June) and thus the sowing period. For practical reasons, I start with the hot, dry season, because Dogon activities and experiences of that season enable me to better circumscribe and explain the way people engage with the weatherscape of the wintering season.

4. In 2011, in Burkina Faso, chemicals were sprayed from airplanes to make rain. This triggered floods that ravaged Burkina Faso and Mali.
5. This Fulbe term is often used throughout the Dogon region.
6. An imported fertiliser containing high concentration of potash is used in this case (for those who can afford it).
7. *Guiera senegalensis*
8. Access to water is restricted by certain prohibitions, such as not wearing any red items, being clean, not wearing shoes, moving silently and calmly in the reservoir, and not fetching water with a jar with a small opening that provokes a bubbling at the surface that wakes the water spirit. The colour red might symbolically refer to blood and therefore the idea of impurity. (This prohibition is also applied when pots are fired collectively.)

Chapter 7

1. Because of a lack of space, I propose here a schematic and summarised definition of the compound. The Dogon social organisation as it is objectified in the built environment is more complex, as shown by Paulme (1988) and (Lane 1986).
2. In French: *A l'intérieur des murs tu trouves qu'il y a une famille qui vit là. C'est là où on est né et çà appartient à nos ancêtres.*
3. Witchcraft also occurs in the compound itself—for example, through a rival cowife.
4. Daily tasks define the temporality of the homescape. The passage of daytime is also felt through the changing intensity of the light and heat of the air between sunrise and sunset. Temporal devices such as the clock and Gregorian calendar are hardly used by people to read time.
5. In French: *Ceux qui construisent une chambre avec de grandes portes n'ont rien compris. C'est-à-dire que les gens peuvent rentrer directement et même voir à l'intérieure. . . . Aussi, en t'abaissant, tu laisses les mauvaises choses à l'extérieur et tu amènes les bonnes choses l'intérieur.*
6. *Oruni sɔ ɛju oyé sanw ama ŋen ɛmɛni sɔ ɛju o, ŋein donɔ marun dudaga tenguru sɔ ɛju ŋen ya ɛmɛni jɛrɛ jamu din ni uju.*
7. In early 1980, Bouju demonstrated the effects on the village of the temporary migration of Dogon youth in town to earn cash and bring back modern goods. He showed that youth embraces Islam learned in town, adapting it as a means to confront the local system (Bouju 1984).
8. *Urginea altissima Baker.*
9. Tamkuba or *Detarium senegalensis* (*cesalpiniacae*).

Chapter 8

1. A first version of this chapter was published in *The Journal of Material Culture* 12(3) in 2007. This chapter includes sections of the earlier version, as well as unpublished ethnographic materials.

2. Sheep and goats. Cow manure is generally produced at the bottom of the scree, where most of the Dogon large cattle are gathered. In the Bankass area (Séno Gondo plain), donkey excrement is not added to the manure because of its high level of potash.

3. In addition to this domestic manure, some Dogon welcome Fulani cattle herders to set up their camp in Dogon fields in the dry season. In exchange, Dogon fields are fertilised by the excrement of the cattle.

4. In some villages, bird manure (known in the West as guano) is collected from the highest parts of the cliffs, where birds nest. This manure is a fertiliser rich in nitrogen and phosphorus; it is added to onion fields.

5. This practice also exists among the Fulani, Bambara, and Mossi people, who called the practice *pága sagdá sɔlɲé*. Yet, different symbolic meanings are attached to it.

6. In some compounds, ashes are thrown away, depending on the occupier's needs and use.

Chapter 9

1. Generally, a man builds his own granary. However, he can be assisted by family members to transport the material to the construction site and to build the walls.

2. The building was undertaken by a 35-year-old man with whom I observed the building of the granary during 12 consecutive days, three times per day. Generally, the building of a granary takes about seven days; in this case, the extension resulted from a miscalculation. The length for each stage was relatively random.

3. Iroko has shown the various uses of termite earth in the making of crafts in Africa, such as building blast furnaces (1996, 133) and habitat (1996, 134–43), creating ceramics (1996, 145–50), and making spinning spindles (1996, 152), as well as providing the inspiration of a mound shape in building mosques (1996, 245).

4. Other material can be added to the mix, such as dung, wild raisin pulp, and, very rarely, shea nuts, to improve its waterproofing quality. A well-constructed granary with material made from a mix of consistent texture can last for about seven years.

5. The ground of the granary was filled with stones and clay-pot fragments collected in the scree between the compounds, on top of which he layered some thick and moist red clay that would prevent mice, ants, and termites from entering the granary.

6. The repertoire consists of first sticking one ball of wet mud onto the existing wall, attaching it onto the *áma* cone and extending the wet mud ball back onto the existing portion of dry wall by pulling it toward the body while simultaneously pressing it down on the structure. Second, the mud is pinched to extend it. Third, it is smoothed down as a means of fusing it completely into the wall and of creating a symbiosis between the existing mud and the new matter. Fourth, the mud is smoothed upward by watering it gently and adding, if necessary, new pieces of mud. Earth containers bring together human and environmental life cycles, along with their essential matter or substance, by objectifying them.

7. The walls were constructed, one row at a time, three times a day, at around 06.30 in the morning, before lunch (at 12.00), and finally late in the afternoon (at 16.45). However, this schedule remained flexible since basically schedules are designed around the builder's free time. The gaps in the schedule allow the walls to dry out before a new set of two to three layers is begun. According to my source, it is important to keep to the same direction, clockwise or counterclockwise, for each section of the walls built as a row. In his view, it gives more strength to the construction, ensuring continuity and coordination on a practical level. The walls are wetted-down repeatedly to smooth the wall surface by filling in its irregularities.

8. Dogon male granaries have one door (at the top) and one or two windows (below). While the first serves men to get in, the second enables men to bring in millet ears. The second door, called *áŋa dóɲu*, used to be called *doru kã* ('the mouth of the penis').
9. Alternatively, the juice of the wild raisin can be used, mixed or not with ashes, to offer a prayer.
10. Sometimes, when the building is finished, some builders add a series of decorations on the walls. These consist mostly of geometric patterns, which are plastered on the wall surface. No particular meaning is attached to the patterns, which occur in many parts of the Dogon land. Decorations are added purely for aesthetic reasons, as well as to consolidate the walls and the door frame. In other words, it is done to testify to the act of building, to being successful in life, and, of course, to being recognised by the villagers as such. Thus, it indicates the builder's capacity to be active in life and to gain social status and repute.
11. The granary is eventually topped by a thatched 'hat', and its walls are decorated.

Chapter 10

1. The basket called *taju* contains about 13 kg of millet ears, which provide about 10 kg of grain.
2. *Ba i: man wo yù: séré karan yù: man dei bira mɔɲu mané biré.*
3. Jolly has discussed the depletion of millet for the production of millet beer (Jolly 2004, 307–12).
4. *Nuwanu daga gugɔ ni yuwa lé yù: dodonugo jé yù: guyan lé i: wɛ ni ya lé do dorɔ̃n jé ma ga paná bira lé ɲo ɲonugo jé.*
5. *Si tu vois une femme qui marche avec les pieds qui partent à l'exterieur, c'est qu'elle gaspille. Mais, si une femme marche avec les pieds qui rentrent, c'est qu'elle fait attention.*
6. *Les gens n'aiment pas qu'on voit qu'ils sont pauvres. Si le mari va mal gérer sa famille, c'est la femme qui part. Donc, il est seul, malheureux et sa réputation est mauvaise, parceque les gens parlent mal sur lui.*

Chapter 11

1. Millet (*Pennisetum spicatum*), called by the Dogon in French *petit mil*, is a crop that reaches between 1.7 and 3 m in height and that grows in sandy soil. The following millet types are found in Tiréli: *yù: ɛɲɛ bojó* (greenish spikes found among other millet plants); *yù: ana* (has itchy hairs); *bobo yù:* (are big grains). Millet is sown in different kind of soils: *sɛdjɛ yù:* (is cultivated at the bottom of and in the scree); *manu yù:* (is cultivated in the sandy plain); *dono yù:* (grows on harder soils, such as in the village surroundings). In terms of the harvests, *yù:dæ̃* (millet that has fallen on the ground, stopped growing, is of a low quality) is the first that people collect; then, they collect the *yù: ana* or *yù: èdju* (the best) and *yù: buburu*, which have fewer grains on their spike and are mature.
2. In the Dogon region, cereal banks exist but, as people say, very few families use them, because they can hardly manage to pay the banks back. As a consequence, Dogon people often have their carts and cattle repossessed by banks. Tourists and local NGOs provide bags of rice and millet, but these do not suffice.
3. In a Dogon view, fruits and vegetables constitute a Western idea of diet that is neither valuable nor nourishing for a Dogon, whose energy for daily hard physical work is found in the hàrd millet paste. Although they are consumed, tomatoes and

salad are still referred to as food for tourists and are eaten not as part of a meal but as a light snack.

4. *Yù: dogum paná i: ɛmɛni paŋà ojé yù: yi: la lé biré ga biré bɛ jinu.*

5. Once millet spikes are harvested, the cattle are moved to the fields, where they eat the remaining leaves of the stalks and trample the stalks, mixing it with their dung. After a while, this mixture becomes manured compost (Chapter 8).

6. The consumption of meat such as mutton or pork occurs mostly on market day, when it is sold as a snack, and during sacrificial rituals and religious celebrations.

7. Even mechanical grinders do not grind millet grains completely. Thus, women have to regrind the remaining *sagi* afterward (about 1 kg of *sagi* in 5 kg of millet). In addition, tiny bits of metal can sometimes be found in the mix.

8. Another technique consists of washing the grains four times before pounding them. (However, the product contains fewer vitamins, and its texture is also lighter.) The water is given to the sheep, because it contains the bran's nutrients.

9. Which she also does by making the first fire. The wood that is commonly used for cooking is *kirɛ (Prosopis Africana)*.

10. Similarly, the establishment of the anvil in the village smithy signifies the attachment and the activity of the blacksmith. The act of establishing the fireplace in a compound is also materialised through the first fire, made with the wood of the *ponu* tree or the tamkuba (*Detarium senegalensis [cesalpiniacee]*) when the couple is newlywed, as an expression of 'starting a compound' that is their dwelling. This uniquely scented wood is also burned while a woman is giving birth.

11. The taste for thick, strongly flavoured and oily sauce is yet not specific to the Dogon, as Stoller describes in his ethnography about Songhai cuisine (1986). Thick and slimy sauces are perceived as prestigious and thus, as Stoller explains, are often served in a Songhai context to guests and at times of celebrations.

12. Aluminium cooking pots, plastic basins, and enamels tend today to constitute a more practical, yet relatively costly choice that appears as an idiosyncratic signifier of modernism and thereby of social prestige (Cunningham 2009), social mobility, and aesthetic tastes (Gosselain, Zeebroek, & Decroly 2008/2009).

13. The Dogon generally have a reputation for poor cuisine. However, Dogon people living in town always prize the food cooked in their family as being of higher quality than food bought in town, which is more expensive.

14. It also constitutes a form of respect toward millet by ensuring its stability through fixed consumption.

15. Prices in 2003–2004; they have almost doubled today.

16. See Dieterlen and Calame-Griaule for an exhaustive list of grains that Dogon people consume in times of food shortage (Dieterlen & Calame-Griaule 1960, 48). In his thesis, Jolly also lists various wild plants, such as *Crateva Adansonii, Balanites aegyptiaca, Cassia tora,* consumed by Dogon people as food supplements (Jolly 1995, 82).

Glossary of Dogon Terms

adurɔ (*adunɔ*)	the world, the nature.
adurɔ woyoji (*adurɔ wohyi*)	to inhabit or to live in the world (to live in a house).
aɲi: gúyɔ	granary that contains hibiscus harvest (*Hibiscus Sabdariffa*).
Áma (Amma)	the name of God.
áma	shrine or altar generally made of earth; magic to protect properties; mud cone used in building the corners and thus the walls of a granary.
ámiru	head of the village; the oldest man (word of Arab/Fulani origin).
àna	village.
àna dà (*dàrã*)	top of the village.
àna bɛrɛ	broader inside of the village.
àna dóɲu	'bottom' of the village.
àna kɛrigu	outside of the village.
àna kóro	inside of the village; area around the site of the foundation of the village.
àna kɔ̃se	council of elders.
ándãŋa	baobab seed paste used to overcome hunger (term used in the *tɛɲe kan* area).
ándugɔ	cult of rain.
áŋa	mouth.
áŋa diyɛ (*áŋa darã*)	granary's wooden door, generally decorated with carvings.
áŋa dóɲu	bottom door of a male granary, formerly called *dorɛ̃ kã* ('mouth of the penis').
án(r)ã (or *ána*)	rain.
ánrã dí: (*korosolu*)	period of the start of the rainy season.
ánrã gába	heavy rains.
ánrã mà	drought ('dry rain').
ánrã mɔɲu	destructive rain.
ánrã pogu	'to attach the rain', a rite to stop the rain.
ánrã pɔ:lɔ	the first rain after which people start sowing.

ánrã vɛru	light/thin rain.
ára	rice.
atɛmu	the ancestors' law; the Dogon 'tradition.
bà bínu	ancestor of the clan.
ba-do (*korosolu*)	period of transition between hot dry and rainy season; period of the first rains.
bà: iré	ritual leader for the *ɛnɛ girú amá* shrine.
bàga taɲu	upright wooden fork on which rests the eating bowl.
baɲá	carved wooden bowl.
Bella ódiu	trade route through Seno Gondo plain used by the Bellah and Touaregs.
bɛrɛ	stomach or entrails.
bínu kédinɛ	priest responsible for rites in connection to the regeneration of nature.
binugu	manure.
bobo yù	big millet grains.
bóduru	to keep things for oneself.
bɔdɔ	to ferment, to decompose, and therefore 'to bring back to life'. See also *ɔmɔgu*.
bɔjɔ	human excrement.
bɔjɔ boji	toilets in the scree.
bomu	name of the inhabitants of 'the edge of the cliffs', given by the Dogon of the plain.
bo senŋe	form of red gravel used in building and in making 'Dogon cement'.
búgu	gun powder.
búlo (*búlu*)	name of the sowing-feast.
dableni	red juice made with hibiscus flowers (also called *bisap*).
damá	prohibition.
da(m)ba	hoe (the Bambara word *daba* is commonly used).
dará	rooftop.
dɛ̃ dé:lie ji	chatting and resting places for women.
di: yoi	floods.
digɛ paná	supper.
dɔgɔ sɔ	Dogon daily and ritual practices, and therefore usages and customs.
dɔnɔ sɔ	Dogon linguistic area; region located in center of the Bandiagara Plateau.

dɔmbay	the last day of the five-day week; market day.
dono yù	millet growing on harder soils.
doru kā	the little mouth that refers to a lower granary door (in the *tɛɲe kan* area).
dorí	vestibule.
dudum (gɔgow)	dune.
dugɔ	magic, amulets.
dugɔ dugu	witchcraft.
ɛ:	potash from millet straw.
ɛ: já	millet-based meal with potash.
ɛ: tɛguru	pierced clay pot to filter potash.
ɛɲɛgiré (also *yógudiyé*)	rachis of millet spikes.
ɛmmɛ	sorghum (*Sorghum bicolor*).
ɛnɛ girú amá	shrine to protect domestic animals.
fonio	a crop, tiny grains (*Digitaria exilis*), called *pɔ̃*.
gɛ tóni	rain-making ritual based on people's reconciliation.
Gimeto	Tiréli settlement in the plain.
gindɔgɔ táru	roughcasting the outside walls of the house.
gíni (diyɛ), gírun, gínu, denw	house; room (bedroom).
gínna (gínu na)	family house; compound; first house of the lineage.
gínna dagi	'little *gínna*' from which a *gínna* develops.
gínna minɛ	lineage fields.
gínna tomoɲu	cold dry season; the cold that is creeping into the house (term used in the *tɛɲe kan* area).
gínu	compound that stems from the *gínna dagi*, a room.
gínu gonɔ	courtyard.
gínu gonɔ jeɲe	compound's fence.
gínu kòro	house in ruins (the house that no longer exists).
gínu múnɔ (gírum múnɔ)	shrine that protects the village
gínu munú ãɲa	entrance.
gínu tɛru	compound site or the original site built.
gínu woyoji	to inhabit a house.
giyɛ	hunger.

gojú diaramú	name of the ritual 'to sweep bad things' when a woman breaks a pestle while pounding millet.
gono (Guiera senegalensis)	tree to protect the house against thunder.
gòrò (ɔru sɔmo)	the cultivated bush.
góro piru	river.
gujɔ	'room' of a bachelor, from which the young man generally starts to build his compound.
gúnu	sterile women.
gùr	vomit.
gúyɔ ana	millet granary.
gúyɔ bɔlɔ	'under the granary'.
gúyɔ kú: yɔnɔ	head of the granary.
gúyɔ té	granary foundation.
gúyɔ togu	patriarch granary for resting and storing altars and magic.
gúyɔ ya	female granary.
Hogon	highest Dogon spiritual authority.
íbɛ	market.
ídu	fish.
íɛ kɔmɔ	crack, fissure, or hollow used as a cemetery.
igɛ:ru para	'height of a person (standing up)'; a measurement.
ilɛ	pungent smell; also something ripe or cooked.
jà: ɔgu yómu	recycled millet porridge served for breakfast as a quick and light meal.
já:bu	soul of a person who died in particular circumstances.
jába	flattening walls with the palm of the hands.
jinɛ	rainy season or wintering.
jinu (jinagu)	bush spirits (may come from the Arabic term *jinn*).
jo	small parcels of land of poor quality.
jú	(*Ceiba pentandra*); silk cotton tree.
júgu	Dogon week of five days.
ká:lu	the cold dry season.
kãwã	condiment made with fermented hibiscus seeds (*hibiscus sabdariffa*).

kara (*béne*)	granary walls.
káru	granary dividers, internal compartments.
karú	sound produced by clicking fingers on the edge of a pestle handle.
kɛbɛlɛ	fragment of calabash.
(*àna*) *kɛrigu, kɛrgu*	outside of the village; the side of the village.
kínɛ	concealment; to conceal.
kine dɔrɔgɔ	living and active, something vital; breath.
kirɛ	type of wood (*Prosopis Africana*).
kirɛ dungɔ	cultivated bush space in the plain characterised by a *kirɛ* tree.
kòdu pílu	calabash used to collect grains in winnowing.
kòdu sí	calabash used in winnoying.
kɔkɔ	escarpment.
kɔmɔ ódiu	path leading to the cemetery.
kóro	container.
kú: màrun	forming/closing the head of the granary.
kukusum	'erasing traces'; a rite of purification of the land.
kú(y)nà: nà	large wooden mortar.
kú(y)nà: í	'child of the mortar'; a pestle.
lá:ra	village's proximate surroundings, or the 'hip' of the bush.
lɔbɔ (*lɔwɔ*)	mythical ancestor that represents earth and the vegetal world; a chtonian entity responsible for the regeneration of the cultivated land; shrine dedicated to the *lɔbɔ* ancestor and that was established at the foundation of the village.
lɔbɔ dalá	site where *lɔbɔ* ritual paraphernalia is kept.
lɔbɔ minɛ	field of the *lɔbɔ* ancestor; the Hogon's field.
ló:do (*lɔgɔ lòro*)	kneading earth with the hands and the feet.
lɔgo	detritus, waste in general.
lɔgo eju	useful waste.
lɔgɔ mán	frothy mud used for building granaries.
lɔgo mɔniu	waste that cannot be transformed.
lɔgɔ páru	plastering the granary.
lòy	empty water jar; fetal envelope.
mà:	dry.
maniu	saddle-billed Stork (*Ephippiorhynchus senegalensis*).

manù   the plain (Seno Gondo).

manù yù   millet cultivated in the sandy plain.

mɛ kúnu tóroy   clay pot containing the umbilical cord and the pla-
                                centa of a newborn.

mí miɲɛ   a very light rain.

minɛ poroba   collective, or lineage, fields.

minɛ sɔ̃ŋɛ̃   erosion.

mɔɲu ɔ̃ŋɛ̃   the place (cemetery) of the bad soul.

muna ɑ̃ŋa go jin   the exit of the compound.

múnɔ   'scream of the fox'; shrine named after the divina-
                                tory power of the fox.

ɲama (ɲaman,   ambivalent reactive vital force, energy, or fluid in
ɲawan, yawan)   people, animals, and things.

nadulɔ   magic artefacts placed above the door to protect the
                                house.

naɲu   brewing area.

naní: ancestor who transmits his vital force to a newborn,
                                who bears a sign of this transmission on his
                                body.

naun   'struggle', 'misfortune', or difficulty in one's life.

nay bánu   'red sun', 'hot sun'; designates the hot dry season.

nème   dirt.

níŋɛ tóroy   small clay pot to cook sauce.

niɲi goro   open-air kitchen.

niɲu girun   room (house) occupied by an elder.

noɲo   plant bulb (*Urginea altissima Baker*) placed in the
                                foundation of a compound to guarantee the conti-
                                nuity of life of its occupiers.

nɔmmɔ   water spirit.

nùmɔ tà:nu   length of the forearm up to the finger tips.

ódiu dì   'the road of water', a rock (path) where libations to
                                attract good fortune are made.

ɔgɔ   spiritual leader enacting as an environmental officer.

o:ɲɔ̃ bánu   'the big dust wind', a sand storm.

o:ɲɔ̃ gába   strong and frequent winds of the rainy season of the
                                West African monsoon.

o:ɲɔ̃ já:bu   the Harmattan wind.

o:ɲɔ̃ mɔɲu   destructive dust wind occurring at the end of the
                                winter.

o:ɲɔ̃ simu	whirlwind that contains the souls of the dead.
olubɛm	spirits of the bush.
ɔmɔ	state of purity; also means 'living'.
ɔmɔ daga loso	rain of lucky people that falls in some places.
ɔmɔgu:	to decompose; to ro—for example, manured compost or the rotting of wet mud used in building (see also *bɔdɔ*).
ɔmna (sɛ sámu)	fairly clear area of the wild bush, pastureland.
ɔmɔlɔ	magico-religious system characterised by sacrifices.
ómulu	tamarind tree (*Tamarinus indica*).
ɔrɔ	baobab tree (*Adansonia digitata*).
ɔrɔ nĩɲɛ	baobab leaf sauce.
ɔru	bush (general).
ɔru dɔ̃y	(also *lá:ra*) the hip of the bush; fields nearby the village.
ɔru gobi	waist or belt of the cultivated bush.
ɔru kú:	head of the bush.
ɔru mà:	the Sahel, 'the dry bush'.
ɔru múnɔ	shrines protecting the cultivated bush.
paŋà niɲi	vital, physical force (general).
pága sagdá sɔlŋé	Mossi term that refers to the practice of interring the umbilical cord and placenta of a newborn in a corner of the compound.
pàlukile	long wooden spatula.
paná biri	place of the kitchen.
paná káyi	eating places (for men—*an(r)ã paná káyi*; for women and children—*paná káyi ɲaw*).
paná tori	pounding place.
pɛgu	shrines referring to the act of fixing and the continuity of life.
pèlu	type of wood (*Khaya senegalensis*).
pélugó: (pélugú:)	weaving with a calabash held by both hands.
pɔ̃ sɛmi	fonio straw.
púno(ɔgu), (púnu)	millet cream.
ponu	tamkuba tree (*Detarium senegalensis* [*cesalpiniacee*]).
púno	millet flour.
pùnu	menstruation.

pùnulu diju	contamination of culinary materials (effect of menstruation).
pùru	impure, impurity.
sá	African grape tree body oil (*Lannea microcarpa*).
sá toɲɔ̄	small clay pot for women's African grape tree body oil (*Lannea microcarpa*).
sagi	pounded hard envelopes of millet grains.
sagujá (*tô*)	pounded millet-based dish with a sauce generally made of baobob leaves.
saguru	to sieve.
sala (*sara*)	territory.
sãmu	vomit.
saraka	(Fulbe term) 'generous earth'; celebration of the harvests and thus of the feeding earth.
Saye (*Say*)	Tiréli people's family name.
sɛdjɛ yù	millet cultivated at the bottom of and in the scree.
sò mò	forceful waterfall.
sógu múnɔ	shrine that brings, stops, and protects against excessive rains.
sumbala	condiment obtained from the fermentation of African locust bean (*Parkia biglobosa*).
taɲa	'the movement of going beyond' that indicates going to the other side of the river.
táru	roughcasting/plastering walls with wet mud.
tɛɲu: (*tɛraɲu:*)	hibiscus or *aɲu* fields cultivated by old women.
tɛgu	remote area of the plateau where people cultivate onions.
tíbi kú:	the plateau.
tíbu tène	piled-up stones used to build the foundation of a granary.
timu dɔ̄	sacred trees located in the cultivated bush space and in the scree.
tire gínna	group of *gínna* (ancestor house).
tire tɔgú	group of family units (father, wives, and children) with the same ancestor (*tire*).
titɛ̃	name of a water reservoir in the cliffs.
tɔgú	family or compound.
tógu	shelter; a village's district.

tógu na	men's meeting house.
to ɲɔ̃ dàni	place below the cemetery entrance where objects of a deceased person are placed.
tólo	star.
tɔro	inedible pieces of herbs, thorny branches, leaves.
tɔrɔ sɔ	Dogon linguistic area, region of the Bandiagara cliffs.
údiu dé	artefact that protects trees against thieves; also described as an *áma*.
uguru	sacrifice ritual to stimulate growth crop sprouts.
únɔ	ashes.
wagem	ancestors.
wagi minɛ	field of the ancestors.
we ɲɛ̃	type of wood (*Ficus lecardii*).
wa ɲu na lɔgɔ	mud from pounds used for building work.
wanaŋet	'black work', meaning 'hard work'; body dirt.
woru minɛ	fields of medium-quality bordering Tiréli's neighbouring villages.
ya pilú	avenging souls of women who died in pregnancy or while giving birth.
ya yɛrɛ	ritual to make rain, by women.
yàlu úlo	the Milky Way.
yèbɛnɛ (yéban, yenew)	chtonic spirits.
yòdiu	plant that marks the fields' boundaries.
yógo (sé)	millet chaff.
yógo di(y)é (yógudiyé, yógo tí:, yógo tíé:)	remains from pounded millet spikes.
yóro (yólo)	millet bran.
yù:	millet spike (*Pennisetum spicatum*).
yù: ana (yù: èju)	spikes with itchy hairs, the best quality.
yù: bé:lu	millet straws.
yù: bòtun	roots of millet straws.
yù: buburu	mature grains.
yù: denwɛ	the 'millet house' used as storage instead of a granary.

yù: doɲo	poundings millet ears.
yù:dæ̃	low-quality millet.
yù: ɛɲɛ bojó	greenish spikes found among other millet plants.
yù: i	millet grain.
yù: keru	millet straw.
yù: ku	millet spike.
yù: kurɔ	millet leaves.
yù: nà í: (*yù: naw*)	grinding stone.
yù: pèdu	shelling grains through pounding.
yù: toru (*tólu*)	to pound hard millet envelopes (*sagi*).
yù: wɛyi	wind winnowing with two calabashes.
yugurú búmo	sand divinations.
yù:sa gúyɔ	female granary (*gúyɔ ya*) used by men.

References

Abramson, A., & Holbraad, M. 2012. Contemporary cosmologies, critical reimaginings. *Religion and Society: Advances in Research* 3(1), pp. 35–50.

Antongini, G., & Spini, T. 1997. Earth shrine: Lobi. In P. Oliver, ed., *Encyclopaedia of Vernacular Architecture of the World I*. New York: Cambridge University Press, pp. 755–56.

Apter, A. 2005. Griaule's legacy: Rethinking 'la parole claire' in Dogon studies. *Cahiers d'Etudes Africaines* 177(1), pp. 95–129.

Arnaud, R. 1921. Notes sur les Montagnards Habé des cercles de Bandiagara et de Hombori. *Revue d'Ethnologie et des Traditions Populaires* 2, pp. 241–314.

Balandier, G. 1988. *Le désordre: Eloge du mouvement*. Paris: Fayard.

———. 1992. *Le pouvoir sur scènes*. Paris: Balland.

Barth, F. 1987. *Cosmologies in the Making: A Generative Approach to Cultural Variation in Inner New Guinea*. Cambridge, NY: Cambridge University Press.

———. 2002. Sidney W. Mintz lecture for 2000: An anthropology of knowledge. *Current Anthropology* 43(1), pp.1–18.

Bayart, J.-F. 2005. *The Illusion of Cultural Identity*. London: Hurst & Company.

Bedaux, R. M. A. 1972. Tellem, reconnaissance archéologique d'une culture de l'Ouest africain au Moyen-Âge: Recherches architectoniques. *Journal de la Société des Africanistes* 42, pp. 103–85.

———. 1988. Tellem and Dogon Material Culture. *African Arts* 21(4), pp. 38–45.

Bedaux, R. M. A., & Lange, A. G. 1983. Tellem, reconnaissance archéologique d'une culture de l'ouest africain au Moyen-Âge: la poterie. *Journal de la Société des Africanistes* 53(5), pp. 5–59.

Bedaux, R. M. A., & van der Waals, J. D. (eds.) 2004. *Regards sur les Dogon du Mali*. Gent: Snoeck, pp. 7–13.

Berthoz, A. 1997. *Le Sens du movement*. Paris: Odile Jacob.

Berthoz, A., & Petit, J.-L. (eds.) 2006. *Phénoménologie et physiologie de l'action*. Paris: Odile Jacob.

Bilot, A., Bohbot, M., Calame-Griaule, G., & N'Diaye, F. 2003. *Serrures du pays dogon*. Paris: Editions Adam Biro.

Blench, R., & Mallam, D. 2005. *A Survey of Dogon Languages in Mali: Overview*. OGMIOS: Newsletter of Foundation for Endangered Languages 3.02(26), pp. 14–15.

Blier, S. The role of earth shrines in the socio-symbolic construction of the Dogon territory: Toward a philosophy of containment. *Anthropology & Medicine* 18(2), pp. 167–79.

———. 1987. *The Anatomy of Architecture: Ontology and Metaphor in Batammaliba Architectural Expression.* New York: Cambridge University Press.

Borges, J. L. 2004. *The Aleph and Other Stories.* London: Penguin Books.

Bouju, J. 1984. *Graine de l'homme, enfant du mil.* Paris: Société d'ethnographie; Nanterre: Service de publication du Laboratoire d'ethnologie et de sociologie comparative, Université de Paris X.

———. 1995a. Fondation et territorialité: instauration et controle rituel des frontières (Dogon Karambe, Mali). In J.-F. Vincent, D. Dory, & R. Verdier, eds., *La Construction religieuse du territoire.* Paris: L'Harmattan, pp. 352–65.

———. 1995b. Qu'est-ce que l'ethnie dogon? *Cahiers des Sciences Humaines* 31(2), pp. 329–63.

———. 1995c. Tradition et identité: la tradition dogon entre traditionnalisme rural et néo-traditionnalisme urbain. *Enquête* 2, pp. 95–117.

———. 2003. La culture dogon: de l'ethnologie coloniale à l'anthropologie réciproque contemporaine. *Clio en Afrique* 10, http://www.up.univ-mrs.fr/wclio-af/d_fichiers10/ sommaire.html, accessed May 16, 2005.

Bouju, J., & Ouattara, F. 2002. *Une anthropologie politique de la fange: conceptions culturelles, pratiques sociales et enjeux institutionnels de la propreté urbaine à Ouagadougou et Bobo-Dioulasso.* Rapport final. SHADYC-Marseille/GRIL-Ouagadougou, http://www.pseau.org/epa/gdda/Actions/Action_A04/Rap_final_A04.pdf, accessed January 26, 2006.

Bouju, J., Tinta, S., & Poudiougo, 1998. Approche anthropologique des stratégies d'acteurs et des jeux de pouvoirs locaux autour du service de l'eau: Bandiagara, Koro et Mopti (Mali); Ministère de la Coopération Projet PS/Eau FAC-IG n° 94017700.

Bourdier, J.-P. 1997. Dogon: Bandiagara. In P. Oliver, ed., *Encyclopaedia of Vernacular Architecture of the World II.* New York: Cambridge University Press, pp. 2123–24.

Bourdieu, P. 1977. *Outline of a Theory of Practice.* New York: Cambridge University Press.

———. 1990. *The Logic of Practice.* Redwood City, CA: Stanford University Press.

———. 1993. *The Field of Cultural Production: Essays on Art and Literature.* Cambridge: Polity Press.

Brasseur, G. 1960. Une maison dogon de la région de Bandiagara. *Notes Africaines* 86, pp. 48–52.

———. 1968. *Les Etablissements humains au Mali.* Tome I & II. Dakar: IFAN.

Bril, B., & Roux, V. 2002. Regards croisses sur le geste technique. *Revue d'Anthropologie des Connaissances* 14(2), pp. 7–28.

Calame-Griaule, G. 1954. Notes sur l'habitation du plateau central Nigérien. *Bulletin de l'IFAN* B 17, pp. 477–99.

———. 1955. *Bulletin de l'IFAN* 17 B, pp. 3–4.

———. 1968. *Dictionnaire Dogon: dialect Toro So.* Paris: Librairie C. Klincksieck.

———. 1996. Valeurs symboliques de l'alimentation chez les Dogon. *Journal des Africanistes* 66(1–2), pp. 81–104.

Cartry M. 1987. Le suaire du chef. In M. Cartry, ed., *Sous le masque de l'animal: Essais sur le sacrifice en Afrique noire.* Paris: PUF, pp. 131–231.

Cazes, M. L. (ed.) 1993. *Les Dogon de Boni: approche démo-génétique d'un isolat du Mali.* Paris: Presses Universitaires de France.

Ciarcia, G. 2003. *De la mémoire ethnographique: l'exotisme du pays Dogon,* Paris: EHESS, collection «Cahiers de l'Homme».

Cissé, L. 2003. La préservation d'un site du patrimoine mondial. In R. M. A. Bedaux & D. van der Waals, eds., *Regards sur les Dogon du Mali.* Gent: Snoeck, pp. 207–12.

Cissé, O. 2007. *L'argent des dechets: l'economie informelle a Dakar.* Paris: Karthala-Crepos.

Cissoko, S. M. 1985. Les Songhay du XIIe au XVIe siècle. In D. T. Niane, ed., *Histoire générale de l'Afrique: L'Afrique du XII au XVIe siècle, tome IV.* Paris: UNESCO, pp. 213–40.

Clifford, J. 1988. *The Predicament of Culture: Twentieth-Century Ethnography, Literature, and Art.* Cambridge, MA: Harvard University Press.

Colson, E. 1997. Places of power and shrines of the land. *Paideuma* 43, pp. 47–57.

Coppo, P. 1998. *Les Guérisseurs de la Folie: Histoires du Plateau Dogon.* Paris: Les Empecheurs de penser en rond.

Coupaye, L. 2009. Ways of enchanting: *Chaînes Opératoires* and yam cultivation in Nyamikum Village, Maprik, Papua New Guinea. *Journal of Material Culture* 14(4), pp. 433–58.

Coupaye, L., & Douny, L. 2009. Dans la trajectoire des choses. *Techniques & Culture* 52–53, pp. 12–39.

———. 2010. Within the trajectory of things: Editorial. *Techniques & Culture* 52–53, pp. 12–13.

Courtright, P. 1987. Shrines. In M. Eliade, ed., *The Encyclopedia of Religion,* London: Macmillan, pp. 299–302.

Croll, E., & Parkin, D. (eds.) 1992. *Bush Base: Forest Farm—Culture, Environment and Development.* London: Routledge.

Cunningham, J. J. 2009. Pots and political economy: Enamel-wealth, gender, and patriarchy in Mali. *JRAI* 15(2), pp. 276–94.

Dawson, A. (ed.) 2009. *Shrines in Africa: History, Politics and Society.* Calgary: University of Calgary Press.

de Bruijn, M. E., van Beek, W. E. A., & van Dijk, J. W. M. 2005. Antagonisme et solidarité: les relations entre Peuls et Dogons du Mali central. In M. E. de Bruijn & J. W. M. van Dijk, eds., *Peuls et Mandingues: dialectique des constructions identitaires.* Paris: Karthala, Afrika-Studiecentrum, pp. 243–65.

de Ganay, S. 1937. Notes sur le culte du lébé chez les dogon du soudan français. *Journal de la Société des Africanistes* 7, pp. 203–11.

———. 1949. Notes sur la théodicée Bambara. *Revue de l'Histoire des Religions* 135(2–3), pp. 187–213.

———. 1951. Une graphie soudanaise du doight du createur. *Revue de l'Histoire des Religions* 139(1), pp. 45–49.

———. 1995. *Le Sanctuaire Kama Blon de Kangaba: histoire, myths, peintures pariétales et cérémonies septennales.* Ivry: Nouvelles du Sud.

Descola, P. 2005. *Par-delà nature et culture.* Paris: Gallimard.

Desplagnes, L. 1907. *Le Plateau Central Nigérien: une mission archéologique et ethnographique au Soudan Français*. Paris: Larose.

de Surgy A. 1994. *Nature et fonction des fétiches en Afrique noire: Le cas du Sud-Togo*. Paris L'Harmattan.

Dieterlen, G. 1941. *Les Ames des Dogon*. Paris: Institut d'Ethnologie.

———. 1947. Mécanisme de l'impureté chez les Dogon. *Journal de la Société des Africanistes* 17, pp. 81–90.

———. 1957. The Mande Creation Myth. *Africa: Journal of the International African Institute* 27(2), pp. 124–38.

———. 1959. Mythe et organisation sociale au Soudan français. *Journal de la Société des Africanistes* 25, pp. 39–76.

———. 1982. *Le titre d'honneur des Arou (Dogon, Mali)*. Paris: Mémoire de la Société des Africanistes.

Dieterlen, G., & Calame-Griaule, G. 1960. L'alimentation dogon. *Cahiers d'Etudes Africaines* 3, pp. 46–89.

Dieterlen, G., & de Ganay, S. 1942. *Le Génie des eaux chez les Dogons*. Miscellanea Africana Lebaudy (Cahier no. 5): Paris.

Dolo, S. O. 2001. *La mère des masques*. Paris: Le Seuil.

Doquet, A. 1999. *Les masques Dogon: ethnologie savante, ethnologie autochtone*. Paris: Karthala.

———. 2002. Se montrer dogon: Les mises en scène de l'identité ethnique. *Ethnologies Comparées* 5, http://alor.univ-montp3.fr/cerce/r5/g.c.htm, accessed May 15, 2005.

Douglas, M. 1966. *Purity and Danger: An Analysis of the Concepts of Pollution and Taboo*. London: Routledge & Kegan Paul.

———. 1967. If the Dogon . . . *Cahiers d'Études Africaines* 28, pp. 659–72.

———. 1972. Deciphering a meal. *Daedalus* 101(1), pp. 61–81.

———. 2003. *Natural Symbols: Explorations in Cosmology*. London: Routledge.

Dougnon, I. 2007. *Travail de blanc, travail de noir: la migration des paysans dogons vers l'Office du Niger et au Ghana (1910–1980)*. Paris: Karthala.

Douny, L. 2007a. *A Praxeological Approach to Dogon Material Culture*. Ph.D. dissertation. UCL: University of London.

———. 2007b. The materiality of domestic waste: The recycled cosmology of the Dogon of Mali. *Journal of Material Culture* 12(3), pp. 309–33.

———. 2011. The role of earth shrines in the socio-symbolic construction of the Dogon territory: Toward a philosophy of containment. *Anthropology & Medicine* 18(2), pp. 167–79.

——— 2014. Wild silk textiles of dogon people of Mali: Wrapping and unwrapping material identities. In S. Harris & L. Douny, eds., *Wrapping and Unwrapping Material Culture: Archaeological and Anthropological Approaches*. Walnut Creek, CA: Left Coast Press.

Douyon, D. 2010. *Parlons Dogon: langues et culture Toroso d'Ireli (Mali)*. Paris: L'Harmattan.

Drackner, M. 2005. What is waste? To whom? An anthropological perspective on garbage. *Waste Management & Research* 23(3), pp. 175–81.

Ermert, E. 2003. Le Musée communautaire de Nombori: une nouvelle stratégie pour la conservation locale de la culture. In R. M. A. Bedaux & D. van der Waals, eds., *Regards sur les Dogon du Mali*. Gent: Snoeck, p. 213.

Espinas A. 1897. *Les origines de la technologie.* Paris: F. Alcan.

Forde, D. C. 1954. Introduction. In D. C. Forde, ed., *African Worlds: Studies in Cosmological Ideas and Social Values of African Peoples.* London: Published for the International African Institute by the Oxford University Press, pp. vii–viii.

Gado, B. A. 1993. *Une histoire des famines au Sahel: étude des grandes crises alimentaires, XIXe–XXe siècles.* Paris: L'Harmattan.

Gallais, J. 1967. *Le Delta intérieur du Niger: étude de géographie régionale,* Vol. 1. Dakar: IFAN.

———. 1975. *Pasteurs et paysans du Gourma.* Paris: CNRS.

Geertz, C. 1973. *The Interpretation of Cultures: Selected Essays.* New York: Basic Books.

Gibson, J. 1979. *The Ecological Approach to Visual Perception.* Boston: Houghton Mifflin.

Giddens, A. 1984. *The Constitution of Society: Outline of the Theory of Structuration.* Cambridge: Polity Press.

———. 1991. *Modernity and Self-Identity: Self and Society in the Late Modern Age.* Cambridge: Polity Press.

Gonzalez, P. 2001. Desertification and a shift of forest species in the West African Sahel. *Climate Research* 17, pp. 217–28.

Goody, J. 1971. The impact of Islamic writing on the oral cultures of West Africa. *Cahiers d'Études Africaines* 11(43), pp. 455–66.

Gosselain, O. 2000. Materializing identities: An African perspective. *Journal of Archaeological Method and Theory* 7(3), pp. 187–217.

Gosselain, O., Zeebroek, R., & Decroly, J.-M. 2008/2009. Les tribulations d'une casserole chinoise au Niger. *Techniques & Culture* 51, pp. 18–89.

Graves-Brown, P. M. (ed.) 2000. *Matter, Materiality and Modern Culture.* London: Routledge.

Griaule, M. 1948. L'arche du monde chez les populations nigériennes. *Journal de la Société des Africanistes* 18, pp. 117–28.

———. 1949. L'image du monde au Soudan. *Journal de la Société des Africanistes* 19, pp. 81–88.

———. 1952. Le savoir des Dogon. *Journal de la Société des Africanistes* 22, pp. 27–42.

———. 1966. *Dieu d'eau: entretiens avec Ogotemmêli.* Paris: Fayard.

———. 1994. *Masques Dogons.* Paris: Institut d'Ethnologie.

Griaule, M., & Dieterlen, G. 1951. *Signes graphiques soudanais.* Paris: Hermann.

———. 1954. The Dogon. In D. Forde, ed., *African Worlds.* Oxford: Oxford University Press, pp. 83–110.

———. 1965. *Le Renard pâle.* Paris: Institut d'Ethnologie.

Guindo, I., & Kansaye, H. 2000. *Nous les Dogons.* Bamako: Le Figuier.

Haudricourt, A. G. 1968. *La Technologie, science humaine: recherches d'histoire et d'ethnologie des techniques.* Paris: Éditions de la Maison des Sciences de l'Homme.

Hawkins, G. 2005. *The Ethics of Waste: How We Relate to Rubbish.* Lanham, MD: Rowman & Littlefield Publishers.

Hawkins, G., & Muecke S. (eds.) 2003. *Culture and Waste: The Creation and Destruction of Value.* Lanham, MD: Rowman & Littlefield.

Heidegger, M. 1971. *Poetry, Language, Thought.* Translations and introduction by Albert Hofstadter. London: Harper and Row.

Hochstetler, J. L., Durieux, J. A., & Durieux-Boon, E. I. K. 2004. *Sociolinguistic Survey of the Dogon Language Area.* SIL International, http://www.sil.org/silesr/2004/silesr2004-004.pdf, accessed March 15, 2006.

Holder, G. 2001. *Poussière, ô poussière!: la cité-état sama du pays dogon, Mali.* Nanterre: Société d'Ethnologie.

Huet, J.-C. 1994. *Villages perchés des Dogon du Mali.* Paris: L'Harmattan.

Ingold, T. 2000. *The Perception of the Environment: Essays on Livelihood, Dwelling and Skill.* London: Routledge.

———. 2004. Culture on the ground: The world perceived through the feet. *Journal of Material Culture* 9(3), pp. 315–40.

———. 2005. The eye of the storm: Visual perception and the weather. *Visual Studies* 20(2), pp. 97–104.

———. 2007. Earth, sky, wind and weather. *JRAI (N.S.)* 13(1), pp. 19–38.

———. 2010. Footprints through the weather-world: Walking, breathing, knowing. *JRAI (N.S.)* 16(1), pp. 121–39.

———. 2012. Toward an ecology of materials. *Annual Review of Anthropology* 41, pp. 427–42.

Insoll, T. 2007. 'Natural' or 'human' spaces? Tallensi sacred groves and shrines and their potential implications for aspects of northern European prehistory and phenomenological interpretation. *Norwegian Archaeological Review* 40(2), pp. 138–58.

Iroko, A. F. 1996. *L'Homme et les Termitieres en Afrique.* Paris: Karthala.

Izard, M. 1985a. *Le Yatenga précolonial: un ancien royaume du Burkina.* Paris: Karthala.

———. 1985b. *Gens du pouvoir, gens de la terre: les institutions politiques de l'ancien royaume du Yatenga (Bassin de la Volta Blanche).* Cambridge, NY: Cambridge University Press.

Jackson, M. 1995. *At Home in the World.* Durham, NC: Duke University Press.

———. 1996. Introduction: Phenomenology, radical empiricism, and anthropological critique. In M. Jackson, *Things as They Are: New Directions in Phenomenological Anthropology.* Bloomington: Indiana University Press, pp. 1–50.

Johnson, M. 1994. Ordering houses, creating narratives. In M. P. Pearson & C. Richards, eds., *Architecture and Order: Approaches to Social Space.* London: Routledge, pp. 170–77.

Jolly, E. 1995. *La bière de mil dans la société Dogon.* Thèse de doctorat, Université de Paris X-Nanterre.

———. 2001. Marcel Griaule, ethnologue: la construction d'une discipline (1925–1956). *Journal des Africanistes* 71(1), pp. 149–90.

———. 2004. *Boire avec esprit: bière de mil et société Dogon.* Nanterre: Société d'Ethnologie.

Jousse, M. 1974. *L'Anthropologie du Geste.* Paris: Gallimard.

Julien, M.-P. et al. 2006. Le corps: matière à decrier. *Corps* 1(1), pp. 45–52.

Julien, M.-P., & Rosselin, C. (eds.) 2009. *Le Sujet tout contre les objets . . . tout contre.* Ethnographies des cultures matérielles. Paris: CTSH.

Julien, M.-P. & Warnier, J.-P. (eds.) 1999. *Approches de la culture matérielle: corps à corps avec l'objet.* Paris: L'Harmattan.

Julliard, A. 2000. Quand dieu souffle: vent, respiration et notion de personne chez les Diola-Adiamat (Guinée-Bissau). *Archives de Sciences Sociales des Religions* 111, pp. 7–24.

Kawada, J. 1991. Notes on 'the techniques of the body' among West African peoples. *Journal of the Anthropological Society of Nippon* 99(3), pp. 377–91.

Kearney, M. 1975. World view theory and study. *Annual Review of Anthropology* 4, pp. 247–70.

———. 1984. *World View.* Novato, CA: Chandler & Sharp.

Knappett, C. 2012. Materiality. In I. Hodder, ed., *Archaeological Theory Today*, 2nd ed. Cambridge: Polity Press, pp. 188–207.

Kuba, R. 2000. Marking boundaries and identities: The precolonial expansion of segmentary societies in southwestern Burkina Faso. *Berichte des Sonderforschungsbereichs* 268(14), pp. 415–25.

Lakoff, G., & Johnson, M. 1980. *Metaphors We Live By.* Chicago: University of Chicago Press.

———. 1999. *Philosophy in the Flesh: The Embodied Mind and Its Challenge to Western Thought.* New York: Basic Books.

Lane, P. 1986. *Settlement as History: A Study of Space and Time among the Dogon of Mali.* Unpublished Ph.D. thesis, University of Cambridge.

———. 1987. Reordering Residues of the Past. In I. Hodder, ed., *Archaeology as Long-Term History.* New York: Cambridge University Press, pp. 54–63.

———. 1988. Tourism and social change among the Dogon. *African Arts* 21(4), pp. 66–69, 92.

———. 1994. The temporal structuring of settlement space among the Dogon of Mali: An ethnoarchaeological study. In M. Parker Pearson & C. Richards, eds., *Architecture and Order: Approaches to Social Space.* London: Routledge, pp. 196–216.

———. 1997. Dogon: Anthropomorphic symbolism. In P. Oliver, ed., *Encyclopaedia of Vernacular Architecture of the World I.* New York: Cambridge University Press, pp. 2124–25.

———. 2003. Banani Kokoro: habitat, architecture et organisation sociale. In R. M. A. Bedaux & D. van der Waals, eds., *Regards sur les Dogon du Mali.* Gent: Snoeck, pp. 75–82.

———. 2006. Household assemblages, lifecycles and the remembrance of things of the past among the Dogon of Mali. *South African Archaeological Bulletin* 61(183), pp. 40–56.

Lane, P., & Bedaux, R. 2003. L'Attitude des Dogon vis-à-vis des déchets. In R. M. A. Bedaux & D. van der Waals, eds., *Regards sur les Dogon du Mali.* Gent: Snoeck, pp. 83–92.

Lauber, W. (ed.) 1998. *L'Architecture Dogon: constructions en terre au Mali.* Paris: Adam Biro.

Lebeuf, J.-P. 1961. *L'habitation des Fali Montagnards du Cameroun Septentrional.* Paris: Hachette.

Lemonnier, P. 1976. La Description des chaines opératoires: contribution a l'analyse des systèmes techniques. *Techniques et Culture* 1, pp. 100–51.

———. 1992. *Elements for an Anthropology of Technology.* Ann Arbor: Museum of Anthropology, University of Michigan.

————. 1993. Introduction. In P. Lemonnier, ed., *Technical Choices: Transformations in Material Cultures since the Neolithic*. London: Routledge, pp. 1–36.

Lentz, C. 2009. Constructing ritual protection on an expanding settlement frontier: Earth shrines in the black Volta region. In A. C. Dawson, ed., *Shrines in Africa: History, Politics and Society*. Calgary: University of Calgary Press, pp. 121–52.

Lettens, D. 1971. *Mystagogie et mystification: évaluation de l'oeuvre de Marcel Griaule*. Bujumbura/Burundi: Presses Lavigerie.

Leroi-Gourhan, A. 1943. *Evolution et techniques: l'homme et la matière*. Paris: Albin Michel.

————. 1945. *Evolution et techniques: milieu et techniques*. Paris: Albin Michel.

Liberski-Bagnoud, D. 2002. *Les Dieux du territoire: penser autrement la genealogie*. Paris: CNRS Edition/Editions de la Maison des Sciences de l'Homme.

Lifszyc, D., & Paulme, D. 1936. Les Fêtes des semailles en 1935 chez les Dogon de Sanga. *Journal de la Société des Africanistes* 6(1), pp. 95–111.

MacEachern, A. S. 1994. 'Symbolic reservoirs' inter-group relations: West African examples. *The African Archaeological Review* 12, pp. 205–24.

Marchand, T. H. J. 2009. *The Masons of Djenne*. Bloomington: Indiana University Press.

Martinelli, B. 1995. Trames d'appartenance et chaînes d' identité: entre Dogons et Moose dans le Yatenga et la plaine du Seno (Burkina Faso et Mali). *Cahiers des Sciences Humaines* (Paris) 31/2, pp. 365–405.

Masquelier, A. 1994. Lightning, death, and the avenging spirits: 'Bori' values in a Muslim world. *Journal of Religion in Africa* 24(1), pp. 2–51.

Mather, C. 2003. Shrines and the domestication of the landscape. *Journal of Anthropological Research* 59(1), pp. 23–45.

Mauss, M. 1936. Les Techniques du corps. *Journal de Psychologie* 22, pp. 363–86.

————. 1974 [1939]. Conceptions qui ont précédé la notion de matière, exposé présenté a la Onzième Semaine Internationale de Synthèse (1939). Oeuvres 2. Représentations collectives et diversité des civilisations. Paris: Editions de Minuit, pp. 161–68.

Mayor, A. 2011. *Traditions céramiques dans la boucle du Niger: ethnoarchéologie et histoire du peuplement au temps des empires précoloniaux*. Frankfurt am Main: Africa Magna Verlag.

Mayor, A., Huysecom, E., Gallay, A., Rasse, M., & Ballouche, A. 2005. Populations dynamics and paleoclimate over the past 3000 years in the Dogon Country, Mali. *Journal of Anthropological Archaeology* 24, pp. 25–61.

McIntosh, R. J. 1989. Middle Niger terracottas before the Symplegades Gateway. *African Arts* 22(2), pp. 74–83, 103–04.

————. 2000. Social memory in Mande. In R. J. McIntosh, J. A. Tainter, & S. Keech McIntosh, eds., *The Way the Wind Blows: Climate Change, History, and Human Action*. New York: Columbia University Press, pp. 141–80.

McIntosh, R. J., Tainter, J. A., & Keech McIntosh, S. (eds.) 2000. Climate, history, and human action. In R. J. McIntosh, J. A. Tainter, & S. Keech McIntosh, eds., *The Way the Wind Blows: Climate Change, History, and Human Action*. New York: Columbia University Press, pp. 1–42.

Merleau-Ponty, M. 1962. *Phenomenology of Perception*. London: Routledge & Kegan Paul.

Meskell, L. (ed.) 2005. *Archaeologies of Materiality*. Malden, MA: Blackwell.

Miller, D. (ed.) 2005. *Materiality*. Durham, NC: Duke University Press.

Naji, M., & Douny, L. 2009. Editorial. *Journal of Material Culture* 14, pp. 411–32.

N'Diaye, F. 1970. Contribution a l'étude de l'architecture du pays dogon. *Objets et Mondes* 12(3), pp. 269–86.

Nelson, R. K. 1983. *Make Prayers to the Raven: A Koyukon View of the Northern Forest*. Chicago: Chicago University Press.

Nooter, M. H. (ed.) 1993. The Visual Language of Secrecy. In M. H. Nooter, ed., *Secrecy: African Art That Conceals and Reveals*. New York: Museum for African Art, pp. 138–46.

Norberg-Shulz, C. 1985. *The Concept of Dwelling: On the Way to Figurative Architecture*. New York: Rizzoli.

Norris, L. 2010. *Recycling Indian Clothing: Global Contexts of Reuse and Value*. Bloomington: Indiana University Press.

Nouaceur, Z. 2004. Brume sèche, brume de poussière, chasse-sable et tempête de sable. *Norois* 191, pp. 121–28.

Palau-Marti, M. 1957. *Les Dogon*. Paris: Presses Universitaires de France.

Parlebas, P. 1981. *Lexique commenté en sciences de l'action motrice*. Paris: INSEP.

———. 1999. *Jeux, sports et sociétés: lexique de praxéologie motrice*. Paris: INSEP.

Parkin, D. 2007. Wafting on the wind: Smell and the cycle of spirit and matter. *JRAI (N.S.)* 13(1), pp. 39–53.

Paulme, D. 1937. La Divination par les chacals chez les Dogon de Sangha. *Journal de la Société des Africanistes* 7, pp. 1–13.

———. 1940. Sur quelques rites de purification des Dogon (Soudan français). *Journal de la Société des Africanistes* 10, pp. 65–78.

———. 1988. *Organisation sociale des Dogon*. Paris: J.-M. Place.

Pecquet, L. 2004. The mason and banco, or raw material as a power for building a Lyela home (Burkina Faso). *Paideuma* 50, pp. 151–71.

Petit, V. 1995. Les Ana Yana, ceux qui partent au loin, migrations internationales des Dogon (Mali). *Revue Européenne des Migrations Internationales* 10(3), pp. 27–48.

———. 1998. *Migrations et société Dogon*. Paris: L'Harmattan.

Prussin, L. 1982. West African earthworks. *Art Journal* 42(3), pp. 204–09.

———. 1999. Non-Western sacred sites: African models. *The Journal of the Society of Architectural Historians* 58(3), pp. 424–33.

Rasmussen, S. 1999. Making better 'scents' in anthropology: Aroma in Tuareg socio-cultural systems and the shaping of ethnography. *Anthropological Quarterly* 72(2), 55–73.

Rathje, W., & Murphy, C. 1992. *Rubbish! The Archaeology of Garbage*. New York: HarperCollins Publishers.

Richards, P. 2003. *Imina sana: masque à la mode: A study of Dogon Masquerade at the Turn of the Millennium*. Ph.D. dissertation, SOAS: University of London.

Rouch, J., & Rosfelder, R. 1950. *Cimetières dans la falaise*. CNRSAV, Paris.

Rowlands, M. 1985. Notes on the material symbolism of Grassfields palaces. *Paideuma* 31, pp. 103–213.

———. 2003. The unity of Africa. In D. O'Connor & R. Reid, eds., *Ancient Egypt in Africa*. London: UCL Press, pp. 55–77.

Rowlands M., Warnier J.-P. 1996. Magical iron technology in the Cameroon grass-fields. In M.-J. Arnoldi, C. Geary, & K. Hardin, eds., *African Material Culture*. Bloomington: Indiana University Press, pp. 51–72.

Sangaré et al. 2002. Effect of type and level of roughage offered to sheep and urine addition on compost quality and millet growth and production in the Sahel. *Nutrient Cycling in Agroecosystems* 62, pp. 203–08.

Sartre, J.-P. 1958. *Being and Nothingness: An Essay on Phenomenological Ontology*. London: Routledge.

Schijns, W. 2009. *L'Architecture vernaculaire des Dogon du Mali: l'évolution typologique et l'avenir d'un patrimoine mondiale*. Amsterdam: Gopher.

Schlanger, N. 1991. Le fait technique total: la raison pratique et les raisons de la pratique dans l'œuvre de Marcel Mauss. *Terrain* 16, pp. 114–30.

———. 2011. *Marcel Mauss: Techniques, Technologie et Civilisation*. Paris: PUF, pp. 74–78.

Schutz, A. 1967. *The Phenomenology of the Social World*. Evanston, IL: Northwestern University Press.

Sigaut, F. 2002 [1994]. Technology. In T. Ingold, ed., *Companion Encyclopedia of Anthropology*. London: Routledge, pp. 420–59.

Sillar, B. 2009. La saisonnalité des techniques: Saisonnalité et spécialisation artisanale dans les Andes. *Techniques & Culture* 52/53, pp. 90–119.

———. 2010. La Saisonnalité des techniques. *Techniques & Culture* (52–53), pp. 90–119.

Sofaer, S. 2007. *Material Identities*. Malden, MA: Blackwell.

Spini, T., & Spini, S. 1976. *Togu Na*. New York: Rizzoli International Publications.

Steinkraus, K. H. (ed.) 1996. *Handbook of Indigenous Fermented Foods*, 2nd ed. rev. and expanded. New York: Marcel Dekker.

Sterner J. A. 1992. Sacred pots and 'symbolic reservoirs' in the Mandara Highlands of Northern Cameroon. In J. A. Sterner, N. David, eds., *An African Commitment: Papers in Honour of Peter Lewis Shinnie*. Calgary: University of Calgary Press, pp. 172–79.

Strasser, S. 1999. *Waste and Want*. New York: Metropolitan Books, Henry Holt and Company.

Teme, A. 1997. *Paganisme et logique et logique du pouvoir dans le Toro, en pays dogon*. Paris: ANRT.

———. 2002. Omolo, la religion dogon. In M. Konaté & M. Lebris, *Les Mondes dogon* (Abbaye de Doualas), pp. 44–61.

Temple, R. K. G. 1976. *The Sirius Mystery*. London: Sidgwick & Jackson.

Thibaud, B. 2005. Enjeux spatiaux entre Peuls et Dogon dans le Mondoro (Mali). *Science et Changements Planetaires/Secheresse* 16(3), pp. 165–74.

Thompson, M. 1979. *Rubbish Theory: The Creation and Destruction of Value*. Oxford: Oxford University Press.

Tilley, C. 1994. *A Phenomenology of Landscape: Places, Paths and Monuments*. Oxford: Berg.

———. 1999. *Metaphor and Material Culture*. Oxford: Blackwell.

———. 2004. *The Materiality of Stone*. Oxford: Berg.

van Beek, W. E. A. 1991. Dogon restudied: A field evaluation of the work of Marcel Griaule. *Current Anthropology* 32(2), pp. 139–67.

———. 1992. Becoming human in Dogon, Mali. In G. Aijmer, ed., *Coming into existence: Birth and metaphors of birth*. Göteborg: IASSA, pp. 47–70.

———. 1993. Processes and limitations of Dogon agricultural knowledge. In M. Hobart, ed., *An Anthropological Critique of Development: The Growth of Ignorance*. London: Routledge, pp. 43–60.

———. 2003a. African tourist encounters: Effects of tourism in two West African societies. *Africa* 73(2), pp. 251–89.

———. 2003b. La Vie et l'au-dela: organisation sociale des Dogon. In R. M. A. Bedaux & D. van der Waals, eds., *Regards sur les Dogon du Mali*. Ghent: Snoeck, pp. 93–103.

———. 2004. Haunting Griaule: Experiences from the restudy of the Dogon. *History in Africa* 31, pp. 43–68.

———. 2005a. The Dogon heartland: Rural transformations on the Bandiagara escarpment. In de Bruijn et al., eds., *Sahelian Pathways: Climate and Society in Central and South Mali*, research report 78. Leiden: African Studies Centre, pp. 40–70.

———. 2005b. Walking wallets? Tourists at the Dogon falaise. In S. Wooten, ed., *Wari Matters: Ethnographic Explorations of Money in the Mande World*. Münster: LIT Verlag, pp. 191–216.

van Beek, W. E. A., & Banga, P. M. 1992. The Dogon and their trees. In E. Croll & D. Parkin, *Bush Base: Forest Farm—Culture, Environment and Development*. London: Routledge, pp. 57–75.

van Binsbergen, W. 1981. *Religious Change in Zambia: Exploratory Studies*. London: Kegan Paul.

Vincent J.-F., Dory, D., & Verdier, R. (eds.) 1995. *La Construction religieuse du territoire*. Paris: L'Harmattan.

von Mises, L. 1949. *Human Action: A Treatise of Economics*. London: Hodge.

Walther, O. 2001. *Stratégies et dynamiques spatiales du tourisme chez les Dogon du Mali: mémoire de licence*. Université de Lausanne: Institut de Géographie.

———. 2006. *Le Développement du tourisme dans les Monts Hombori (Mali)*. Rapport de mission rédigé pour le Projet Hombori, Université de Neuchâtel, Suisse, http://www.hombori.org.

———. 2010 [2006]. *Le développement du tourisme dans les Monts Hombori (Mali). Rapport de mission 2006*. Université de Neuchâtel, Suisse. http://www.hombori. org, accessed October 2012.

Warnier, J.-P. 1999. *Construire la culture matérielle: l'homme qui pensait avec ses doigts*. Paris: PUF.

———. 2001. A praxeological approach to subjectivation in a material world. *Journal of Material Culture* 6(1), pp. 5–24.

———. 2006. Inside and outside: Surfaces and containers. In C. Tilley et al., eds., *Handbook of Material Culture*. London: Sage, pp. 186–96.

———. 2007. *The Pot-King: The Body and Technologies of Power*. Leiden: Brill.

———. 2009. Technology as efficacious action on objects . . . and subjects. *Journal of Material Culture* 14(4), pp. 459–70.

Weiss, B. 1996. *The Making and Unmaking of the Haya Lived World: Consumption, Commoditization, and Everyday Practice*. Durham, NC: Duke University Press.

Williamson, K., & Blench, R. 2000. Niger–Congo. In B. Heine & D. Nurse, eds., *African Languages: An Introduction*. New York: Cambridge University press, pp. 11–42.

Zedeño, M. N. 2008. The archaeology of territory and territoriality. In B. David & J. Thomas, eds., *The Handbook of Landscape Archaeology*. Walnut Creek, CA: Left Coast Press, pp. 210–17.

Index

About the Author

Laurence Douny is an honorary research fellow at UCL Anthropology. Since 2001 she has been conducting research on the social construction of the landscape and domestic material culture in the Dogon region of Mali in West Africa. Since 2008 she has been researching wild silk and indigo materials, techniques of production, trade, and social usages in Mali, Burkina Faso, Northern Ivory Coast, and Nigeria. She has written several papers on West African land shrines, domestic waste, wild silk textiles, and the anthropology of techniques.